'This is another handbook aimed at helping Christian leaders in both agencies and churches to be efficient and effective in their work. It is comprehensive, practical and thorough, written in an accessible style with points of application clearly shown. It is certain to become a standard for the genre of reference publications.'

Dr Peter Brierley
Church consultant

'I believe that Christian organizations are called to manage themselves "decently and in order", and the ways we express these responsibilities can serve as signs of God's well-ordered kingdom of which we are servants. I commend this indispensable guide for those associated with the governance and management of Christian charities.'

David Coffey
President of the Baptist World Alliance

'This book is warmly to be welcomed. It brings between two covers a wealth of vital information for charity trustees and managers. It deserves to become an essential handbook.'

David Cornick
General Secretary, United Reformed Church

'In the past, churches have been subject to a minimum of external regulations – whether in respect of employment, financial, health and safety, legal, or trust matters. That is now all changing, and this book will go a long way towards preparing church officers for these changes.'

Eric Cousins
Grace Baptist Trust Corporation

'Over the last twenty years it has become increasingly evident that charities in Britain are often mired in the nineteenth century. They bumble along, often making huge errors, not out of wickedness, but out of innocent ignorance. Paul Martin has done all charities, especially church charities, in Britain an enormous favour. He has written an eminently practical book about the proper conduct of trustees, and the governance of charitable trusts and non-profit corporations. He writes not only as a lawyer, but also with the accumulated wisdom of thirty-six years of service as a trustee. Consequently, this book is not presenting obscure information strangled by pages of legalese. Simple enough for the most ordinary vicar to understand, his book has performed a great service for the church in England. May it be used to prevent others from making stupid mistakes and falling foul of an increasingly complex area of law. My expectation is that it will become an indispensable aid for churches and charities. I heartily commend it.'

Eric Delve
St Luke's Church, Maidstone

'Paul Martin is to be commended for drawing together this helpful guide. Charity law is hugely complex and changes fast, and I have no doubt that this volume will be warmly welcomed by those who have to pick their way through the jungle of charity regulations.'

Jonathan Edwards
General Secretary, Baptist Union of Great Britain

'This book could not have come at a better time. It is a comprehensive tool for those involved in the running of charitable organizations.

Based on many years of practical experience in this area, Paul has simplified every aspect of running a charity. It really is an answer to the cry for help from many pastors who want to do what is right but don't know how. I would highly recommend this book, and, in the light of recent developments, I particularly recommend it to the evangelical churches who have wondered how to run their churches properly and efficiently.

Certainly an excellent book!'

Agu Irukwu, senior pastor of Jesus House, London
Head of the Redeemed Church of God (RCCG) UK
and member of the council of the Evangelical Alliance

'An easy-to-read, valuable reference tool containing good practical advice. Clearly based on an in-depth knowledge of the area, this book is a great resource for almost anyone in the charity sector, but particularly for newcomers.'

Andrew James
Director of Campaigns & Marketing, Scope

'What an extremely helpful guide to operating a Christian charity "professionally" and "achieving compliance with excellence" in the minefield of modern legal requirements. From his thirty-six years of experience, Paul Martin manages to include a wealth of detail on all manner of issues from governance and employment to finance and IT, and all presented in plain simple English. He includes a handy list of perceptive questions and addresses – "what to do when". If you are multi-tasking within a small-medium charity and don't have the time and resources to be a legal specialist, this book will be an invaluable reference for you. My office manager said "This is a gem", and I agree.'

J. John
Philo Trust

'Effective Christian ministry includes the wise management of people and resources, and sometimes one mistake can torpedo the work of a church or Christian organization. Here is a comprehensive manual full of professional advice and godly wisdom. I welcome its publication wholeheartedly – every church and Christian agency needs this essential resource.'

Jonathan Lamb
Director, Langham Partnership International

'Running a charity used to be so simple, but now the multitude of legislation seems to make it so complicated. Paul helpfully brings together many of the key issues of running a charity under one umbrella. Christian charities need to be at the cutting edge of good practice and this is a key resource for anyone in the sector.'

Martin Lee
Director, Global Connections

'Seeking to navigate a charity responsibly is rather like trying to find your way through a maze strewn with landmines. That is why this comprehensive and highly practical guide to "everything charity" is so welcome and timely. Written with the minimum of jargon and the maximum of common sense, it will be a constant source of reference and guidance for all who want to do more than pray that they do the right thing.'

Peter Meadows
Director of Giving and Communications, Bible Society

'This handbook is an essential part of a Christian charitable trustee's toolkit. It spells out the legal requirements and pitfalls in clear and simple terms so the layman can easily grasp the issues. Paul and Jayne have provided invaluable help to the LCF in recent years and have now transferred their considerable combined experience and expertise into print. This book could not have come out at a more opportune moment with the Charities Act 2006 coming into force so recently. There is no doubt that operating in the charitable sphere is going to prove increasingly challenging for Christian charities who wish to maintain a distinctive biblical witness. This book will prove an essential tool to prepare for the difficult times ahead. Forewarned is forearmed!'

Mark Mullins
Barrister
Public Policy Chairman
Lawyers Christian Fellowship

'Not all charities are the same – but they are in law. This handbook brings a new dimension to the growing charity literature by balancing the distinctive issues of the religious charity sector within the wider environment.'

Professor Paul Palmer
Cass Business School, London

'How very timely this book is. The past years have been a time of apprehension, waiting for details of the New Charities Act to surface. Paul has now provided an excellent trustees road-map for all of us "enthusiastic amateurs" to be good stewards in the responsibility of trusteeship.

Using language we can all understand, the book provides a guide to the choice of paths that trustees need to consider and take. It will give confidence to trustees as they tackle all the complex responsibilities of governance.'

Colin B. Saunders
Executive Chairman, Christian Resources Exhibitions

'*The Christian Charities Handbook* does two important things. It encourages people to think about being trustees and directors of charities – the body of Christ needs a new generation of trustees and directors of charities. Secondly, this book helps everybody who is a trustee or director to understand clearly what it is they have to do. Paul's experience and understanding are a fantastic resource. I highly recommend it.'

Laurence Singlehurst
YWAM

'Running a charity requires increasing professionalism, given the complexity of legislation and the growing demands made on trustees, Paul Martin's work should be essential reading for all involved in the governance and administration of charities, whether church, mission or aid agency. This handbook provides an invaluable resource in understandable English to help busy trustees grasp the requirements of the spiritual, ethical and legal requirements of their role.'

Dr Patrick Sookhdeo
International Director, Barnabas Fund

'It's getting tougher to do charitable work these days – if for no other reason than the massive legal hurdles and regulations. Thanks to my friend Paul Martin, whose legal credentials are top-notch, we now have this handy and understandable guide through the choppy waters of doing business the right way. When it comes to doing charitable business correctly, it's not *who* you know but *what* you know that will keep you out of jeopardy ... although, come to think of it, if Paul Martin is who you know, then what you know will be solid and safe!'

Joe Stowell
Teaching Pastor, Harvest Bible Chapel, Chicago, Illinois, USA
Former President, Moody Bible Institute

'Paul Martin has advised the church here at King's consistently and helpfully for the past decade. I would like to endorse this very practical and accessible handbook, which is timely in providing a resource to handle the legal complexities of running a Christian charity.'

Steve Tibbert
Senior Pastor, King's Church Catford, and part of the Newfrontiers leadership team

'In these days of growing regulation, with its swelling tide of daunting obligations, being involved in the management of churches or charities can seem like an intolerable nightmare.

What we need to meet this challenge is a comprehensive explanation of the world of charity, presented in a user-friendly way, which takes away the fear that threatens to overshadow this complex sector of our national life. With this book, Paul Martin has furnished us with exactly that. Subject by subject, he guides us unswervingly through all that we have to do – and why we have to do it.

All Christian service should be undertaken well and wholeheartedly, and the author provides not only the tools for the task, but also an infectious enthusiasm which will inspire managers, trustees and administrators, whether they are "professionals" or willing volunteers, to approach their responsibilities with joy.'

Richard Underwood
General Secretary
The Fellowship of Independent Evangelical Churches

'As Christian charities increase in number and the complexities multiply, this is an essential guide to the sector. Those contemplating charity status would do well to read this and count the cost. Those who are already operating will find this a useful checklist for efficiency. Those who are avoiding compliance will be soundly rebuked. Paul Martin has encapsulated his years of experience in this area to produce a helpful and all-encompassing overview that will benefit us all and drag us into the new reality of charity legislation.'

Dr Chris Wigram
National Director, OMF International (UK)

'Paul J. Martin is a very experienced charity lawyer, whose wealth of expertise has been instrumental in the smooth running of many Christian charities in the UK. He is a special adviser to Christ Faith Tabernacle International Churches and Prophetic Voice Ministers in the UK. I would like to recommend this handbook as a must-have for every Christian charity.'

Apostle Alfred T. B. Williams
President, Afro-Caribbean Evangelical Alliance, and General Overseer, CFTI

The
CHRISTIAN
CHARITIES
HANDBOOK

To my wife Claire. Together we have served in charities for over thirty years, and her encouragement and understanding have made this book a reality.

And to Jonathan and Elisabeth, who, having experienced the charitable sector via their parents, have now gone on to greater involvement themselves.

PAUL
MARTIN

THE
CHRISTIAN
CHARITIES
HANDBOOK

THE ESSENTIAL GUIDE FOR TRUSTEES AND MANAGERS

ivp

INTER-VARSITY PRESS
Norton Street, Nottingham NG7 3HR, England
Email: ivp@ivpbooks.com
Website: www.ivpbooks.com

First published 2008

British Library Cataloguing in Publication Data
A catalogue record for this book is available from the British Library.

ISBN: 978-1-84474-276-9

Set in Monotype Garamond 11/13pt
Typeset in Great Britain by Servis Filmsetting Ltd, Manchester
Printed and bound in Great Britain by Cromwell Press, Trowbridge

- the need to use its resources in the most efficient, effective and economic way;
- the principles of best regulatory practice;
- the desirability of facilitating innovation by or on behalf of charities;
- such generally accepted principles of good corporate governance as is reasonable to regard as applicable to it.

Charity Tribunal

Before the Charities Act 2006 came into force, it was difficult to appeal against a decision of the Charity Commission. Charities that had the appetite (and resources) for a hearing in the High Court were able to choose that route for certain types of appeal, but it was a relatively slow and very expensive course of action.

The establishment of a Charity Tribunal has been widely welcomed across the sector, although it was among the final parts of the Charities Act to be brought into force, involving much work within government departments (including the drafting of supporting legislation) and the recruitment of staff. It was also partly dependent upon how other parts of the Charities Act were implemented.

Whilst it is quicker and easier to take an appeal to the Charity Tribunal than before, in practice it may be that the cost will still prohibit many charities from doing so. In exceptional cases, public funding may be granted under the Access to Justice Act 1999, but only 'if the case merits it'. If the issues involved are particularly complex and require legal representation, the Attorney General can take a case to the Tribunal and this would take away the burden from the charity of paying for the matter to go to the Tribunal. However, he is only likely to do this in high-profile cases or those that have involved legal complexities. In addition, controversial cases will still need to be heard by the High Court in order to test existing case law and create new legal precedents where necessary. These mechanisms are embodied in the new Charities Act.

That said, it is important that charities for the first time have an independent tribunal to hear appeals against, and reviews of, decisions, directions and Orders of the Charity Commission. It acts as a charity's first port of call if a charity is unhappy with a decision of the Charity Commission, for example, a decision not to recognize a particular purpose as being charitable, and should increase the Charity Commission's accountability to the charities it regulates. The Charity Tribunal will not deal with 'customer service' complaints in relation to the Charity Commission. These will continue to be dealt with by the Charity Commission's internal complaints system and the Independent Complaints Reviewer. Details of how these work can be found on the Charity Commission's website.

Whether or not the Charity Tribunal will be successful in the long term will entirely depend on the ability of charities to exercise their right of appeal in a way that is affordable and straightforward. This will need to be monitored and reviewed to ensure that those with legitimate appeals are not prevented from bringing an appeal simply on the grounds of cost.

Registration of charities

All charities, apart from exempt and excepted charities (see below), are required to apply for registration if their gross annual income exceeds £5,000. This provision, together with the removal of the requirements for charities that hold Permanent Endowment or occupy land to register, regardless of their income, has removed the requirement to register with the Charity Commission from around 30,000 charities.

However, existing registered charities with a gross annual income below £5,000 will remain on the register unless they ask the Charity Commission to remove them.

By section 9 of the Act, both 'excepted' charity status and 'exempted' charity status are withdrawn.

Exempt charities

The Charities Act 2006 divides exempt charities into two categories: those that have a defined 'principal regulator' and those that do not.

The first category are exempt charities that are already regulated by a body other than the Charity Commission, and that body has agreed to take responsibility for ensuring that the charities meet charity law. These charities continue to be exempt and are regulated by their current regulator, now known as a 'principal regulator'. The Charity Commission will be able to investigate these charities at their principal regulator's request, and the charities will also be subject to the Charity Commission's protective powers.

If it is not possible to identify a principal regulator, then previously exempt charities with annual gross income in excess of £100,000 have a compulsory requirement to apply for registration with the Charity Commission.

Those under the £100,000 threshold currently do not have to apply for registration, although they do come under the Charity Commission's jurisdiction. The £100,000 threshold is an interim level and may be reduced in the future, but this will not be until there is a review of the Charities Act.

These new provisions also affect exempt charities under the Places of Worship Registration Act 1855. The Registrar General maintains the record of these places of religious worship by adding those newly certified and cancelling those that are disused.

Excepted charities

Under the Charities Act, excepted charities with annual gross income in excess of £100,000 must apply for registration with the Charity Commission and fulfil the resulting obligations. Those under the £100,000 threshold will continue to be excepted charities, although this will be kept under review.

Excepted charitable status applies to the following churches:

Church of England
Church in Wales
Presbyterian Church in Wales
Methodist Church
United Reformed Church
Congregational Church
Baptist Church
FIEC churches (Fellowship of Independent Evangelical Churches)
Religious Society of Friends (Quakers)

It is important to note that any other churches will be required to apply for registration with the Charity Commission if their gross annual income exceeds £5,000.

It should be noted that Church of England and Roman Catholic parishes are affected quite differently by the new rules regarding exempt and excepted charities, both from each other and from other Christian denominations. Much of this is because of their history, but there are some important distinctions to be drawn on their treatment in terms of charity law.

An outline of the main Christian denominations, and particularly how they are regarded as far as charity law is concerned, is included in section 1.

As with the Charity Tribunal, the parts of the Charities Act 2006 dealing with exempt and excepted charities are among the last parts to be brought into force, in recognition of the fact that all parties affected by these provisions needed time to prepare for the changes being introduced.

The Charity Commission expects to have to register large numbers of charities that previously held exempt or excepted charity status. In addition, if exempt or excepted charities that do not have to register wish to apply for voluntary registration, the Charity Commission has the discretion to accept such applications. However, once all the exempt and excepted charities that must be registered have been registered, then the Charity Commission will have an obligation (not a discretion) to register any previously exempt or excepted charity that applies for registration.

Charitable Incorporated Organisation

The Charities Act 2006 introduced a new legal form called a 'Charitable Incorporated Organisation' (CIO). Charities that want a corporate structure currently have to register both as charities and as companies, and therefore have to meet the dual regulatory burdens of both the Charity Commission and Companies House. The CIO is a new vehicle for charities and will have the advantages of a corporate structure, such as reduced personal liability for trustees, without the burden of dual regulation. Mechanisms are contained in the Charities Act 2006 to allow most existing charities to convert to a CIO relatively easily.

Mergers

Part 2 of the Charities Act 2006 contains a number of provisions to facilitate mergers. One of the most significant measures relates to legacies. Where legacies are made to a charity that subsequently merges with another charity, such legacies will be able to benefit the new or merged charity provided the merger has been registered with the Charity Commission. This is discussed in more detail in section 27.

Other provisions

The provisions of the Act concerning trustee remuneration are discussed in more detail in section 7. The provisions concerning trustee indemnity insurance are discussed in more detail in section 25, and those concerning the power to spend capital are discussed in sections 21 and Appendix 1.

Part 3: Public charitable collections

Part 3 deals with public charitable collections, professional fund-raisers and the regulation of fund-raising activity. This is discussed in further detail in section 22.

Part 4: Miscellaneous and general

Part 4, as it suggests, deals with miscellaneous matters, such as the establishment of a regulator in Northern Ireland to exercise functions that are similar in nature to the functions exercised in England and Wales by the Charity Commission. It also deals with the appointment of a person to review generally the operation of the Charities Act.

The review will have to address the effect of the Charities Act on:

- excepted charities;
- public confidence in charities;
- the level of charitable donations;
- the willingness of individuals to volunteer;
- the status of the Charity Commission as a government department;
- any other matters considered appropriate.

Part 4 also includes administrative details such as the ability to make Orders, as well as amendments to other legislation and transitional provisions.

SECTION 4 THE ROLE OF THE CHARITY COMMISSION

The Charity Commission acts as both 'friend' and 'policeman' (i.e. adviser and regulator) to charities. The fact that charities are regulated more strictly than, say, non-charitable social enterprises is seen by some as a disadvantage of charitable status. The Charity Commission, and probably the public at large, sees its role very much as the regulator as well as the registrar for charities.

Charitable status does confer benefits – most notably tax advantages and the assurance of accountability to the Charity Commission. But enterprises operating as charities must also accept the obligations that come with charitable status, including:

- the requirement to satisfy the 'public benefit test' (see section 3);
- the need to justify any payment to charity trustees (including directors of charitable companies);
- rules on trading and investment that can significantly limit the charity's activities;
- tougher regulation, since it is aimed at protecting the rights of beneficiaries, donors and other stakeholders who do not have enforceable rights and may have limited information.

Charities receive the majority of public donations and therefore there should be robust mechanisms to make them accountable to the same public.

The Charity Commission sees its role very much as sustaining the public's trust and confidence in the sector as a whole. The Charity Commission has a 'gateway' procedure when it assesses an organization's initial application for charitable status. This effectively means that the Charity Commission alone determines what constitutes sufficient public benefit to be charitable.

Regulator

The Charity Commission is the independent regulator of charities in England and Wales, although it is a non-ministerial government department. However, it is neither part of the Cabinet Office nor is it subject to the direction or control of Ministers. That said, Cabinet Office Ministers do have some functions in relation to the Charity Commission. Examples include appointing the Charity Commission board members, replying to questions in Parliament about the Charity Commission, and making Orders to give effect to changes in charities' constitutions that are regulated by Acts of Parliament and have been agreed by the Charity Commission.

The Charity Commission describes its role as regulator as including securing compliance with charity law and dealing with abuse and poor practice, enabling charities to work better within an effective legal, accounting and governance framework, keeping pace with developments in society, the economy and the law, and promoting sound governance and accountability.

The Charity Commission promotes legal compliance through its publications and casework, with higher expectations of compliance placed on larger charities that have paid staff and access to professional advice. The Charity Commission is increasingly employing the 'name and shame' concept to encourage charities to provide the information required by the appropriate deadlines.

Investigations

The Charity Commission is also active in intervention and enforcement, working with other regulators as necessary. It evaluates complaints against charities and if it believes things have gone seriously wrong, it will open a formal investigation. Examples include where there has been serious misconduct or mismanagement, or where charitable assets are at risk of loss, damage or misuse. The Charity Commission's stated aim is to ensure that 'the charity is back on track to carry out its work for the future', although that is not always apparent to charities at the brunt end of an investigation. The Charity

Commission also publishes reports of all its inquiries 'to help other charities learn lessons'. This in turn can sometimes fuel high media attention, particularly if the subject of the investigation has already attracted significant media coverage. Investigations involving churches or Christian charities that caught the eye of national and local media include the Victory Christian Centre in Bath (inquiry report published in April 2007), Christian Life Bible College (April 2005) and The King's Ministries Trust (October 2005).

Review visits

As well as carrying out investigations, the Charity Commission also visits several hundred charities each year to review their activities, constitutions and administration. A review visit is not an Audit or an investigation, but neither is it an accreditation. Rather, it is an opportunity for the Charity Commission to examine key aspects of the charity, including its activities, governance and finance, to understand any issues in context, and to provide advice on legal requirements and good practice (see Appendix 1, paragraph 17).

Work with faith-based charities

In 2007, the Charity Commission established a 'Faith and Social Cohesion Unit' to work with and support faith charities, strengthening their governance and accountability, with funding provided by the Department of Communities and local government. At that time, there were over 23,000 faith charities on the central Register of Charities. These include charities established specifically to advance a particular faith, as well as charities whose faith or religious belief is the motivation for the charitable activity undertaken.

The Unit co-ordinates the Charity Commission's work in providing advice, guidance and capacity-building support to faith charities in a number of key areas, including trustee duties and responsibilities, governance, finance, and working with children and vulnerable beneficiaries. The Unit is building on the work carried out in recent years by the Commission's Faith Groups Project.

SECTION 5 THE IMAGE OF THE CHARITY

The charity's name

Naming the charity can be a challenge. Some names are descriptive of the activity of the charity (Youth With A Mission), some define the charity's area of operation (London City Mission) and some invoke a scriptural theme (Good Shepherd Ministries).

When selecting a name for a charity the following should be taken into consideration:

- The name must be distinct from other registered charities so as not to cause confusion with the public.
- The name should not include words or phrases that would cause offence.
- A name that includes certain words may be more difficult to register (e.g. Royal or International) and some words may not be allowed by law.

Before registering an organization as a charity, the Charity Commission will review the proposed name against those existing on the Register of Charities (an applicant can do this beforehand at www.charity-commission.gov.uk). If it is identical or too similar to an existing name, then the Charity Commission will ask for the name to be changed before they complete the registration.

The registration of a name does not give the charity any rights to that name under general law. Furthermore, the Charity Commission will not guarantee the continued use of that name following registration. A name is always open to a subsequent challenge by others who may claim to have used the name (even as a 'working name') over a long period in respect of an unincorporated charity. For example, the charity 'British Province of the Unitas Fratrum' protects the name 'Moravian Church' and would preclude its use by a subsequent charity.

The Charity Commission has the power to require the charity to change its name if:

1. the registered name is the same as or too similar to the name of an existing charity;
2. the charity's name is likely to mislead the public as to the true nature of the purposes or activities of the charity;
3. the charity's name includes a word or expression that in the Charity Commissioner's opinion is likely to mislead the public as to the status of the charity (for example, words which denote national or international status or royal patronage);
4. the charity's name is likely to give the impression that it is connected in some way with H M Government, a local authority or some other body to which, in fact, it is not connected;
5. the charity's name is offensive.

If the Charity Commission order the charity to change its name after registration, then, notwithstanding that the name may have been available at registration, they will not indemnify the charity against the costs of the change or the reprinting of any stationery or marketing material.

If the organization is to be a charitable company then similar restrictions will exist with regard to its name. A prior review of the Companies House website is advisable (www.companieshouse.gov.uk).

Use of sensitive names

'Royal'	To include this word in the title of a charity will be extremely difficult. Prior consent to use the name would need to be obtained from the Department of Constitutional Affairs before the Charity Commission would register.
'International'	Evidence of the proposed charity's activities (or intended activities) in at least two overseas countries will be required.
'Charity'/'Charitable'	The use of these words in the title requires the approval of the Secretary of State for Trade and Industry, and, in the case of a registration as a charitable company, Companies House will require the Charity Commission's prior written consent as well.

Name change

Many charities change their name without remembering to notify the Charity Commission. As a result, difficulties can arise.

For any charity to change its name, the law requires a resolution to be passed. For a charitable company this will require a 'special resolution' of the company. For an unincorporated charity it will require an ordinary resolution to be passed by the trustees.

For an unincorporated charity

An unincorporated charity's name as contained in its governing document (e.g. 'Sovereign World Trust') is part of the charity's trusts, and any unauthorized alteration is therefore technically a breach of trust! Such a breach can be remedied as follows:

1. If the unincorporated charity has power in its governing document to change its name, then an ordinary resolution should be passed by the trustees and, subject to the new name being acceptable to the Charity Commission, the Charity Register can be changed.
2. If the unincorporated charity does not have power in its governing document to change its name, it will require a Scheme of the Charity Commission as it is effectively changing the trust of the charity. However, the Charity Commission are unlikely to be enthusiastic about such an application given that Charity Commission Schemes are usually reserved for more serious issues.
3. The pragmatic approach (often suggested by the Charity Commission) is to allow the charity to use the new name as a 'working name' and to keep the old name as the registered one. The new name is also entered onto the Charity Register as part of the required details of the charity, and the charity is then free to use the new name on its letterheads, reports and published documentation.

For a charitable company

A special resolution to change the name of a charitable company must first be filed with the Registrar of Companies, and the change will not be completed until the Certificate of Incorporation on Change of Name has been issued by the Register of Companies. The registrar of companies retains the power to object to a new name and therefore any name change should be checked in advance with the Companies House Register (www.companieshouse.gov.uk) as well as with the Charity Commission (www. charitycommission.gov.uk).

A copy of the special resolution is then filed with the Charity Commission who, subject to agreeing the name, will change the register to reflect the change. It is advisable to check the Charity Commission website to see that the new name is available beforehand.

Many charities decide to use a shortened version of their name or a 'working name' to be the name by which the charity will be known in every-day activity (e.g. RCCG are the initials by which the charity Redeemed Christian Church of God is known). The abbreviated name will usually be entered on the Register by the Charity Commission. The charity cannot use as an abbreviated or trading name a name that it has been prevented from registering due to its similarity to an existing registered charity.

Publicity

It is wise for every charity or charitable company to include its full name and charity number on its letterheads, publicity material and website. Furthermore, under the Charities Act 1993 a registered charity (providing its gross income for the last financial year exceeded £10,000) should include the fact that it is a registered charity on:

a. all notices, advertisements and other documents issued by and on
   behalf of the charity to solicit money or other assets for the benefit of the
   charity;
b. all cheques, promissory notes, endorsements and other orders for money
   or goods, signed on behalf of the charity;
c. all bills rendered by it and in all its receipts and letters of credit.

Any person (trustee and/or senior staff of the charity) falling foul of (a) and (c) above or any persons signing a document falling within (b) above is guilty of an offence and liable to a fine if prosecuted.

Publicity for a charity should be produced with the object of advertising the charity and work that it does. It is considered unwise for a charity to take a 'position' on certain political international and otherwise controversial issues simply because that is unlikely to be the main object for which the charity exists.

Care should also be taken when third-party material is offered on a charity's website or otherwise endorsed by the charity's publications, as again the charity could suffer from being too closely aligned to a particular stance. The Charity Commission have upheld complaints concerning the endorse-ment made by some charities (and opened formal enquiries into the charity's activities), ultimately requiring the charity to disassociate from certain publications that had been promoted by it.

The above guidance is to be distinguished from instances where, for example, the charity's Object is to advance the Christian faith by reference to a particular set of beliefs. It would be entirely consistent for the charity in those circumstances to take a particular position on conduct or beliefs that are inconsistent with the stated beliefs of the charity.

In the case of an unincorporated charity, its trustees are well advised to ensure some degree of influence over the charity's position on certain subjects, as ultimately they are responsible.

Logos and trademarks

In instances where the charity's officers wish to protect its name beyond the very limited protection given by its very existence on the Register of Charities, they may wish to consider registering either the charity's name and/or its logo as a trademark. Registration in this way would be a deterrent to those who might otherwise try to plagiarize the name for fund-raising or marketing purposes.

Registration of a trademark is possible on a DIY basis (www.ipo.gov.uk); otherwise it is wise to consult a specialist intellectual property firm who can advise on the best forms of registration, particularly if the name to be protected is to be used worldwide (see also section 15).

SECTION 6 GOVERNANCE AND MANAGEMENT

What is governance?

The charity's effectiveness in both the achievement of its Objects and the way in which it functions will depend largely upon the ability of its board of trustees or directors to govern efficiently.

Many of the issues encountered by charities in both their administration and function (some of which require Charity Commission intervention) can trace their origins back to deficiencies within the governance and management structure of the charity.

Governance has been defined as 'the process by which a governing body ensures that an organisation is effectively and properly run . . . Governance is not necessarily about doing; it is about ensuring things are done' (Sandy Adirondack: *The Good Governance Action Plan*, National Council for Voluntary Organisations, 2002).

Primarily, governance is the responsibility of the board of trustees (or directors), and it includes setting policy and long-term strategy, establishing and monitoring the charity's core values and evaluating the performance of the charity towards achieving its stated objectives.

The trustees have certain specific roles, which are discussed in section 7. However, the principle is that trustees govern, and managers manage.

It is vital that the trustees work to develop a good relationship between themselves and those who are primarily carrying out the objectives of the charity (staff or volunteers). There are certain relationships that are key:

- between the chairman of trustees and the Chief Executive or pastor;
- between the trustees themselves – particularly if they bring key skills to the organization, which they could use to monitor certain of the staff and volunteers (for example, finance, legal or human resources).

For the trustees to be effective in their governance role, they will need to take time together to reflect on the 'bigger picture'. There does not exist an ideal model of governance for charities, simply because charities come in various sizes and have different approaches. However, for a fuller discussion on various model forms of governance, the National Council for Voluntary Organisations (NCVO) has published helpful material on the subject.

Many smaller charitable organizations do not have full or part-time staff, and therefore it is not practical for the board to concentrate exclusively on governance, as they need to be involved in both management and implementation. However, even in smaller charities the fundamental role of the trustee does not change – it is just that they have other responsibilities as well! It is suggested that trustees in small charitable organizations should identify those activities for which they have a governance role, those for which they have a management role and those for which they have a volunteer role.

Conflict between trustees and management

If the board and the management have carefully defined their respective roles and have worked on building a good working relationship, then the possibility of conflict is minimized. However, both the trustees and the management should recognize that relationships and responsibilities are an evolving process, and from time to time areas of potential conflict can arise. Good governance is demonstrated when those issues can be identified and addressed before they become a significant distraction.

In a great many charities, however, the pressure of the day-to-day activity together with the limited amount of time that the board of trustees can invest in the work can mean that there are areas of responsibility that have never been correctly agreed and defined, and problems can arise. This is particularly illustrated when a growing charity hires its first administrative employee. The trustees may continue to work on various management and practical issues, and the new employee is therefore unclear as to their own area of responsibility. The challenge for the board of trustees will be to delegate the day-to-day management (within clearly defined limits of authority) to the new employee, and refocus their energies on the governance issues.

Governance responsibility of a trustee or director of a charity will include ensuring:

- that the charity pursues its Objects within its governing document;
- financial integrity;
- compliance with laws;
- that management are held accountable;
- long-term strategy;
- stewardship of the resources of the charity;
- appointment (and dismissal) of the Chief Executive;
- decisions on major issues that have a significant impact on the charity.

Managers are responsible for:

- implementation of plans or policy whereby the charity pursues its Objects;
- reporting fully to the trustees;
- guiding trustees on compliance;
- the delegated authority for the implementation of financial policy, performance evaluation process and risk management process.

The American author, John Carver, is noted for his development of the policy model for boards of directors.[1] Carver's model distinguishes between the organization's goals and the means that the organization employs to obtain those goals. In his model, it is the board's job to decide the goals, and the Chief Executive's job to determine the means to achieve the goals.

The founder trustee

In the charitable sector, it is often the case that the energy and vision behind the establishment of a charity derives from one person – 'the founder trustee'. Many of today's high-profile charities trace their origins back not to a committee or to a business plan but to an individual who had both the

---

1 John Carver, *Boards that Make a Difference: A New Design for Leadership in Nonprofit and Public Organizations*, 2nd edn (San Francisco: Jossey-Bass, 1997).

vision about how change could be brought about and the drive and commitment to ensure that an organization was birthed to achieve that vision.

In both the birth and the establishment of the charity, the founder's zeal, single-mindedness and ability to attract resources, often in the face of significant opposition, is probably the single reason why the charity exists. However, notwithstanding all those great qualities that enabled the charity to be established and to grow, in the longer term, the founder has to relate to fellow trustees, management and staff of the growing charity if the new charity is to be sustained and be accountable to its beneficiaries, rather than being the personal project of the founder trustee.

Most charities and churches at some stage have to face the fact that the entrepreneurial single-minded visionary leadership that gave birth to the organization is not the only skill that is required to take the organization forward. Sooner or later, qualities of team-building, delegation, participatory management and accountability are those that have to be developed in the charity, if the work is to be sustained and the baton passed to a new generation.

In cases where these issues are not addressed by the board at an early stage, the result can be that the founder trustee continues to lead an organization which is his own personal domain, and either the management (perhaps under another leader) rises up and challenges the founder or the founder continues until he can continue no longer and the organization falls away.

It is difficult for trustees, who may have been appointed by the founder trustee, to challenge the structure and style that the founder has established. However, just as there are parallels in both the business and political worlds where leaders have overstayed their time, the same can apply in the charitable sector.

An examination of some of the instances where the Charity Commission have intervened in the affairs of a charity shows that a number of them had boards of trustees and staff positions that were populated by the founder trustee and his family and friends. In such cases the Charity Commission have often found that the founding trustee is virtually unchallenged or not held accountable by fellow board members, and an unhealthy and possibly dangerous situation exists. In my experience of over thirty years of legal representation of charitable organizations, the following principles have been observed:

- It is not advisable for both a husband and wife (or two other persons from the same household) to be trustees of the same charity.
- A pastor or minister of a church should not automatically be made a trustee of the church charity, unless there is a good reason for doing so.

- If the pastor/minister is salaried by the church, albeit he is not a trustee, then his wife should not be a trustee of the church charity.
- Members of the founding trustee's family (siblings, brothers and sisters) should not be on the board of the charity unless they are clearly outnumbered by independent trustees.

The relationship between the church pastor and the trustees of the church is a very special one and is worthy of further consideration, as it exists as a cameo to illustrate the different perspectives that both the pastor and the trustees bring to the issue.

The trustees are accountable to the authorities (Charity Commission, Companies House and the HMRC) for the charity. The provisions of the charity's governing document show that they have control of the charity, its property and assets, and are responsible to govern the charity in such a way as the assets are used towards achieving the Object for which the charity was set up. The pastor as an employee of the church will be employed upon terms that are agreed and monitored by the trustees.

The pastor considers that he is accountable to God for fulfilment of the call on his life and the responsibility for the people under his care in the church. Difficulties can arise when the trustees, in order to meet their responsibilities, appear to control the pastor ('after all, he is our employee'). The pastor, however, reacts to this by bypassing the trustees and trying to make their position irrelevant.

The challenge is as follows:

For the trustees – how can they ensure they are discharging their responsibilities to the authorities without creating unnecessary friction with the pastor?

For the pastor – how can he operate responsibly within the constraints placed on him by the trustees, without compromising his call and ministry or operating in a way that makes the trustees feel irrelevant?

When the pastor has felt threatened in his position, some typical reactions have included:

- The keeping of the church's cash, instead of allowing it to be paid into the bank or allowing an independent person to monitor it.
- Intimidation of the trustees to submit to his will.
- Refusing to attend trustees' meetings to explain his vision, plan and budget.
- Keeping the church's account as a personal account, sometimes as sole signatory, or ensuring that a trustee signs blank cheques for him.
- Operating a parallel administration to sidetrack the trustees.
- Openly preaching about the problems of the trustees from the pulpit.

The reactions of the trustees have included:

- Seizing the accounts, account documents and frustrating the pastor's effectiveness.
- Deciding to instigate the removal of the pastor.
- Speaking ill of the pastor to third parties.

Pastoral responsibility against legal responsibility

The power play illustrated above between the trustees (those legally responsible) and the pastor (spiritually responsible) for a church begs a fundamental question: who is ultimately responsible in the charity?

Clearly as far as the UK law is concerned, the trustees of the charity are answerable for the charitable trust that they govern and for all the activities that go on within it. As stated above, the pastor or spiritual leadership are responsible to a higher call and there are occasions when the spiritual direction in which they are taking the church can result in strains and stresses. For example:

- The spiritual leaders decide that the church no longer needs an annual general meeting as they seek to downplay the ability of the membership to vote on major issues. That is likely to conflict with the charity's governing document and potentially puts the trustees in breach of the law.
- The spiritual leadership decide to embark on a major expenditure (for example, the purchase of a new building), the complexity and expense of which causes some disquiet amongst the trustees. Given that the trustees would need to be a party to the acquisition and any associated financial arrangements (the latter probably involving them in personal liability), they feel that it is beyond the historical performance of the charity to date to support the project that the leadership envisage.
- The trustees feel that they need to make an executive decision – perhaps on a staff matter – which the spiritual leadership do not agree with.
- The spiritual leadership are running the church and taking important decisions without consulting with or otherwise informing the trustees, and the trustees feel that, as ultimately they are responsible, they cannot allow the spiritual leadership to commit them to obligations they are unaware of or unwilling to enter into.

The above are just some examples of issues that can separate those who are legally responsible and those who are spiritually responsible. If conflict and a possible split are to be avoided, then both parties need to establish principles in the early days of the relationship that would prevent the establishment of 'camps'. These could include:

- Ensuring that at least one or more of the spiritual leadership also serve as trustees (but probably not the pastor).
- Shared vision and commitment to mutual accountability.
- The inclusion of a clause similar to that set out in section 10 above being included in the charity's trust deed.
- Clear definition and agreement of roles of the trustees and of those who are responsible for the spiritual life of the church.
- An accountability/mentoring relationship to an outside third party for those responsible for the spiritual side (e.g. an outside pastor), who can bring wisdom and objectivity into the scenario.

Appointment of Chief Executive/pastor

The Chief Executive/pastor is accountable to the board of trustees as a whole, although the board chairman should work to establish a good personal working relationship with the Chief Executive/pastor.

It has been suggested above that the pastor should not also be a trustee. However, he or the charity's Chief Executive (if not a trustee) can and should be invited periodically to trustees' meetings both to report on the progress of the organization and so that he can understand the trustees' perspective on some of the decisions that they are seeking to make.

The roles and responsibilities of the chairman of the board and the Chief Executive/pastor should clearly be defined and agreed at the outset.

Given that there may well be a degree of suspicion between the board as a whole and the Chief Executive/pastor, the relationship between the chairman of the board and the Chief Executive/pastor is critical to overcome such suspicion. Their relationship should include regular meeting times and agreed methods of communication between those meetings.

Whilst the chairman of the board should not be too involved or interfere with the day-to-day running of the organization, he needs to be aware of what is going on in order that he can in turn report back to the board. The chairman will be responsible for the annual appraisal of the Chief Executive.

It would be wise for the board to consider whether the relationship between it and the Chief Executive/pastor should be covered under an applicable contract. This contract should be professionally produced to ensure that it deals with all the issues that the charity should properly be concerned with. For example, if the Chief Executive/pastor is allowed to take outside speaking invitations and is given an honorarium, does that belong to the charity or to the Chief Executive/pastor? In like manner, if the pastor writes books (albeit in the charity's time), is he to be allowed to keep the royalties or do they belong to the charity? Failure to deal with these issues in the proper way has been the grounds upon which the Charity Commission have investigated charitable organizations.

The setting of the remuneration of the Chief Executive/pastor is not without its challenges. The charity will wish to pay at a level that is sufficient to recruit suitable candidates, yet remuneration levels in charities are historically lower than those in the commercial world. Clearly the final decision is one for the board of trustees as a whole, and salary levels may differ from charity to charity. Organizations such as The Reward Group (www.reward-group.co.uk) publish the median salaries for most types of occupation and can provide guidelines to charity trustees who are seeking to discover the 'going rate'. It can also be a useful evidential back-up for instances when the charity is specifically asked, 'Who set the level of remuneration of the pastor/Chief Executive?'

Larger charities are beginning to replicate the commercial world by the establishment of remuneration committees comprising representatives of the board and senior management. If such committees are to be utilized, it is recommended that the charity trustees produce an appropriate protocol that governs the setting up and function of the committee.

SECTION 7 THE BOARD

The point has already been made that 'the board' is made up of the people who form the governing body of the charity. Depending on the nature of the charitable organization, they may be known as trustees, directors, board members, council members, governors or executive committee members (for the remainder of the book I will call them collectively 'trustees').

Most trustees volunteer for the role and receive no payment (other than reimbursement of any necessary out-of-pocket expenses incurred in carrying out their trusteeship). As trustees they have the ultimate responsibility for running the charitable organization. It is therefore vital that charities give high priority to the recruitment, selection and training of the trustees.

Role and recruitment

The trustee's role can be summarized as follows:

- To understand the charitable organization, its structure and the purpose for which it exists.
- To protect the assets of the charity and ensure that they are applied exclusively for the charitable purposes of the organization.
- To act at all times in the best interest of the charity and its intended beneficiaries.

- To be accountable to the other members of the board, the donors, the beneficiaries and to the law.

If the organization is a charitable company, then although the board members are called directors, they function as trustees for the purposes of the Charities Acts. In the case of a charitable company, care should be taken by anyone who is not on the board, yet who seeks to issue directions to the board as to how they should act. Such a person may well be a Shadow Director and therefore found to be responsible for sharing the liabilities of trusteeship (for example, he would share the liability for wrongful trading with the other trustees).

Many charities find the process of recruitment of new trustees a difficult task. As a result there is the temptation to recruit a board (perhaps from amongst friends or close contacts) and leave that board in place until someone retires. Given that today there is a significant weight of responsibility imposed upon charity trustees (and boards need to ensure that they can act in an effective way), often this will necessitate recruiting additional trustees who will bring skills of different disciplines to the board table.

Many charities undertake a basic skills survey amongst their board members in order to determine:

- what is needed to make the board as effective as it can be;
- whether it has the right mix of skills, experience, ethnic background and age to enable it to deliver its service to its intended beneficiaries.

Very few charities who conduct a skills survey settle for the status quo. There then follows the task of sourcing and recruiting new trustees.

Traditionally charities have recruited new trustees through personal connections and/or word of mouth. The Charity Commission have published some helpful material on trustee recruitment in which they recommend other recruiting methods, such as advertising.

The following guidelines are suggested to assist in the recruitment process:

- Decide which member(s) of the board will take ultimate responsibility for leading the charity in the recruitment process.
- Prepare a job description for the trustee position that the charity is seeking to fill. Be realistic in the job description as to the time commitment and responsibilities required. New trustees cannot be expected to react positively if they find that the time and responsibility commitment is significantly above that which was represented to them.

- Prepare a pack that includes the job description, a copy of the charity's governing document, a copy of its most recent Annual Report and accounts, together with an executive summary of the organization and all recent publicity.
- Identify the target audience. Decide whether the position will be communicated by word of mouth and/or advertised.
- Prepare a comprehensive induction programme that can be offered to the new recruit to enable them to transition smoothly into the position.

When a potential candidate has been identified and they are responding to the initial overtures being made, seek (with the candidate's consent) to take up at least one reference on the candidate (unless they are personally known to one or more of the existing trustees).

A formal offer to the candidate should be subject to receipt of the aforementioned reference, proof that the candidate is eligible to act as a trustee (see section 9) and possibly subject also to a Criminal Records Bureau (CRB) check (see Appendix 1, paragraph 2).

Qualities in a charity trustee

Willingness to take responsibility. This comes from an understanding of the governing document, an acceptance of the Objects for which the charity is set up and a willingness to discharge the role of trustee effectively.

An ability to work with others. A board of trustees is made up of individuals but together they comprise a team. The overriding requirement on a charity trustee to act in the best interest of the charity is that he or she forgets personal considerations if they conflict with the good of the charity.

Willingness to give the appropriate time. To serve on a board of trustees is not something that can be done adequately by giving 'an hour or so each month'. In addition to the scheduled board meetings, a trustee will need to take time to read briefing papers, give specific input from his or her specialization to staff members of the charity and visit the charity's beneficiaries (this can include travelling overseas if the charity conducts its work there), in order to fully understand and evaluate the charity's performance.

The confidence to ask awkward questions from time to time. Given that a charity trustee's primary responsibility is that of governance, they must be free to challenge and hold executive staff accountable. If the trustee has any doubts or suspicions about the charity's function or personnel, he or she must be confident to share these concerns with the chairman of trustees and if necessary put them in writing.

Work to understand and develop the trustee's role within the organization. Following the completion of an induction course, the role of trustee will evolve with the organization and each trustee is responsible for moving ahead with the organization to ensure that it achieves its stated Objects.

Demonstrate the integrity that the charity is expected to model. If the charity's success is in a large part dependent upon the effectiveness of the trustees, then it must follow that sloppy behaviour amongst the trustees is likely to lead to a poorly functioning charity.

The contribution that each trustee brings to the charity depends largely on the mix of trustees on the board. However, in general terms it will include the contribution of:

Adviser – bringing the trustee's personal experience and qualification to advise
    the other members of the board and the staff of the organization.
    Generally providing leadership for the organization.
Ambassador – making contacts and linking the charity's staff to outside persons
    and bodies who can assist in the charity's development. Generally
    supporting the Chief Executive and senior staff.
Advocate – acting as a voice for the charity. The trustee will often be a visionary
    able to enthuse others towards achieving the objects for which the charity
    was set up.

The effectiveness of the trustee board is something that the trustees themselves should take time to review from time to time (see section 28). For many charitable organizations, the demands of fund-raising, motivating and managing staff, and striving to achieve the charitable objectives are more than sufficient for the board to cope with. To those trustees, 'effectiveness' is perhaps measured in terms of whether or not the organization is still existing at the end of the year!

Trustees should act within the powers that are set out in the charity's governing document. It is essential, therefore, for each trustee to be given a copy of the charity's governing document, and the board should ensure that a copy is available at every board meeting as the definitive guide to trustees' decision-making.

The trustees owe a duty of care to the charity, which includes acting reasonably and prudently. Trustees should understand the legal, financial and management issues that affect the charity, and from time to time, they may need to seek specialist advice on issues where they do not have a personal expertise. Where professional advice is taken, then a copy of that advice should be preserved with the charity's minutes to support the decision that was subsequently made. Charity trustees are responsible for compliance with the applicable Charity Law and, in the case of a charitable company, with Company Law.

Induction and training

An induction programme is an essential prerequisite of any aspiring trustee. There are two reasons for this:

1. Potential trustees can be effective only when they understand the organization, its aims, its culture and what contribution the trustee is expected to bring.
2. The charity needs to understand clearly the skills and contributions that the trustees individually and collectively can be relied upon to contribute.

A common reason for charity managers to express frustration with the board of trustees (and vice versa) arises out of an unrealistic expectation of the other. Very often this can be traced back to the absence of a clear induction policy.

There are two essential qualities that a new trustee must have at the outset of their period of service:

1. A good understanding of the objectives of the charity and a positive desire to identify with those.
2. The appropriate amount of time to contribute to the charity and fulfil their responsibilities as a trustee.

Given that the charity trustee is responsible for the charity's assets and has a clear duty to act at all times in the charity's best interests, a prospective trustee would be unwise to take up responsibility unless he or she had read and considered:

- a copy of the charity's governing document;
- copies of the last three years' audited accounts;
- copies of minutes of trustees' meetings for the same period.

In addition, a new trustee should be encouraged to meet with a cross-section of the staff and volunteers of the charity and to read some project reports or maybe even visit a project and interact with some of the beneficiaries, in order to get a good understanding of the way in which the charity functions.

It is also suggested that new trustees should receive:

- a copy of the original positional description, amended as necessary;
- a copy of any organizational structure;
- details of all other trustees together with their contact information;
- copies of any strategic plans;
- copies of any major fund-raising proposals/grant applications;
- a copy of any trustee code of conduct.

In addition to the written information, a structured induction programme could include:

- informal time with other trustees and senior staff of the charity;
- visits to one or more of the charity's projects;
- an opportunity for new trustees to feed back what they have seen and heard and any conclusions concerning the charity and its work.

Remember that a new trustee is to be valued for the fresh ideas and views that they may bring to the board. Just because the charity has run in a certain way for many years does not mean that those ways are the best. It follows that new trustees must feel valued and feel that the contributions they make (particularly new insights) will be well received and evaluated rather than dismissed with a 'we've always done it this way' response. A disillusioned new trustee will not serve the charity well and will gradually withdraw from meetings and contributions they would otherwise bring. This in turn brings resentment amongst the other trustees and distracts the board of trustees from their essential work.

It is likely that new trustees will be particularly disillusioned by:

- trustees' meetings that do not focus on key issues and are badly run;
- the lack of proper reports and detailed information that is passed to the board by the charity's workers;
- poorly thought out plans for fund-raising and financing the charity's ongoing operations;
- estranged relationships between the trustees themselves or the trustees and the key staff.

The chairman of the charity has a key role both in making new trustees feel welcome and also in drawing them out at trustees' meetings and ensuring their effective participation in the governance of the charity as a whole. It is suggested that the chairman can usefully schedule time to meet with a new trustee during their first year, to ensure their expectation of the charity and the charity's expectation of them is still intact.

For a fuller consideration of this subject, I recommend the publications of The National Council for Voluntary Organisations, and also Andrew Hind's excellent book, *The Governance and Management of Charities* (although currently not in print).

Meetings and records

It is vital that trustees' meetings are fully and accurately minuted. For this purpose it is suggested that an independent person is invited to be a minutes secretary, so they can concentrate exclusively on capturing the important points without having to join in the discussion.

Comprehensive minutes are vital for the following reasons:

* to confirm the discussions held and the decisions made;
* to record the agreed action and the responsibilities for carrying out those actions;
* to inform those trustees who did not attend the meeting, yet are bound by decisions made by the board;
* to remind those who did attend the meeting what they agreed to do.

Following the meeting, the minutes should be prepared quickly (whilst events are still fresh in the mind) and checked with the chairman of the meeting, and thereafter circulated to all who attended and those who were entitled to attend but could not.

Whilst it is important that the draft minutes are checked with the chairman of the meeting, they should not be altered in any way that reflects a discussion or decision that did not in fact take place. The minute secretary should refuse to have any further part in the publishing of minutes that did not in fact reflect the discussion and decisions that had been reached at a properly convened meeting.

Once the minutes have been circulated it will not be until the next meeting of the trustees that they can formally be accepted (by means of a vote) and signed off by the chairman of the meeting, at which time they will be taken as being a true and accurate record and placed in the charity's minute book.

The courts have held that a valid meeting normally consists of the quorum of trustees who can both see and hear each other. Telephone conference calls cannot normally be used to transact business if the governing document or the law itself requires a face-to-face meeting. For larger charities, particularly where the trustees are spread around the country or overseas, the governing document may permit video conferencing whereby all trustees can see and hear each other.

Obviously not all the business of the charity has to be conducted at meetings. There may be times when trustees will conduct business by telephone, fax or the Internet, or by the circulation of papers (for example, the written resolution procedure that can be utilized by a charitable company).

The chairman

The chairman is usually also a trustee. The terms of his appointment as chairman are usually governed by the governing document. The chairman is responsible for leading the trustees' meetings through the business items that are on the agenda. Sometimes the governing document also gives the chairman a casting vote in the event of a deadlock.

At the outset of a trustees' meeting, the chairman should announce whether or not the meeting has a quorum (i.e. the minimum number of people that the governing document says must be present in person in order to make a valid decision at the meeting). If there are not enough trustees to form a quorum, then the meeting has no standing and the chairman should adjourn it.

Trustees' meetings will be greatly assisted if an agenda is circulated to all participants beforehand, together with copies of any briefing papers or other reports or documents that the trustees will be considering. In that way trustees can prepare thoroughly before attending the meeting.

Some chairmen decide that the element of surprise is an essential ingredient to a major decision and fear that announcing a proposal in advance of the meeting will allow time for opposition to the proposal to be mounted. Trustees in turn seldom like being surprised and may react to the surprise by deferring a decision!

It is for the chairman of the meeting to decide how much time will be allocated to each item on the agenda, and it is helpful if the chairman also indicates to the meeting whether a decision is being required on a particular matter at the meeting or whether the item is there for information only at that stage.

In advance of the meeting the chairman and the secretary can usefully spend time preparing for the meeting in the following way:

- considering how the room should be set out and whether an overhead projector/flip chart/laptop and projector would be of assistance;
- creating a seating plan around the table;

- deciding whether refreshments will be offered before or after the meeting (it is suggested in any event that mineral water be placed on the table for the trustees to use during the meeting);
- setting the anticipated finishing time for the meeting (it is good practice to announce the timetable at the beginning of the meeting).

The chairman conducting the meeting needs to have a clear grasp of the procedural requirements of the charity's governing document and also must ensure that all discussions are channelled through the chair, so the chairman can exercise a degree of control over the meeting. If persons other than trustees are to be invited to come in and contribute to a section of the trustees' meeting (for example, a Chief Executive who is not on the board), then that person should be brought in at the appropriate time and should leave as soon as their part of the agenda has been completed.

The chairman should also ensure that before a vote is taken the proposal is clearly summarized so that all board members understand what they are being asked to vote on.

If the meeting is adjourned before it is completed, then it can be reconvened at a later date and time without the need to circulate fresh notice.

At the beginning of a meeting, any trustee who has a personal interest in one of the items on the agenda should declare that and withdraw from the meeting when that item is discussed and voted on. An example of this would be where an executive of the charity who is also a trustee attends a board meeting at which their terms of employment are to be discussed. (See section 24 with regard to trustees' conflicts of interest.)

The minutes of the meeting should record in reasonable detail the substance of discussions that led to major decisions being made. If the trustees have sought outside professional advice on a particular matter, then that advice should be alluded to in the minutes and a copy of the advice appended to the finalized minutes themselves. An example of this would be where the trustees resolve to make a major purchase (say a property) and advice was sought from a surveyor and perhaps the charity's accountants as to the charity's ability to fund such an acquisition. Remember the decision affects not just the trustees who actually take it, but also their successors as trustees, who may carry the ramifications in the event that the decision taken proves to be a wrong one. If the minutes record a clear reasoning for the decision and show that the trustees took all possible advice before coming to a reasonable decision in all the circumstances, then the trustees are unlikely to be criticized by the Charity Commission.

If a trustee is unable to agree that the draft minutes are an accurate record of the meeting, they should draw their issue to the attention of the chairman before those minutes are signed. If the trustee is ultimately unable to agree the minutes, then their dissension on a particular issue should be noted and recorded as an addendum to the minutes before they are signed.

Minutes of a trustees' meeting should be provided to all of the charity's trustees. It is wise to provide a copy of the minutes of the annual general meeting to the charity's auditors. It is not necessary to make the minutes of trustees' meetings available for public inspection.

The minute book of the charity should be retained by the charity's secretary and should be kept in a safe place. It is recommended that the minutes of trustees' meetings should be kept for the entire life of the charity. A charitable company is permitted to retain its statutory books on computer.

Remember that although the trustees can invite non-trustees to a meeting (for example, a professional adviser or a staff member), those people cannot vote. Furthermore, charity trustees cannot nominate someone to vote on their behalf.

Code of conduct

Increasingly charities are beginning to use a trustee code of conduct to improve the governance of the charity. The National Council for Voluntary Organisations publishes a model trustee code of conduct, which is in effect a contract between the trustee and the organization whereby the trustee promises to observe the organization's values, avoid conflicts of interest, protect the organization's reputation and participate professionally in board decisions. The benefits of such a code of conduct include:

- defining the role of the trustee;
- improving the day-to-day governance;
- minimizing the risk of misconduct against the organization;
- highlighting certain dangers, such as conflicts of interest;
- enabling the chairman to get alongside a trustee who is not complying with the code and thereby minimizing 'non-performance' by a trustee.

'Blue sky thinking'

Given that trustees serve in a voluntary capacity and use up some of their valuable free time to do so, it is highly unlikely that they will have additional time that can be donated to the charity for what may be considered unproductive endeavours. Despite this, however, many charity boards are now finding the benefit of being able to create a block of time (perhaps on an annual basis) when they can be together and think strategically without a specific agenda.

The Americans call this 'blue sky thinking'. Usually one of the trustees will be a prime mover for such an activity, which takes board members out of the boardroom environment with its detailed agendas and time constraints. Blue sky thinking enables the board to:

- review its performance as a board – perhaps against an agreed checklist (see section 28);
- review the performance of the charity against its stated Objects. In advance of this, it will be helpful to obtain some specific 'beneficiary feedback' from those who are the direct recipients of the charity's activities.
- invite a guest speaker who can speak either on the specific area in which the charity is operating or perhaps on governance and management issues;
- interact with the key staff who may also be invited to participate in all or part of the day;
- have a small group discussion and review of case studies;
- share a meal or other fun activity;
- perhaps invite the Chief Executive of another charity working in a similar field to come and speak to the group and facilitate a sharing of ideas.

Fundamentally, a healthy board that is committed to the growth and development of the charity needs to take time to reflect, think and understand the environment that the charity is working in and to project future trends. Perhaps the old maxim can be applied specifically to charity trustees by saying 'trustee boards that fail to plan, plan to fail'.

Payment of a trustee

The general principle of charity law is that trustees are not entitled to receive any payment from the charity other than the reimbursement of their reasonable out-of-pocket expenses. However, the charity's governing document may permit the remuneration of one or more employees who may also serve as trustees. An example of this would be where a church employs its pastor who also sits on the board of trustees.

If the charity wishes to remunerate an employee (in either a part-time or full-time capacity) who will also be a trustee then the following issues are relevant:

1. A check of the charity's governing document should be made to ensure that specific permission is given to the trustees to make such a payment.
2. Any discussions about the need to remunerate that person should be held without that person being present at the meeting. Neither, for that matter, should the spouse or child of that person participate in the trustees' meeting, even if they are a trustee in their own right.
3. A clear offer letter should be issued by the board setting out the terms and conditions of the employment (conceivably offering a specific contract of employment – see section 16) and setting out the remuneration package (guidance as to the level of remuneration can be sought from the charity's accountants or trustees of similar charities).
4. The accountants of the charity should be advised so that they can oversee the setting up of the appropriate PAYE system in the charity's accounting records.
5. A correctly drawn contract of employment should be prepared for the employee to sign ('boiler-plate' agreements available on the web or from the law stationers are not advised).

The Charities Act 2006 allows for a trustee to be paid by a charity for providing goods or services to it if certain conditions are satisfied. This provision does *not* include a payment for a person serving as a trustee or payment made to a trustee under a contract of employment with the charity. The provision does, however, allow a trustee (and those connected to them either by marriage or close business relations) to be paid, provided that the goods and services provided clearly benefit the charity.

The conditions that need to satisfied before such a payment is made are:

1. The remuneration must be set out in a written agreement and not exceed what is reasonable.
2. Before entering into the agreement, the charity trustees need to agree that it is in the best interests of the charity for the proposed goods/service to be provided by the trustee.
3. The trustee concerned, together with any other charity trustee who is also remunerated, constitute a minority of the persons on the board of the charity.
4. The governing document of the charity must not contain any provision that prohibits the payment of the remuneration to the trustee concerned.
5. Trustees who stand to benefit should take no part in any decision about the agreement.

It is important that this provision, which allows for payment in these circumstances, is not abused by charities. If the governing document does not permit a trustee to be remunerated, then an application can be made to the Charity Commission for specific consent. The Charity Commission will need to be persuaded as to why a specific authority should be given (see Charity Commission guidance note 'Payment of Charity Trustees').

Delegation to committee and sub-groups

The governing document of most charities will permit the trustee board to set up sub-committees. These are small groups to which the board assigns a particular task or area for them to focus on. The tasks delegated can include finance, administration, staff welfare, relocation or other major project. Their role is purely an advisory one, and ultimately they will report back to the board, who will make a decision as to whether or not to implement their findings.

The make-up of these sub-committees can contain non-board members, although it is advisable for a sub-committee to have at least one board member represented thereon.

Some boards also set up advisory groups. This is an opportunity for the charity to benefit from specialist knowledge and experience from people who do not otherwise have the time to commit to full board membership. These groups are usually comprised of non-board members and, whilst they have no official role or decision-making ability, they provide advice to the board based on their knowledge and experience. Often a charity will set up an advisory group that is comprised of specialist professionals who operate in the field that the charity is working in.

Some charities have a Council of Reference or a Board of Governors. Generally speaking, these are well-known people who agree to lend their name to be associated with the charity. They add a degree of kudos and authority to the charity. As with an advisory group, they have no official role or decision-making powers. As a rule, charities who have Boards of Governors or Councils of Reference should ensure that they keep those people updated with the activities of the charity, perhaps on a half-yearly basis. It can be embarrassing if a member of the public approaches one such person, only to be told that they have not heard from the charity for some time!

Andrew Hind, in his book *The Governance and Management of Charities*, makes a persuasive argument for the reduction in the number of sub-committees that the board of a charity set up. He expresses the opinion that in most cases a charity should have no more than four sub-committees:

1. An executive committee
2. An investment committee

3. An Audit committee
4. A remuneration committee

If a charity is to set up a sub-committee, then the trustees must ensure that each committee has clear terms of reference and that the committee comprises people who have the required skills base and experience to enable the sub-committee's deliberations to benefit the charity.

Lastly, it must be remembered that final decisions concerning a charity must be taken by the trustees acting together.

Financial responsibilities of the board

The trustees' financial responsibilities include:

- ensuring that the charity properly administers its income and expenditure;
- approving the annual budget and monitoring the charity's performance against budget;
- establishing the charity's fund-raising policy and monitoring its fund-raising activities;
- ensuring that any investments are made in accordance with the charity's governing document, are made with the benefit of professional advice, and do not put the charity's assets at risk;
- ensuring that the charity's capital and income are used exclusively in furtherance of the charity's stated objectives;
- overseeing any trading activities and ensuring that all tax implications are properly managed;
- having correct systems in place within the charity to minimize the risk of fraud, money laundering or other irregularities;
- ensuring that correct systems are in place concerning the expenditure of the charity's monies;
- approval of the annual accounts.

When the Charity Commission inquire into the affairs of a charity, often the financial management of the charity occupies most of their attention.

Whatever the size of the charity, it is suggested that the following should be observed:

- Provisions to ensure that every cheque or other money transfer document is signed by two different people. Ideally it should be two trustees, but the Charity Commission now recognize that this may be impractical (particularly in the case of small charities that do not have a functioning day-to-day office, thereby necessitating the cheque or other document being transported several miles to find another signature). However, one of the signatures should be by a trustee. Whatever system is in place, the Charity Commission look to the trustee to be ultimately responsible. Therefore, any system for signing cheques and other orders that departs from the 'two trustees principle' needs to sit comfortably with all of the trustees.

- The Charity Commission recommend that blank cheques should not be signed in advance and given to another trustee to countersign.
- No one person (trustee or otherwise) has sole authority to bind the charity, order goods or services without sanction of the board of trustees (save for small items of up to, say, £1,000).
- A policy to ensure that any cash or cheques received by the charity is counted and recorded by two individual people (neither of whom should be the treasurer). This is particularly important in the case of churches where offerings are very often received in cash. It is not acceptable for one person to take the cash home after a service, count it and then pay it into the bank. The offering should be counted before it leaves the building by at least two independent people, who should agree the total and sign a record to that effect. Those records should be kept and passed at the end of the year to the Auditor, who compares them with the paying book. These comments are not intended to suggest any impropriety but rather that trustees must be prepared to go the extra mile to show that there is little or no opportunity of any irregularity taking place.
- The charity's post should also be opened in the presence of two people.
- The charity's assets are protected at all times (for example by adequate insurance policies).

Liability of trustees

If trustees act carefully, lawfully and in accordance with the charity's governing document, then any liabilities they incur as trustees can be properly met out of the charity's resources. If the trustees do not so act, then they may be in breach of trust and can be personally responsible for the liabilities that have been incurred by the charity. As the trustees act together as a board, they will usually be responsible as a board to meet any liability to a third party.

The above principle holds true regardless of the legal structure of the charity. For example, in the case of a charitable company, although the company is a separate legal entity to its directors, the directors will still be liable under charity law if they fail in their duty and a breach of trust occurs. An example of a breach of trust could include:

- spending the charity's monies on activities that are not permitted by the charity's governing document;
- making a bad investment decision – entering into a contract or liability that is out of all proportion to the charity's resources at a time when there is no realistic prospect of the charity having the necessary funds;
- undertaking a course of action that was contrary to professional advice that the trustees had received.

In addition, the directors (trustees) of charitable companies can also be liable for wrongful or fraudulent trading.

The Charities Act 2006 permits the Charity Commission in circumstances where a charity trustee (or its Auditor or Independent Examiner) is or may be personally liable for a breach of trust or a breach of duty, but that he has acted honestly and reasonably, to make an Order relieving that person wholly or partly from any liability. However, this relief does not apply in relation to any personal contractual liability of a charity trustee. Conceivably, therefore, the charity trustee who signs a mortgage deed in favour of a lender to charge the charity's asset to that lender as security for a loan may, if the charity defaults, be excused from liability by the Charity Commission. However, if he signed a personal promise to pay the mortgage under the mortgage deed, he could still be held liable in that personal capacity to the lender.

Charity trustees may be permitted under the governing document to effect trustee indemnity insurance (see section 25). However, the Charity Commission are keen to ensure that if a trustee acts with a total disregard for their responsibility as a trustee, they should not be protected by trustee indemnity insurance. An area of high risk to charity trustees is where the charity has a subsidiary trading company, and great care needs to be exercised in the supervision of the activities of that company.

Succession policy

This is one area in which most charities struggle. The point has already been made that it is difficult enough to recruit trustees for small to medium-sized charities, and the thought of having to find replacement trustees fills most boards with a degree of concern.

However, there are many charities existing today that have on their board people who may have served in that capacity for twenty-five or thirty years, in circumstances where it is questionable whether they can take an objective view about the charity's competencies and activities. Such a person may, by weight of their longevity on the board, be a limiting factor for the board moving forward, and act as a disincentive to new trustees who would otherwise bring fresh ideas and experience to the charity.

Possible solutions to the issue would include:

Enforcing a fixed retirement age: the charity's governing document may require a charity trustee to step down when they reach a certain age. Given that people today often retire from their jobs at between sixty and sixty-five years of age, many of them are open to serving on a board of trustees once they have retired. They undoubtedly bring the great benefits of experience and time, and it would be short-sighted to exclude them from serving by having a retirement age that was the same as the normal retirement age in business. Equally, to have trustees still on the board when they reach eighty years of age could be stretching things a little too far. Perhaps a compromise at, say, seventy-two years of age (the retirement age for judiciary) would be acceptable.

Agreeing service of a trustee for a fixed period: this would apply if the charity were to adopt the rotational method set out below.

A systematic rotation policy: this is a methodology favoured by the Charity Commission, whereby one third of the members of the board automatically come up for retirement at each AGM. They can offer themselves for re-election to serve for, say, two more periods of three years, after which they must leave the board. (See also section 9.)

Whichever methodology is ultimately adopted, the charity needs to weigh carefully the benefits of having new people and ideas refreshing the board on a regular basis with the burden of the lack of continuity in the critical mass of the board caused by constant change.

Perhaps other factors such as demographics (whereby people are less likely to stay in one place for life) means that there will naturally be a rotation in board members, although whether this is enough to ensure that the board of trustees remains invigorated and focused is something that the board in each charity will need to decide for themselves.

There may be a temptation to think of offering the founder of the charity a seat on the board for life. For reasons already discussed in section 6, this is not a good idea. However, he or she could always be offered the position of Patron, which is a largely ceremonial position with little opportunity to influence decisions.

What if?

The board of trustees need to review their 'What if?' strategy on a regular basis – perhaps annually. For example:

What if . . . the Chief Executive leaves? Does the charity have people who are being groomed to take on such a responsibility? What would be the effect on the charity and its programmes? Should there be Key Man Insurance on his life?

What if . . . the charity failed to raise sufficient funds to discharge its obligations for the current year? Can the activities be scaled back and restricted to the level of income that could be raised?

What if . . . a major donor or a major grant provider were to withdraw their patronage? Could the charity disengage from contractual responsibilities without penalty? Would the trustees need to borrow monies to disengage?

What if . . . a claim was made against the charity by an ex-employee, or by the family of a worker who was killed or kidnapped overseas?

What if . . . there was a fire at the charity's headquarters and all the records were lost? Is the system backed up? Could the charity continue to function from another base?

The above are only a sample of the contingencies that could arise. More detailed analysis of risk management is contained in section 25.

The important principle for charity trustees is that where considerable reliance is placed on people, systems and the goodwill and cooperation of third parties, trustees would be unwise to pretend that everything will turn out just as they planned.

Corporate trustee

Remarkably, it seems possible for a corporate trustee to be appointed as one of the trustees of a charity. This would seem to be at variance with the basic provision in charitable organizations whereby trustees can be personally liable for breach of trust (whether they are trustees of an unincorporated charity or directors of a charitable company).

It is possible for a corporate body (i.e. a company) to be the sole trustee of a charity. The responsibilities and liabilities of trusteeship are with that corporate body, but the body itself needs to act through individual persons in order to express its will, although those persons are not themselves trustees of the charity.

The directors of the corporate trustee company will not be held liable by the charity itself, although they could be held liable to the company for any liability the company has incurred in respect of the charity. The directors of a corporate trustee should therefore be familiar with the charity's governing document, and also with the general requirements affecting charity trustees.

It is important to ensure that the governing document of the charity allows for the appointment of a company as a trustee, whether jointly with other individual trustees, or as a sole trustee. If the governing document does not permit this, it may be possible to modify the deed either under the provisions of s74 of the Charities Act 1993, or upon application to the Charity Commission. It is also important to ensure that the corporate body that is to be appointed to act as a charity trustee has the power under its own Memorandum and Articles to do so.

Fundamentally, the test before effecting the appointment of any corporate trustee is to consider whether the appointment will be in the best interests of the charity. Possible grounds for such an appointment would include:

- if the charity is having difficulty in appointing individual trustees and considers that such difficulties will continue into the future;
- if the appointment of a corporate trustee will bring to the charity the benefit that corporation has had either with similar charities, or in the specific field in which the charity is operating;
- if the charity has a separate charitable body that holds the title to the charity's premises and seeks a corporate trustee to be the sole trustee of that charitable body.

For further discussion on the advantages and disadvantages of a corporate trustee, the reader is directed to the Charity Commission guidance paper on the subject.

Custodian trustee

This is defined as a corporate body that has been appointed to have the custody of the trust property of a charity. As such, the custodian trustee holds the title to land, shares, etc., receives the income and remits it to the trustees. The actual functioning of the charity is then carried out by the managing trustees.

An example of this arrangement is where a body holds the ownership of a church building yet leaves the day-to-day running of the church itself in the hands of the local managing trustees.

Official Custodian for Charities: In circumstances where there is likely to be a regular rotation of trustees of a charity, it may be decided that the title to any freehold or leasehold property should be vested in the official custodian who will hold it on trust for the charity. The Official Custodian will have no power to take part in managing the land vested in him. This procedure avoids the need regularly to update the ownership details at the Land Registry.

Trust Corporation: A Trust Corporation is a particular type of corporate trustee being one either appointed by the court or under the Public Trustee Act 1906 to act as a custodian trustee.

SECTION 8 ACCOUNTABILITY

Charitable organizations exist not for the benefit of the founders or the trustees but for the benefit of others. Charities themselves have the potential for exercising considerable power or influence, yet at the same time risk failure of one form or another if they are unclear to whom they are answerable.

Accountability can be defined as being responsible to a person or persons and giving account as to motives, decisions, activities and performance in pursuing the charity's stated goals. Perhaps above all accountability is an attitude.

It is helpful to explore two specific areas of accountability within a charitable organization.

Accountability of the leader (CEO/pastor)

Myles Munroe makes the valid point that 'the key to good leadership is the power to influence through inspiration not manipulation. The danger of leadership is its potential for wielding power without answering to anyone else. Dictatorship can materially occur in the absence of a leader's submission to an authority.'

Arguably, in faith-based charities there is a greater need for accountability, given that leadership in such organizations often includes the element of 'calling' or 'vocation'. In some organizations, the notion that the leader should be accountable to others does not sit comfortably with their position as leader of the organization. However, as we have seen in section 6, an unnecessary stand-off between the trustees and the leader can follow the perception that one or other party is acting in an independent way.

The essential protection of the leader (to say nothing of the charity and its beneficiaries) is in the voluntary submission of the leader to a trusted authority. A leader seeking to be accountable should consider establishing a group of mature, experienced and willing people, who are prepared to spend time with the leader, to understand his/her vision, the charity itself and the constraints under which he/she works, and as a result to offer counsel, challenge, rebuke, correction, encouragement and example. It is suggested that for the relationship to work the following principles will be relevant:

- The group should be of no more than four people.
- The group should function in the same geographical community as the leader in order that they can observe and understand the wider picture.
- The group, or perhaps individuals from it, should meet with the leader regularly to build a relationship and interact.
- The leader should be willing to trust the group implicitly and heed their input.

A wise leader who is prepared to be accountable in this way will find that it forms a secure base from which he or she can operate, and it will enable the leader to innovate and take the appropriate risks, which are the hallmark of those who seek to lead charities.

Accountability of the board of trustees/directors

Trustees are accountable for:

- the exercise of their powers to govern the charity;
- utilizing the resources that they have within the charity to pursue its stated objectives.

They are legally accountable under Charity Law and to the Charity Commission, for submission of accounts and the annual return.

In the case of charitable companies, they are legally accountable under Company Law and to Companies House for submission of the Annual Return and accounts.

In addition to their 'legal' responsibilities, charity trustees can also be accountable to a variety of people and groups including:

- The charity's donors – whether individuals, local authorities, corporations or government.
- The beneficiaries of the charity's 'service'. Under the Charities Act 2006, charities are now required to demonstrate Public Benefit. However, going beyond that, the modern charity should put in place adequate procedures to assess the impact of its work. Indeed, many large donors now require an independent evaluation of the effectiveness of a charity's programme as a condition to their ongoing support.
- Its members (see section 10).
- The general public who are the potential beneficiaries of the charity's activities. It follows that if the charity is not fulfilling its stated objectives, then its services or facilities will not be taken up to the extent that they could be.

The board will also need to consider how it will hold both staff and volunteers accountable.

A salutary reminder that the principle of accountability has not been universally embraced by Christian organizations can be had by visiting the Charity Commission website (www.charitycommission.gov.uk), and viewing the section entitled 'Inquiry Reports'. Reported cases concerning Christian organizations show that in the majority of cases the issues that have arisen can be traced back to a lack of accountability amongst the leaders and/or the trustees of the particular charity.

If faith-based organizations, given their affinity with biblical principles, cannot give a lead in such matters, then it brings into question their integrity in the eyes of the secular authorities.

SECTION 9 ADMINISTRATION

Address/registered office

It is important for each charity to have a registered address that is notified to the Charity Commission and to which information addressed to the charity can be sent.

The registered address receives official correspondence from the Charity Commission and, in the case of a charitable company, from Companies House. Furthermore, the address is designed to receive service of any legal actions.

Care should be taken if the registered address is that of a residence belonging, say, to one of the trustees. If that trustee moves or resigns from the trusteeship, important documents from the Charity Commission may go unanswered, thereby ringing alarm bells with the Charity Commission, and in the case of a charitable company, possibly resulting in that company being struck off the company's register for non-compliance. The efforts to reinstate the organization can be costly, in terms of both time and expense.

The registered address forms part of the charity's details that are disclosed to the public. A visit to the Charity Commission's website gives access to much information about a registered charity, and this information may even include a telephone number for the charity's registered address or their correspondent.

Some charities appoint their lawyers or accountants to provide their registered address so that official documentation will immediately be passed to the persons who need to act on them. The registered address must be a specific street address and not a post office box.

Appointment of directors/trustees

'The board' is made up of the people who form the governing body of the charity. Depending on the nature of the charitable organization, they may be known as trustees, directors, board members, council members, governors or executive committee members.

The initial trustees are appointed when the charitable organization is first registered. Usually they are recruited by the founder as being people who identify with the aims of the organization and can bring necessary skill, vision, leadership and governance to it.

The governing document of most charitable organizations provides that subsequent trustees are appointed by the existing trustees, although nominations may be submitted to the trustees from other sources. In circumstances where the governing document for the organization does not provide a mechanism for the appointment of subsequent trustees, then an application may need to be made to the Charity Commission for assistance.

It is important that the appointment of trustees is recorded correctly. In the case of a charitable company, this involves the filing of a company form 288a with Companies House, and in the case of an unincorporated charity, the notification is to be given to the Charity Commission using the 'Trustee Update Form' available on their website.

In the case of unincorporated charities who own property, special care should be taken to ensure that those trustees in whose name the freehold or lease was first registered have correctly passed on their title to their successors. For example, the title to a charity's property may be registered in the names of 'A, B and C as trustees for the XYZ Charity'. If any or all of those trustees subsequently resign their trusteeship, then the charity may be in some difficulty when it comes to dispose of the property, particularly if those parties can no longer be found. This issue can be resolved in two ways:

1. By a formal Deed of Retirement and Appointment of New Trustees. This is signed by both the retiring trustees and the newly appointed trustees and is registered at the Land Registry to ensure that the registered title is updated; or

2. By the retiring trustees signing a formal transfer document in favour of the new trustees, which would then be registered at the Land Registry.

In both courses of action a Land Registry fee is payable but not Stamp Duty Land Tax.

Special care needs to be taken if an unincorporated charity holds a lease on a property, as it is likely that this lease will have been granted to 'A, B and C as the trustees of the XYZ charity'. If a trustee retires, then it may be necessary to obtain the landlord's consent to the lease being assigned to A, B and D as the new trustees of the charity. This is because the original trustees will have made covenants in the lease that cannot be released without the landlord's consent. Unincorporated charities proposing to take a leasehold property may therefore consider it wise to incorporate or convert to a CIO or a charitable company status before completing the lease.

In the case of a charitable company, the title to a freehold or leasehold property is invariably registered in the name of the charitable company itself, and therefore when its directors rotate there is no need to change the registered title.

Trustees of an unincorporated charity, who wish to overcome the problems associated with transferring land each time the trustees change, can consider applying to the Charity Commission for a certificate incorporating the trustees as a body corporate. If the Charity Commission consider that it is in the interests of the charity, they can grant such a certificate whereupon the charity becomes a corporate body and may transact business in that corporate name. However, the trustees of the charity, notwithstanding their incorporation, shall still be accountable personally for their own actions and for the due administration of the charity and its assets.

The size and make-up of a board of trustees is critical to the charity's effectiveness. Many charities have too few trustees (three is the absolute minimum, but in the event of one of those retiring, the charity is immediately plunged into crisis until a new trustee can be found and appointed). Alternatively, many other charities have a board of trustees that is too large, and the board therefore lacks flexibility and it is difficult adequately to involve all of the trustees.

There is no definitive answer as to the ideal size for a board of trustees, although it is suggested for most small to medium-sized charities (i.e. gross income of up to £3 million), a board comprising between five and nine trustees would be sufficient. It is suggested that to have an 'odd' number of trustees minimizes the chances of a voting deadlock!

Trustees may be appointed in many different ways. Depending on the governing document, these may include:

- being elected at an Annual General Meeting by a vote from the membership of the charity;
- being co-opted on to the board by the board of trustees themselves;
- being nominated by an outside organization that has a significant interest in the work of the charity, for example, a local authority who funds the charity;
- by virtue of the office (*ex officio*) that a person holds, for example, the CEO of a charity.

Trustees who are either nominated from outside or serve on the board in an *ex officio* capacity should be particularly careful in circumstances where a conflict of interest may arise between their position as a trustee and their responsibilities or loyalties to the organization that has nominated them. Their priority as a trustee must always be to do what is in the best interest of the charity. If the conflict of interest is irreconcilable, then at the very least they will need to withdraw from the discussions concerning the issue in hand or in some cases resign their trusteeship completely.

A person is disqualified from acting as a charity trustee if they:

- have unspent convictions for offences involving deception or dishonesty (a conviction is 'spent' between six months and ten years after conviction, depending on the offence; however, custodial sentences in excess of two and a half years can never be 'spent');
- are an undischarged bankrupt;
- have in the past been removed from trusteeship of a charity by the Charity Commission or the Court;
- are disqualified from being a company director under the Company Directors Disqualification Act 1986;
- fail to make payments under a county court administration order;
- have come to an arrangement with their creditors and have not been discharged.

In addition to the above, a person is disqualified from acting as a director of a charitable company if they:

- have been persistently in default of company requirements for filing accounts and documents;
- have been found guilty of fraud or fraudulent trading.

The charity's governing document may contain a restriction on who may be a trustee, and, for example, require a person to be of a particular religious denomination.

A cautionary tale involves the status of the first trustees of a charitable company. It is likely that the first trustees ('directors') of a charitable company include the person(s) who at registration signed the Memorandum and Articles of Association of the organization in their capacity as 'subscribers'. These subscribers became members of the company. When they eventually resign as directors, it is possible that they will forget to resign their status as members of the company. Given that the members of the company are often those who confirm the appointment of directors of the company, there have been cases where subsequent directors have been held to have been incorrectly appointed, and therefore decisions that the 'directors' have made have not been valid. The authority for appointment had in those circumstances remained with the original subscriber(s), who by then would have very little to do with the organization.

Criminal Records Bureau checks

Charities which are either (a) working with children and/or (b) concerned with the care of vulnerable adults in circumstances where the trustees have access to such vulnerable adults in carrying out their normal duties, need to pay special attention to the requirements for Criminal Records Bureau (CRB) checks on the trustees to ensure that a trustee is not disqualified from working with vulnerable people. Currently the Charity Commission's policy is that trustees (a) must be CRB checked where there is a legal requirement to do so and (b) should be checked where there is a legal entitlement to do so.

Fundamentally, each charity and its trustees must decide whether they are legally allowed to carry out CRB checks or whether they are legally required to do so. The burden is therefore on the charity and its trustees to ensure compliance. It is an offence to offer a regulated position (e.g. the position as a trustee of a children's charity) to an individual who is disqualified from working with children, even if the person offering the position did not know that the candidate was disqualified.

There is a legal *requirement* to carry out CRB checks on trustees in the following circumstances:

1. governors of independent schools;
2. trustees of charities that are 'child care organizations';
3. trustees of charities that work with vulnerable adults who are in a care position.

There is a legal *entitlement* to carry out CRB checks on trustees of:

1. charities working with those under the age of 18 in either children's charities or charities in a further education institution involving regular contact with people under 18;
2. charities providing care services for vulnerable adults or the representation of advocacy services for, or access to, vulnerable adults.

As an illustration of the above principles it is likely that CRB checks will need to be carried out on persons who are trustees of:

- youth groups;
- organizations that run facilities that are used by children or that arrange activities such as sports training for children;
- out of school clubs and playgroups;
- organizations that offer counselling to children.

These requirements clearly have implications for churches as in the majority of cases churches are also charities.

The Charity Commission expect that CRB checks should be renewed every three years, and will monitor or review whether or not charities are checking up on the eligibility of their trustees, both when an organization applies to be registered and thereafter through ongoing monitoring. (See also section 18.)

Retirement/removal of trustees

The governing document of the organization may prescribe a length of time for which a person shall serve as a trustee. Difficulties arise in cases where the governing document is silent on the point, particularly if the trustees of the charity have served in that capacity for many years! This fact in itself can serve as a serious deterrent to new trustees joining the board.

The Charity Commission now favour wording in an organization's governing document limiting the period for which a trustee can serve, although permitting that trustee to stand for re-election for a further period. It is suggested that perhaps an initial period of three years, with the ability to be re-elected for a further three years, is a good starting point. At the end of the six-year period the trustee should be required to stand down from the board for a significant period (probably no less than three years), before offering themselves for re-election. Furthermore, a correctly structured rotational policy for the board means that new faces are continually being recruited and ensures that the board benefits from new ideas and new skills.

The disadvantage of a rotational policy can be that it is difficult for the trustee board (given that it perhaps meets two or three times a year) to gel, as its members are constantly rotating. Furthermore, new persons joining the board feel that their period of service is more akin to being on a conveyor belt than sitting on a board of governance.

If the governing document does not contain adequate provisions for retirement (whether after a set period of service or upon reaching a certain age), then those provisions can be added by a resolution of the board. The governing document will need to be carefully reviewed, as such an alteration may require Charity Commission consent (see Appendix 1 paragraph 12). In the case of a charitable company the Memorandum and Articles of Association duly revised need to be lodged with Companies House after the resolution has been made.

A charity will often need different skills of leadership as it grows in size or when the issues with which it is dealing change.

Other factors such as ill-health or an inability to attend trustees' meetings regularly may cut short a trustee's period of service on the board. Given the responsibilities now placed on charity trustees, it is suggested that any trustee who is absent from three consecutive trustees' meetings may need to seriously consider resigning (for their own sake as well as the charity's).

The Charity Commission have the power to remove a trustee who has been found guilty of an offence under the Child Protection legislation.

If the governing document of the charity permits, then a trustee can be removed from office by resolution of the other board members. If the governing document does not contain the power to remove a trustee, then specialist advice will need to be sought. In the case of a charitable company, the members of that company can vote at an Annual General Meeting for the replacement of all or part of the board. In extreme circumstances, the Charity Commission can remove trustees where they have instituted an Inquiry into the charity and have concluded that there has been misconduct or mismanagement and that it is necessary or desirable for the protection of the property of the charity to remove a trustee whose conduct has contributed to or facilitated it.

In circumstances where there is not a clear majority of trustees to vote for the removal of a trustee (or perhaps that trustee is the only one left on the board), an application to the Charity Commission may be necessary.

The secretary

The responsibilities of the secretary include sending out meeting agendas and board papers, taking the minutes at board meetings and the AGM, and undertaking other duties that may be delegated to the secretary by the board or its chairman. In addition, the secretary will complete and file the annual return with the Charity Commission.

A charitable company may be required by law to have a secretary. In addition to the above responsibilities, a charitable companies secretary is required to keep up to date the register of members, the register of directors, the register of charges, notify Companies House of changes, complete the company's annual return and ensure that the company's documents are kept securely.

Specific details of the secretary's responsibilities include:

1. ensuring that proper notice is given of the charity's meeting (with reference to the charity's governing document and the required period of notice for any particular resolutions that are being proposed);
2. ensuring that when the election of officers is to take place, nominations are received by the appropriate date in advance of the meeting;
3. agreeing with the Chairman the proposed agenda;
4. ensuring that any relevant papers are made available to the charity trustees in good time for a board meeting;
5. at the meeting itself, ensuring that any arrangements for a vote or poll which may be needed are in place, that there is the appropriate quorum present throughout the meeting, that apologies for absence are noted and that all decisions made at the meeting are minuted;
6. the production of the minutes after the meeting, agreement of the same with the chairman and their circulation to all those entitled to receive the same.

The treasurer

The treasurer's responsibility is to oversee the financial affairs of the charity, reporting to the board on the charity's financial viability and ensuring that the correct financial records are maintained. This will include interpreting the accounts and the accounting policies to other members of the board in a way that is easy for them to understand.

The treasurer is responsible for liaising with the charity's Auditors/ Independent Examiners, producing the financial records for Audit, and ensuring the Auditors have all the information and clarification that they require to do their job properly.

The treasurer should have sufficient technical expertise to understand and guide the financial affairs of the charity. In a small charitable organization, the treasurer is likely to prepare the financial reports and budgets.

The responsibility of treasurer is very often given to a member of the charity's board, in order to provide a level of expertise at the board table. Church treasurers are very often deacons and serve in a similar capacity.

In larger charities, where the charity has investments, the treasurer will be the person primarily responsible for liaising with the charity's financial advisers and monitoring the investments on behalf of the board to ensure best possible return.

Larger charities may well have a full-time employee serving as a finance director or chief financial officer. In such cases, the treasurer will provide practical interface between the finance director and the board.

It is suggested that the job description of a charity's treasurer could include the following responsibilities, although depending on the size of the charity, not all of this will be applicable.

- Maintaining the appropriate book-keeping system and a petty-cash system
- Responsibility for making the bank reconciliation
- Maintenance of a system for recording and paying bills
- Responsibility to ensure all income due to the charity is received (this includes legacy income)
- Keeping a record of all vouchers for production to the Auditor/Independent Examiner
- Keeping of the charity's cheque book and possibly acting as one of the (two or more) cheque signatories
- Monitoring of the charity's money held on deposit and ensuring a good rate of interest
- Preparing the annual budget for the charity, together with budgets for any specific projects
- Preparing management accounts for the trustees, showing both the 'budget' and 'actual' figures
- Liaison with the charity's accountants/Independent Examiner in order to obtain the Audit/examination of the accounts
- Ensuring the audited/examined accounts are signed off, presented to the AGM and filed with the Charity Commission (and Companies House if applicable)
- Ensuring appropriate reports are made to the charity's main grant-funders
- Liaison with charity's fund-raisers and monitoring the charity's fund-raising projects
- Monitoring of the charity's payroll scheme and ensuring that all returns are made to the HMRC, and tax/National Insurance is paid
- Ensuring the trustees are fully aware of all issues relating to the employment of staff (salaried, freelance or volunteers)

- Ensuring appropriate insurances are maintained
- Coordinating and monitoring the charity's financial and reserves policies

Annual return

Trustees of all registered charities are required to send an Annual Return to the Charity Commission. Usually this document is sent by the Charity Commission to the charity's registered office, partially completed, and the charity is required to complete and return it within a prescribed period. The Charity Commission maintain a record of charities that are persistently late in filing their annual returns, and have adopted a 'naming and shaming' policy on their website.

With the growth of the Internet, the Charity Commission now send out annual returns by email and are prepared to accept the completed document for filing in a similar format.

Charitable companies are also subject to Company Law, which means they must submit and return a Companies House annual return, again within a prescribed period. This is in addition to the one they will also file with the Charity Commission.

Companies House annual returns tend to be in a fairly rigid format, whereas the Charity Commission vary both the format and the questions asked.

In the case of a charitable company's annual return, this is a public document, a copy of which can be obtained readily from Companies House. At present the Charity Commission have not made a charity's annual return available to the public. The Charity Commission's annual return is due ten months after the end of the financial year, and a charitable company's annual return to Companies House is to be filed within six months of the end of the financial year.

Compliance

Trustees of charities (be they unincorporated charities or charitable companies) have a duty to comply with both charity and Company Law requirements. A brief summary of the main areas is set out below:

- All charity trustees must be eligible to serve as trustees (e.g. not disqualified).
- Charity trustees are responsible for ensuring proper compliance with reporting and accounting requirements.

- Charity trustees must ensure the charity complies with the law relating to trading and fund-raising.
- Trustees of a charitable company are also company directors and therefore subject to the Companies Act requirements relating to directors. In addition to the reporting requirements to Companies House, there is an overriding responsibility on them to act in the best interests of the company and to ensure the charitable company does not continue to trade if the trustee knows or should have known that the charitable company is insolvent.
- If the charity employs staff, then issues relating to employment law, health and safety and taxation will be relevant.
- Trustees of charities owning property need to be aware of environmental issues.
- Charities working with children and vulnerable persons need to comply with the relevant provisions (see section 18).
- Data protection issues may relate to the charity's database and other confidential information.
- Charities that trade are subject to the appropriate trading standards and legislation relating to the supply of goods and services.
- Trustees of charities that have an income of over £250,000 per year need to have a Reserves Policy.

See also the sections on Risk management (section 25), Charities working overseas (section 20), Intellectual Property (section 15) and What can go wrong? (section 24).

Trustees are not expected to have an in-depth knowledge of all the legislation that can affect the charity. However, it is important to be aware that legislation exists, and ignorance of the law is no defence. Trustees should be encouraged to take independent legal and accounting advice on the issues that relate to their particular charity and to retain such written advice with the charity's records and keep it reviewed on a regular basis. It is a good practice to ensure that one of the trustees is responsible for making sure that the charity is both aware of, and complies with, the relevant legislation.

It is not a defence for charity trustees to say that they delegated responsibility for compliance to executive staff or other persons (for further details on this, see section 6).

It is good governance practice for trustees to have written policies covering issues such as health and safety, risk management, kidnap and ransom, reserves and child protection.

The Charity Commission have undertaken a 'compliance campaign' to ensure charities are aware of the issues and have systems in place to respond to them. Should the Charity Commission undertake a review visit, they are likely to ask for a sight of the written policies.

Records

A charity should keep a record of its accounts and the supporting papers for a minimum period of six years from the end of the financial year in question. It is not sufficient to point to the fact that the accounts have been filed with the Charity Commission and/or Companies House; the supporting papers themselves must be preserved. It is good governance practice to keep copies of annual returns, contracts and important correspondence for a similar period.

Although there is no minimum period for which a charity should keep records of minutes of its trustees' or board meetings, it is suggested that these should be kept indefinitely. (I recently had good cause to be thankful that the records for a particular charity included the minutes of a trustees' meeting in 1895. The existence of those records enabled the charity to establish title to a piece of land, the sale proceeds of which greatly enriched the charity!)

Many charities keep their major records on computer in an effort to reduce the dependence on paper. The computers should be backed up on a regular basis and the back-up programs kept off site in case of fire at the charity's main office.

The charity's records should be available for inspection by the current trustees, who should be afforded access to records going back to the period before they were appointed to the board.

Charities are obliged to send copies of their accounts to anyone who asks for them (although they are allowed to make a small charge for copying and postage).

As part of 'risk management', many charities are now backing up their entire accounting records in order that a virtual office could be recreated at another location in the case of destruction of the charity's main office. It is now considered excellent practice for a charity to periodically power up the virtual office in order to ensure that the back-up is fully functional. The purpose of backing up the records is to ensure a seamless transition. In cases of emergency, it would be extremely frustrating if the back-up did not allow the charity to continue to function.

SECTION 10 MEMBERSHIP ISSUES

Who are the members?

In an unincorporated charity, any rules concerning membership of the charity will be set out in the governing document of the charity. The governing document also identifies the founding trustees (who are also the members) and explains the procedure for the appointment of new trustees and the retirement of the existing ones.

The governing document of a charitable company is called a Memorandum and Articles of Association. This document will also define who are the members, stipulate the number of members that the charitable company is to have, and provide that the members are responsible for electing the trustees (usually known as directors) at each annual general meeting.

Those setting up new charities can decide how many voting members the charity will have (i.e. will it be limited to the trustees or to a wider group of people?). Those members in turn determine the composition of the trustee board. It is possible for very large charities with considerable income and influence to be regulated by a small number of members who hold complete power. No outside donor or beneficiary of the charity can become a member unless recruited by the existing members.

The membership of a charity (if distinct from the board of directors or the trustees themselves) can have a significant democratic influence over the activities of the trustees. In other words, the membership can hold the directors/trustees accountable, and this is a function that some major donors and grant-makers to a charity are keen to see.

Some charities maintain a large membership and admit to membership almost anyone who has had any meaningful relationship with the charity, be they a donor, a beneficiary of the charity's activity or those who have expressed a keen interest in the charity's work. It is suggested that a large membership can prove to be unwieldy and potentially damaging to the charity. Given that all members are entitled to attend and vote at the charity's annual general meeting, it makes for not only lengthy meetings, but also the possibility that partisan voting may end up replacing one or more of the trustees at each AGM, resulting in a lack of continuity from year to year.

Small charities restrict the membership to the actual directors or trustees for the time being, in which case those people hold the dual role of directors/ trustees and members.

The issue of trustee accountability is addressed elsewhere in this book, but it is good discipline for the board of directors/trustees to question on a regular basis whether in fact they are held accountable for their actions in a meaningful way by the members of the charity.

Some charities have great difficulty in determining who exactly are the members of the charity. The Charities Act 2006 gives the Charity Commission the power to determine who are the members of a charity, either on the application of the charity itself, or following an inquiry by the Charity Commission.

Some UK charities have established subsidiary charities in other parts of the world and regard those subsidiaries as members of the parent charity. Periodically, the parent charity will convene a conference in which all the subsidiary charities are invited to participate, and very often issues of significance for the whole organization are debated and voted on. In such cases, it is suggested that it would be good practice for the governing document of the parent charity to define exactly what voting influence each subsidiary would have. For example, is it to be one subsidiary one vote, or would the voting rights be in proportion to the number of staff controlled by each subsidiary, or perhaps the amount of money that each subsidiary raises from year to year, etc.?

Alternatively, it may be provided that the subsidiaries have no decision-making power but are considered to have a powerful influence on decision-making by voicing a regional or field-led view on important policy issues.

Confusion may exist: (1) in the current law on membership of charities and (2) in many charities themselves as to the identity and role of their members. The following suggestions reflect current thinking.

Charities seeking to build a high profile in the public (both for fund-raising and to extend their charitable objectives) should consider developing an active and engaged membership. Potential benefits include:

- members help keep the trustee boards fresh and accountable;
- they can help to generate income for the charity because of their perception of being involved;
- an active and engaged membership enables member-led lobbying and campaigning;
- it presents to the general public a clear picture of an open participatory and accountable organization.

However, charities wishing to develop an active and engaged membership should look carefully at their governing documents to ensure the role, rights and obligations of members are clearly defined. (If they are not, then an alteration to the governing document, or an addendum, should be prepared.) If there is to be a clear distinction between voting and non-voting members, that fact needs to be stated clearly in order to prevent any dispute at the AGM.

The Charity Commission estimate that approximately 9,000 charities in the UK now have corporate members (i.e. a commercial body such as a trading company). Benefits of corporate membership to the charity include financial support, expertise and influence. Disadvantages include their lack of attendance at the AGM and perhaps the potential of a conflict of interest between the corporation's aims and the charity's best interest. Many corporations are open to membership of a charity, as it gives them a platform to demonstrate their social responsibilities as well as giving them a real voice in the affairs of the charity.

Remember, however, that ultimately the directors/trustees are responsible for the running of the charity. If the charity is intending to strengthen its membership participation, then the following suggestions are made:

- the trustees should be clear about their role and legal responsibility towards the charity's members;
- the members should be clear about their role and responsibilities towards the charity;
- the membership list should be kept completely up to date;
- the governing document of the charity should clearly set out the respective roles and responsibilities of the members.

There is a corresponding responsibility on charity members to ensure that they exercise their rights to vote in the interest of the charity and abide by decisions that are fairly taken within the rules of the charity.

Church membership

Churches are a good example of charities that take the issue of membership quite seriously. They tend to fall into three categories:

1. 'One member one vote' – these churches tend to maintain an active membership list. Would-be members specifically apply and are formally admitted to membership, which usually carries voting rights. Membership can be lost if the person subsequently leaves the church or fails to be in regular attendance. Major issues are put to the general meeting and each member is encouraged to vote. The annual general meeting votes on the appointment of the main officers of the charity (deacons, treasurer, secretary, and in some cases the minister or pastor).
2. 'Consensus membership' – the qualification for membership is as above. Although regular meetings are held, no specific voting is undertaken on an issue. Decisions tend to be taken on a consensus, which is usually led by the church minister or elders.
3. 'Informal membership' – this covers scenarios where regular attendees of the church are called members, although there is no formal procedure for admitting people to membership, and members are not given any specific rights.

Many non-conformist churches draw a clear distinction between the spiritual leadership of the church (the minister, the elders and deacons) and the membership/trustees. Whilst the membership/trustees can and do appoint deacons and in some cases the minister, many churches have disagreed over the years on the question of church government. A fuller discussion of this is contained in section 6, but many church governing documents would benefit by spelling out the difference in responsibility along the following lines:

> The spiritual government and leadership of the church shall remain with the recognized spiritual leadership of the church fellowship and to the extent to which the trustees are not the same persons as the spiritual leadership, the trustees' power shall be confined to the proper management and administration of the charity in accordance with the provisions of this governing document and charity law, and in so doing they shall have full and proper regard to the spiritual leadership and provided always that they shall not act outside of their powers as conferred by this deed and by the general law.

Furthermore, it is considered helpful if the governing document of the church sets out that church's intentions for the meetings of the church, the membership, the minister/pastor, elders and deacons. Many churches also include a statement of belief in their governing document.

As an alternative to including provisions with regard to church membership and its officers in the governing document, it is possible to refer in the governing document to a constitution which is something the church can develop itself and which exists alongside the governing document. In that way, changes can be made to the constitution without the necessity of having to file new documents with the Charity Commission and Companies House each time a change is made.

Charities meetings

The frequency of other meetings and the methodology for calling them is usually set out in the charity's governing document. The courts have agreed that participants at a meeting should be able to see and hear each other, so telephone conference calls may not be acceptable. A brief summary of the types of meetings and the methodology for calling them is summarized below.

Trustees' meeting

The main strategic decisions are usually made at these meetings. A meeting of the trustees can be called by the secretary at the request of any trustee, but usually on the instruction of the chairman. It is not specifically necessary to give formal written notice, as meetings can be arranged informally so long as all the trustees agree. The period of notice to be given of a meeting should be reasonable, unless all parties agree to convene a meeting at short notice. It is considered good practice to circulate an agenda, together with reports and other documents to be considered in advance of the meeting, to give sufficient time for board members to consider them and be prepared to contribute informatively to the meeting.

If a trustee is absent from the United Kingdom, then whilst the regulations in most governing documents of a charitable company say that it is not necessary to give notice to the absent trustee, the remaining trustees should consider carefully the likely impact on that absent trustee if he/she returns to the UK to find a meeting has taken place without their knowledge and in their absence. The charity trustees may wish to invite non-trustees to some of their meetings in order to bring specific input to particular areas of the charity's activity. The non-trustees cannot vote. Good practice suggests that it would be unwise for non-trustees to be present for that part of the agenda that does not specifically concern them.

The governing document usually specifies the quorum needed for a valid meeting. If it does not, then the Charity Commission recommend it should be a minimum of one-third of the total number of trustees, plus one.

The Charity Commission suggest that charities should aim to hold at least two trustee meetings each year, although ultimately the frequency of meeting will depend on the needs of the particular charity.

Annual General Meeting

Not all charities have members or need to have an annual general meeting. The governing documents of the charity will say whether an AGM is required.

An AGM is a meeting for the trustees of an unincorporated charity or charitable company to explain their management of it to the members. It is for the board of directors to agree the date of the AGM and resolve to call it, although the governing document will state when it should be held. The 2006 Companies Act provides that an AGM need not be held unless the company's Articles of Association require it to hold one.

A charitable company needs to observe the provisions of the Companies Act in calling such a meeting, and these require a formal notice that specifies the date, time and place of the meeting and also the fact that it is the AGM. There is a right for a proxy to be appointed and every notice of a members' meeting must state this. It is possible for charitable companies to dispense with the need to hold an AGM in certain circumstances by passing an elective resolution to that effect.

The suggested[1] period of notice for a company meeting is twenty-one days, but meetings can be called at shorter notice if it is agreed by all the members entitled to attend and vote at the meeting. The Companies Act provides that the notice should be in writing and either posted, sent electronically or given to the members personally (if posted, forty-eight hours should be allowed within the postal system before the twenty-one clear days' notice). Notice should also be given to all directors and to the Auditors.

The Charities Act does not specify a similar procedure for convening an AGM (although the charity's governing document may well lay down a timetable). However, it cannot be wrong for the trustees of an unincorporated charity to follow as nearly as possible the procedure observed by a charitable company for convening an AGM. Many churches give notice by

---

1 The 2006 Companies Act now provides that the notice period for meeting is to be reduced from twenty-one days to fourteen days, unless the company's Articles specifically state twenty-one days, in which case the Articles will need to be changed.

way of including details in the weekly notice sheet, and also displaying a notice on the church notice board. It is considered that the trustees need to do all they can to be certain that notice has been given to all the members of the charity, particularly if proposals are to be put to the AGM that may be controversial and will require the members to vote.

Again, it is considered good practice to circulate Annual Reports and accounts prior to the AGM, as this enables issues to be raised and dealt with and closed off at the annual general meeting. Charitable companies are required by law to send copies of the Annual Report and accounts prior to the AGM.

There are two main advantages in a charitable organization holding an Annual General Meeting. First, it gives the trustees the opportunity to explain their leadership of the charity to the members, and secondly, it gives the members the opportunity to ask questions before they vote on any of the business items on the agenda. The trustees are bound to act on decisions taken by members only where the governing document of the charity stipulates that those matters must be decided at such a meeting. It is worth checking the charity's governing document in order to be clear on that point before the meeting, and if the trustees are not bound to act on decisions taken by members, then perhaps the point should be made at the outset of the AGM.

The business usually conducted at the AGM is as set out in the agenda (which should also be circulated prior to the meeting). If any special resolution is to be passed, then the agenda must state that the resolution is to be proposed as a special resolution, and the exact wording of the resolution itself must be given. If any trustees are to retire or be appointed at the AGM, full details of the candidates should be included in the information sent out prior to the AGM.

Minutes of the AGM must be taken. If they are subsequently signed by the chairman of that meeting (or of the next meeting), then they are considered to be evidence of those proceedings, and unless the contrary is proved, the meeting is deemed to have been properly convened and held, and all the proceedings duly conducted.

Given that an AGM is an open forum where charity trustees and members come together for the purpose of open discussion, the possibility of there being a dispute at such a meeting is probably increased. It is helpful for the trustees to consider in advance of the AGM a procedure for dealing with potential disputes at a meeting, and the following points are suggested:

• The chairman should make it clear at the outset of the meeting that all members' behaviour is expected to be to a certain standard throughout.

- The chairman and the trustees should agree a certain point at which the meeting would be adjourned.
- It should be agreed that no new items for the agenda would be received from the membership at the meeting itself (in that way the trustees have advance notice of the issues that are likely to be raised).

A sample agenda for an AGM is set out below.

Agenda

Of the charity [.........]
to be held at [.........]
on the [...] day of [.........] 200. . .

1. Minutes of the previous meeting
2. Matters arising on those minutes
3. Reports and accounts
4. Appointment of Auditors
5. Appointment of charity trustees (including any retirement and reappointment by rotation permitted in the governing document)
6. Proposed resolutions
7. Chief Executive's annual report
8. Financial report
9. Any other business

Extraordinary General Meeting (EGM) and Special General Meeting (SGM)

Any general meeting of the members of a charitable organization other than an Annual General Meeting is known as an Extraordinary General Meeting (sometimes referred to as a Special General Meeting by unincorporated charities). The directors/trustees may call an EGM whenever they think fit, subject to proper notice. Members can also ask the trustees to call an EGM if they feel the trustees are not fulfilling the charity's aims and objectives or the charity is not being administered effectively. The governing document of the charity may well regulate the procedure for calling an EGM. Usually these are meetings of a charity held to deal with 'one-off' matters of business that require approval of the members of the organization in the months between the AGMs. The same people who are qualified to attend an AGM are usually those entitled to attend an EGM (or SGM).

Members of a charitable company holding one tenth of the voting rights at a general meeting may requisition the calling of an EGM by depositing the request at the company's registered office. Upon receipt of that, the directors must call the EGM within twenty-one days and the meeting itself should be held within twenty-eight days after the date of the notice convening the EGM. The period of notice required for the EGM depends on the business to be conducted – if there is to be a special resolution or resolution appointing a director, then twenty-one days' notice must be given. If not, then only fourteen days' notice is required. Again, the meeting can be held on short notice if this is agreed by a majority of the voting members.

It is considered that the right to call an EGM is one that exists for the members of a charitable company only, as there is, subject to any provisions to the contrary in an unincorporated charity's governing document, no statutory right for the members of an unincorporated charity to call such a meeting.

Proxies

If the articles of association of the charitable company allow a member to appoint a proxy, then that proxy may speak at an AGM and vote on a poll, although he does not have the same right as the member appointing him to demand a poll.

Proxies must be appointed in writing and a copy of the appointment delivered to the registered office of the company forty-eight hours before the start of the meeting.

Resolutions

A resolution is an agreement or decision made by the directors or members of a company. When a resolution is passed, the company is bound by it. The types of formal resolutions that are relevant to a meeting of the charitable company/charity are:

Ordinary resolution

For example, to approve the audited accounts of the organization. This is passed by a simple majority of those members voting in person (or by virtue of a proxy if this is permitted) on a vote. An ordinary resolution requires not less than fourteen days' clear notice of the meeting at which it will be considered.

Special resolution

For example, to change the name of the organization or its Objects. A special resolution is passed by a majority of not less than 75% of those members voting in person (and by proxy if permitted) on a vote taken at the meeting. A special resolution requires at least twenty-one days' clear notice of the meeting at which it will be considered.

Extraordinary resolution

For example, to wind up the company. An extraordinary resolution needs to be passed by a majority of not less than 75% of those voting in person (and by proxy if permitted). The notice period for a meeting at which an extraordinary resolution will be considered requires fourteen days' clear notice.

Written resolutions in place of a meeting

Charitable companies may be permitted under the 1989 Companies Act to undertake by a written resolution anything that may be done by a resolution passed at a general or extraordinary meeting, providing necessary procedures are completed.

   Written resolutions cannot be used to remove a director or Auditor before the expiry of their term of office when they would otherwise have a right to make representations to the general meeting. The procedure by which the company undertakes a written resolution (as opposed to convening a general or extraordinary meeting) is as follows:

1. The board of the charitable company should resolve at a properly convened board meeting to utilize the written resolution procedure to pass (if members think fit) the proposed resolution.
2. The form of the written resolution is then prepared and sent with an explanatory letter to each of the members of the charitable company. This letter explains the reasons for the proposed resolution, encloses any supporting documentation and invites the member to sign their agreement (or otherwise) and return the documentation to the secretary of the company by a specified date.
3. The company then also sends a letter at the same time to the Auditors enclosing a copy of the resolution.
4. The written resolution is effective once all the members have signed it, and it becomes effective from the date upon which the last copy of the signed resolution is received by the company's secretary.
5. An appropriate memorandum is then entered in the company's minute books recording the completion of the necessary procedures.

A written resolution procedure may therefore be attractive to charitable companies that have a small membership.

Elective resolution

Again, this is available only for charitable companies and it enables the company to disapply certain statutory requirements.

There are four circumstances whereby a charitable company can use an elective resolution, and a separate resolution will need to be passed for each circumstance.

1. An election to dispense with the holding of an AGM
2. An election to dispense with the laying of accounts or reports before a general meeting
3. An election to dispense with an annual appointment of Auditors
4. An election to reduce the majority required to sanction short notice of a meeting

The procedure for passing an elective resolution is similar to that for a special resolution, except that all members are entitled to attend and vote at a meeting and the company must agree to the passing of the resolution. Twenty-one days' written notice must be given for the meeting at which the elective resolution is to be passed, and the notice sending out the resolution must state that it is to be proposed as an elective resolution.

SECTION 11 ASSOCIATED CHARITIES

'Daughter' churches

Many churches, particularly in non-conformist streams, expand their work by planting other churches in different geographical locations ('daughter churches'). The question often arises as to whether daughter churches should be registered as independent charities in their own right, or whether they should continue to function under the charity registration of the parent church. Having worked with both models over many years, I have come to the firm conclusion that it is better to register each daughter church as a separate independent charity. There are several reasons for this.

- The trustees can exercise their governance responsibilities more effectively if they are locally based. They are able to help the charity to adapt to meet local needs and able to observe first-hand the workings of the charity. In my view, it is unwise for a board of trustees to try to be responsible for a group meeting in another geographical area in circumstances where they have little or no first-hand contact or information.
- There would be a simplified accounting treatment – this means that the accounts of the daughter church can be prepared and audited locally rather than being subsumed into the parent charity's accounts with all the attendant auditing difficulties.

- Strong local leadership is likely to be built up if the leaders are empowered to control and administer their own independent organization.

Notwithstanding that the daughter church is set up as an independent charity, it is still possible for at least one trustee to be common to both parent and daughter, provided that the majority of trustees of the daughter are independent of the parent.

The parent church and the daughter church can be linked in vision, mandate and operational style by a written agreement. Such an agreement can be set up as akin to a 'licensing agreement', particularly if the parent church has a particular name that it is prepared to allow the daughter church to use provided they respect the vision, mandate and operational style of the parent church.

If the daughter church is established as an independent charity, it is vital that the parent church does not seek to control the daughter church in a way that prevents trustees of the daughter church from being able to control their own affairs. Sometimes this can be difficult to achieve, particularly if the parent church is initially underwriting the costs of the daughter church. However, it is a fundamental rule of charity law that the trustees of a charity must have free and unhindered discretion to exercise their trustee function without control or undue influence from any outside source. The parent church may, however, prescribe the type and contents of the governing document and seek to have some constitutional influence on the daughter church, including:

- a requirement that no change of purpose or style of operation may take place without the 'parent's' consent;
- provisions to disallow the continued use of the 'name' for a specific reason;
- a requirement to approve the disposal of any assets of the 'daughter' upon the winding up of the charity.

If the parent church decides to set up the daughter church without it being an independent charity (i.e. the daughter church will exist under the parent charity's registration), then it is possible for the parent church to exert influence and control on the management and function of the daughter church.

'Overseas cousins'

Some UK charities and mission agencies have been set up by, or closely relate in vision to, an established church or charitable agency registered overseas. While this is perfectly workable, there are some potential pitfalls for the unwary, specifically:

- Whilst the UK charity can include on its board trustees who are ordinarily resident overseas, nevertheless the simple majority of the trustees must be ordinarily resident in the UK.
- Ultimate control and decision-making must rest with the UK trustees. This is so even if the overseas body is actually financing the UK one.
- If the overseas body advances money to the UK charity for a special purpose (for example to buy a property), then it is important for the UK trustees to establish in writing whether the asset purchased will:
  a. belong to the overseas body – with the UK one having use of it, either for a rental or for free;
  b. be purchased by the UK charity but with a mortgage or obligation back to the overseas one in respect of the monies advanced;
  c. belong absolutely to the UK charity, in which case the money advanced will be a gift to the UK charity. This means that if the asset is sold for any reason, the money remains with the UK charity.

If the asset is the property of the overseas body, it is important that it is not shown as an asset on the accounts of the UK charity. If it is, then the UK charity trustees will have some explaining to do when the asset is eventually disposed of!

If the UK charity is to send monies back to the overseas organization at any time, then, unless it is in repayment of a specific loan or liability, the trustees of the UK charity must be convinced that sending the money overseas is exclusively in furtherance of the UK charity's Objects.

Some activities that an overseas organization may undertake may be lawful for them, but not charitable in the UK, for example, political lobbying.

Notwithstanding the need to keep the UK charity and the overseas body 'separate', it is still possible to have a legal agreement between the two organizations that defines their shared vision, mandate and operational style.

SECTION 12 PROPERTY ISSUES

For most charities, a property transaction is likely to be one of the largest, and most demanding, projects that they will undertake. Whether it is the price itself, the complexity of a new build or the sheer emotional drain of the transaction, most charity trustees never forget the property transaction!

The Charities Acts do not put any specific constraints on trustees who are purchasing property, whether freehold or leasehold. However, it is always wise to check that the charity's governing document permits the charity to hold property and raise money on mortgage.

Under the Charities Act 1960, trustees were required to obtain the Charity Commission's specific consent before they could enter into a mortgage, grant a lease of more than twenty-two years, or otherwise dispose of land that had been occupied for the charity's purpose. Thankfully things were simplified somewhat by the Charities Act 1993 and those provisions have been largely unaffected by the 2006 Act.

In the main, a charity's property issues are fourfold.

Acquisition

Whilst there are no specific requirements imposed by the Charities Act on the trustees when a charity acquires a property, charity trustees would be wisely advised to consider an independent valuation on the price to ensure they are getting good value. The valuation will take into account not only the property itself but the permitted planning use and the effect of any restrictive covenants on it. The trustees should ensure that the lawyers instructed to act for the charity in the acquisition are fully briefed as to the intended use of the property. A building with a covenant prohibiting the proposed charitable activity or obliging the property to be used only for a specific purpose that is distinctly uncharitable is of little use to the charity. Surprisingly enough, I have seen examples of charities acquiring such a property notwithstanding!

Registered charities are entitled to relief from Stamp Duty Land Tax (SDLT) on the purchase price. However, this relief is only available if all the purchasers are charities or charitable trusts. Therefore, if any of the 'purchasers' are not a charity or charitable trust, then no SDLT relief is available on the purchase price at all. Relief is only available if the conditions as to the use of the property are satisfied. There is no such relief from Land Registry fees, which are payable at the appropriate scale on the purchase price.

The trustees should decide how the property will be held. For example, will they hold it in their own names upon trust for the charity, or will they use a custodian trustee, or the official custodian of charities? In the case of a charitable company, the property is registered in the name of the charitable company itself and, as discussed in section 9, that avoids the need for constantly changing the registered proprietors when trustees change.

Upon completion of the registration of title, the Land Registry will enter a restriction on the title to the land, effectively preventing a sale by the registered proprietor unless the provisions of s37 of the Charities Act 1993 are complied with.

When the charity is considering acquiring a property on lease there are three specific points to make:

1. The covenants in the lease need to be carefully reviewed (and interpreted by a property lawyer) to ensure that they are not onerous to the charity.
2. A check should be made to see whether the lease has the provisions of s24 to s28 of the Landlord and Tenant Act 1954 specifically excluded. Those provisions normally permit a renewal of the lease at the end of the term on substantially the same terms as the original lease was granted (save for an adjustment in rent). It follows that if the provisions of that Act have been excluded, then the charity will have no automatic right to renew the lease at the end of the term.
3. Careful attention should be paid to any rent review provisions that may be contained within the lease. These allow the landlord to negotiate to increase the rent at various times during the lease (usually every three or five years). The charity trustees will need to take specialist advice from a chartered

surveyor to ensure that any necessary notices are served, and the rent review negotiations are properly handled. It is not for the trustees to agree an increase in rent that may be out of proportion to the average market rents in that area, however encouraging the landlord may have been towards the charity!

Disposal

Registered charities and charities excepted from registration (but not exempt charities) may sell or lease land held by or in trust for it, without an order of the court or the Charity Commission, providing certain conditions are complied with and the sale is not to a 'connected person, or a trustee or nominee of a connected person'. (A 'connected person' is defined as a trustee of the charity, a person who is the donor of any land to the charity, a child, parent, grandchild, grandparent, brother or sister of any trustee or donor, an officer or an agent or employee of the charity, the spouse of any person falling within any of the above, an organization that is 'controlled' by any of the above, or a corporate body in which any connected person has a substantial interest.)

The conditions and the usual procedure for the charity to comply with before it disposes of land (providing it is to a non-connected person) are as follows:

1. The charity trustees must obtain and consider a written report on the proposed sale from a qualified surveyor instructed by the trustees and acting exclusively for the charity.
2. The trustees should advertise the proposed sale in such manner as the surveyor advises in his report, unless in that report he has said it would not be in the best interest of the charity to advertise the proposed sale, and the trustees decide they are satisfied, having considered his report, that the terms of the proposed sale are the best that can reasonably be obtained for the charity.

This procedure covers all 'sales' including surrenders or assignments of leases and the granting of easements.

Once the above conditions have been complied with, the sale contract and subsequent transfer document or lease will contain specific provisions under the Charities Act 1993, which are in effect statements made by the trustees that they have complied with these provisions of the act, whereupon the sale can proceed without the consent of the Charity Commission.

In some instances, the trusts on which the charity holds land stipulate that it be used for the specific purposes of that charity. For example, land may be given to a charity on condition that it is used as a young people's camp ground. In such cases, the trustees cannot sell, lease or dispose of the land unless they have given public notice of the proposed transaction, have invited representations to be made within a set period and have taken into account any representations made to them. This provision does not apply if the purpose of the sale is with a view to acquiring a replacement property that will be held on the selfsame trusts, or the transaction is itself the granting of a lease for a term of two years or under.

The provisions above do not apply:

- to any sale for which a specific authority is given (e.g. a Charity Commission Scheme or Order);
- if the disposal is made to another charity for less than its probable value, provided that the disposal is authorized within the Objects of the disposing charity;
- to a lease to a beneficiary of the charity at less than market rent, provided that the property is to be occupied for the purpose of the charity.

Leases

If the charity proposes to grant a lease for a period not exceeding seven years, then the charity must:

1. obtain and consider advice on the proposed grant of the lease from a person (not necessarily a qualified surveyor) whom the trustees reasonably believe to have the necessary ability and practical experience to provide them with competent advice on the matter;
2. decide that they are satisfied, having considered that person's advice, that the proposed terms for the transaction are the best that can be reasonably obtained for the charity.

The grant of a lease for a period of more than seven years is dealt with in the same manner as the proposed sale of freehold property by the charity (as set out above).

Mortgages

As mentioned above, the Charity Commission's specific consent will not be needed in connection with a loan or grant in situations where the charity trustees have, before signing the mortgage, obtained and considered proper advice given to them in writing addressing:

a. whether the proposed loan or grant is necessary in order for the charity trustees to be able to pursue the particular activity in connection with which the loan or grant is to be taken – for example, to purchase a property;
b. whether the terms of the proposed loan or grant are reasonable in regard to the status of the charity as the proposed recipient of the loan or grant; and
c. the ability of the charity to repay the loan or grant on the terms offered.

The person who provides such advice must be someone who is reasonably believed by the trustees to be qualified by his ability and practical experience of financial matters and who has no financial interest in the making of the loan itself.

The mortgage deed must state the fact that the land is held by or in trust for a charity and contains the appropriate statements under the Charities Act 1993. Furthermore, the mortgage itself must state that the trustees have power under the governing document of the charity to grant the mortgage and that they have considered the advice that has been given to them.

If the mortgage is to secure the discharge of any other proposed obligation, for example, a mortgage that secures a guarantee that may have been given by the charity, the 'proper advice' should address whether or not it is reasonable for the trustees to undertake to discharge that guarantee obligation having regard to the charity's purposes.

There are two specific riders to add to this:

1. In some cases, banks and other financial institutions loaning money to charities take the view that their status is perhaps not the same as a commercial company or a purchaser of a residential property, and this results in the interest rate being a little higher than would be paid by a commercial or residential buyer. The written advice that is given to the trustees should address the issue of the interest rate. If it is unreasonably high (I have seen some that quote a very high rate of interest, which is then reduced substantially provided loan repayments are regularly made), then those unusual provisions need to be reported to the trustees. If in doubt, the trustees must seek the Charity Commission's specific consent before proceeding with the mortgage, as they could be criticized if the charity subsequently failed to make regular repayments and a loss resulted.
2. The trustees of the charity (whether unincorporated or incorporated) need to check carefully the terms of the mortgage deed, as they may be

liable personally on the direct covenant in the mortgage deed. This means that if the bank or financial institution need to repossess the property and subsequently sell the same, and if there is any loss, they may decide to come after the trustees personally for that loss. If the charity has no other assets, the trustees may need to make good the loss.

Miscellaneous

S82 of the Charities Act 1993 allows the trustees to pass a resolution empowering two or more of their number to sign deeds and documents on behalf of all the trustees. This is of assistance when the trustee board is quite large, as it saves documents having to be circulated amongst a number of trustees for signature. Obviously it applies only to unincorporated charities, as charitable companies can sign all documents by one director and the company secretary, or by two directors.

The Charity Commission can make an Order under s26 of the Charities Act 1993 to authorize an action where they are satisfied that the action proposed in the administration of the charity is in the best interests of the charity. This is a useful provision, as under it the Charity Commission can make good any apparent defect in the charity's governing document in order to authorize a particular property transaction. It also extends to general administrative provisions that may need to be specifically authorized and is therefore not limited to authorizing property-related matters.

Compulsory Purchase Orders are binding on a charity in exactly the same way as they would be on an individual or a company. If the charity is the recipient of a CPO, it is essential that professional surveyors are instructed immediately to negotiate on behalf of the charity to get the appropriate level of compensation for the land itself and the costs of relocation.

Special care needs to be taken where charities use or occupy property that belongs to one or more members of its board of trustees. If the use by the charity is entirely 'rent-free' (i.e. no benefit of any kind is passing from the charity to the trustee in return for the use of the premises), then the situation is permissible. However, it is strongly advised that the fact that the use is 'rent-free', together with any other arrangements as to the length of term and restrictions on use, is documented (preferably in the charity's minutes book) so there is no misunderstanding in the future.

In situations where it is proposed that the charity will make a payment of some kind to the trustee, then great care needs to be exercised by the charity. The negotiations between the charity and the trustee in question should be handled by an independent surveyor/valuer, who should then report to the charity on whether this is in their best interests and whether the level of rent or other considerations are reasonable for the locality and type of property concerned. This care is necessary, as it is a fundamental principle of charity law that trustees should not benefit directly from the charity that they are serving. See also section 24 with regard to conflicts of interest.

Church or charity development projects

It is not uncommon today for churches and charities to be involved in development schemes. Based upon my experience of such schemes over the last thirty years, the following points are offered as observations that I have made:

- It is essential for an independent professional to be appointed who can advise on the viability and conduct of the whole project. Many trustee boards have become starry-eyed as to the possibilities, and have overlooked some of the down-side that exists in most development projects.
- It is important to appoint a 'project manager'. It is helpful if that person has also had some experience of property development, but his/her main role is to be the contact point for the trustees and those who are advising or carrying out the project.
- It is impractical for the entire trustee board to be involved in every detail of the project. By establishing a small working group with appropriate skills, who are then given appropriate authority to reach decisions quickly and report back to the full board, it will avoid unnecessary frustrations. It is clearly impractical to call a board meeting every time the builder wants to make a small change.
- It is seldom wise for the pastor or spiritual leader to be the project manager or to be intimately involved in leading the project. His role as the spiritual shepherd could be neglected, as it is all too easy to become intoxicated by the thrill of the project that is going to deliver a sparkling new building to the charity.

A feasibility report is essential, together with appropriate tax/VAT advice. The trustees may well turn this into a formal business plan, which is likely to be required by a bank or other funder as a condition of providing the finance. A bank or other funder will, in addition to being convinced of the viability of the project, require to be satisfied that the church itself represents an acceptable risk for the loan. Churches who have fewer than three years audited accounts, or who have a history of splits and divisions, are unlikely to be accepted by funders on normal commercial terms.

Joint venture arrangements with an outside developer need to be carefully negotiated and documented. Within the same project are two conflicting goals – the developer wishes to make a profit and the church wishes to obtain its facility for little or no money. The church needs to guard against letting the developer have unfettered use of its asset (for example the land) in circumstances where the charity is left unsecured if the developer fails in any way.

The use of a limited company as ' special purpose vehicle' for a development project is often considered a wise way to proceed. The limited liability (albeit that the shares or a proportion of them will be held by the charity) means that the trustees have another level of protection as they enter into the project. All development projects carry a level of risk that is somewhat higher than the traditional purchase or sale of a property. The use of a limited company may also have certain tax and VAT benefits.

Town and country planning

Each type of property is given a 'use class' by the Town and Country Planning (Use Classes) Order 1987. In the case of a shop, it is A1, in the case of an office it is B1, and in the case of a church it is D1.

To 'change the use' of a property involves obtaining consent from the local planning authority to switch the use from one class to another. For the most part this involves a full planning application. Whilst there are national guiding principles given to local planning authorities, the local planning authority is also able to impose its own restrictions on the kind of use that it allows certain buildings in its area.

Local planning authorities have shown a marked reluctance to permit a change of use from commercial or retail to a church property. On the whole, they are not anxious to see the loss of employment opportunities in areas that are primarily commercial, and they consider that if a property is used by a church, then it is likely that less employment opportunities will exist as a result. There is also the small matter of the fact that they will receive a substantially reduced business rate on a property used by a charity than they will on a property used for commercial purposes!

Charity trustees should not proceed with the purchase of, or the taking of, a lease of a property that will involve the change of use from one class to another without having a clear indication from the local authority that in principle such a change would be accepted. Clearly the local planning authority will not give an instant decision and will usually require a full application. However, they will usually say whether such an application would meet with their support or whether, in fact, they would oppose it.

Specialist professional advice on town and country planning issues is essential for the trustees before they commit to purchase or lease a property that would require a change of use. In some cases, it may be possible to negotiate to purchase a property subject to a successful application for change of use. In that case, the contract is exchanged conditionally on the change of use being granted, and completion takes place after the planning consent has been given. If, however, the planning consent is refused, then the conditional contract can be set aside.

In circumstances where the charity is occupying a property within the permitted use under the Town and Country Planning (Use Classes) Order 1987 and then desires to set up other operations in the property that involve a different use class (a mixed use), then the trustees need to be very careful that such a mixed use will not put them in breach of the planning laws. For example, a church that has a bookshop or a coffee shop solely for those visiting the church is unlikely to attract the interests of the planning authority. However, contrast that with a church who wishes to rent off specific parts of its building to outside organizations to use for something the local planning authority are likely to consider to need a change of use.

Enforcement action is when the local planning authority decides that the present use to which the building is being put (in whole or in part) is contrary to the permitted planning use for that property. They will usually give the property owner a period of time to change the use back to the permitted one, and in default of that they will serve an Enforcement Notice. Whilst it is open for the charity to appeal against the enforcement action, ultimately if that appeal fails, then continued use in contravention is a criminal offence.

If a person wishes to appeal against either a refusal of planning permission or service of an Enforcement Notice, then the applicant can request either a public enquiry or an appeal dealt with by way of written representation. In either case, specialist planning and legal advice should be taken. The costs involved in a public enquiry are not for the faint-hearted!

SECTION 13 CHARITY CONTRACTS

Contracts bring benefits, but also responsibilities. Charity trustees should take more than a passing interest in the contracts signed by and with the charity. In the case of unincorporated charities, the trustees could be personally liable!

For the purpose of this section, we shall consider the charity's contracts in two separate sections: those that benefit the charity; and those that benefit others.

1. Contracts that benefit the charity can include:
    1.1 A contract to acquire something for the charity, for example a lease or HP agreement on a vehicle
    1.2 A contract for funding, for example a grant
    1.3 Contracts with the charity's staff
    1.4 Contracts with outside suppliers, for example agencies
2. Contracts that benefit others can include:
    2.1 A contract for the charity to provide services, for example a contract with the local authority for the charity to provide its services
    2.2 A contract with another organization to provide for the charity and that other to pursue a common purpose, for example a joint venture

Looking at each of these in turn:

1.1 Any such contract, which is in effect a long-term financial commitment, should be entered into only after the trustees have determined that the charity can afford the regular payments. As mentioned above, in the case of an unincorporated charity it is likely that the trustees will be personally liable if the charity defaults. Indeed one or more of the trustees may be asked to stand as guarantor under the agreement.

1.2 Grant funding to a charity often comes in an agreement whereby, in return for the payment of money to the charity, the charity is expected to deliver its service to certain standards and pre-agreed timetables. It is important that the charity determines that any such targets are realistic, in order to avoid any claim for repayment. Furthermore, grant making organizations often reserve the right to conduct an audit to determine the way in which the charity has spent the money and the results of the projects that have been funded. It is not uncommon for a charity to be asked to repay all or part of the grant, either because the project could not be completed, or for some error or omission in the way in which the charity accounted for the expenditure.

Furthermore, a worrying trend has developed in recent years, where the grant funders have delayed payments or have altered the terms of the funding during the term of the contract, thereby causing extreme cash flow problems for the recipient charity.

1.3 Staff contracts are some of the most important contracts that the charity will sign. (See section 16.)

1.4 Contracts with outside suppliers need to be reviewed periodically to ensure the charity is getting best value for the services it is purchasing. Such contracts can range from those for the office equipment to human resource agencies.

2 Where the charity enters into a contract to provide its services for the benefit of others, care needs to be taken for the following reasons:

2.1 If the charity is operating under a fixed-price contract, it needs to ensure that it fully understands its cost base and is confident it can provide the service (for the term of the contract), even if it has to buy in outside assistance.

Trustees should be alert to the potential loss of independence for the charity in as much as the charity can look at such contracts as a useful means of income and in due course be dependent on a particular source and subject to the dictates of that funding source. As mentioned elsewhere, it is essential that the charity does not compromise its independence and therefore its ability to be innovative and a real force for change in its chosen charitable objective.

2.2 If the charity is considering entering into a contract jointly with
another charity or organization, then whilst such an arrangement may
spread the financial risk and make the service more effective, the two
organizations need to consider:

- what their individual contributions and duties will be;
- how they will divide both the income and the expenditure between the two
  organizations;
- what happens if the two organizations disagree – who would resolve the
  dispute? How would liability be apportioned between them?
- whether one party has the ability to bind the other into a contract or
  arrangement.

If the joint venture is between a charity and a commercial concern (for
example, where a charity desires to work with a property developer in developing land for the benefit of the charity), care should be taken to ensure that
the charity is not exposed to unacceptable risk. A special purpose company
(a joint venture company) may be preferable (see section 12).

Potential risks

Ultimately, trustees are legally responsible for a contract to which the
employees of the charity may have committed the charity (this may be the
case even when the trustees have not authorized an employee directly to
enter into that contract). Trustees should therefore ensure that internal controls are in place in the charity so that the charity cannot be committed to
significant liabilities under a contract without the trustees' prior approval.
The Charity Commission have a useful guidance (Internal Financial Controls
for Charities), which is available on their website.

Charities need to ensure that the proposed activity to be regulated under
the contract is, in fact, exclusively in furtherance of the charity's stated
objectives. For example, if the charity exists to provide books to church
leaders in Africa, a contract obliging the charity to provide a translator to
translate a book for a South American country would be inconsistent. If
the contract is within the charity's Objects, then liability that arises under the
contract can be settled out of the charity's monies. However, if that contract is for a purpose that is distinct from the charity's Objects, then the
trustees are actually in breach of the trusts of the charity and could be personally liable for the performance of that contract and any liabilities that
arise under it.

NB: It is unlikely that the Charity Commission would permit the objects clause of a charity to be changed so that it could enter into a contract, if the subject matter of that contract was quite distinct from the charity's Objects in its governing document.

Specific areas of risk include:

Cancellation of the contract

This can result in the loss of income to the charity, damage to its reputation, liability for expenses without the corresponding assurance of income, and possibly a claim on the charity for return of all or part of the monies paid under the contract. If the charity cannot deliver the service or the product contracted, the charity is exposed to a potential claim for damages.

Loss of independence

A possible compromise of the charity's independence may occur by virtue of it becoming dependent upon one or more major contracts. Reliance upon the contracting parties' terms and conditions for payment could adversely affect the charity's cash flow. Unless the charity has reserves, it may be forced to borrow monies in order to maintain cash flow.

Possible tax and VAT implications

These could include the withdrawal of the percentage relief from business rates on the charity's property, if the property is no longer being 'wholly or mainly' used for charitable purposes, due to a contract with a commercial concern.

Minimizing risk

A separate company could be established to provide the service under the contract in question. This would be either a company limited by guarantee (without charitable status) or a commercial trading company. Other steps to minimize risk could include:

Insurance

There are three kinds of policy that could be applicable:

1. a commercial insurance policy to cover fire, theft, occupiers liability, or third-party liability;
2. public liability insurance (this provides indemnity if someone is injured as a result of the negligence of one of the charity's employees);

3. indemnity insurance (this would indemnify the contracting party as a result of losses that may come from the failure of the charity or be a policy to indemnify the trustees of the charity against contractual liabilities, which they may have to pay out of their own pocket).

Independent legal advice

This would cover areas such as whether or not the charity's Objects allow it to enter into the contract, the contract itself, and any resultant liability (for example, if the contract obligated the charity to take on a lease of a property). In addition, wording may need to be written into the contract to limit the liability under the contract to the value of the assets that the charity has legally available to meet such liability.

SECTION 14 INFORMATION TECHNOLOGY

Website and email

Using electronic media provides many benefits to charities – speed of communication, research, access to statutory bodies such as Companies House
or the Charity Commission (for filing returns), and the ability to do banking
'online'. However, along with the benefits come responsibilities.

The charity is responsible for the contents of its website – even if it contracted with another company to produce or manage the same. Therefore:

- It is important to ensure that the charity can support all statements,
  opinions and representations that it makes on its website.
- Any resources produced by other organizations and offered on the website
  must be consistent with the charity's Objects. For example, to offer a book
  that contains statements that are controversial and distinct from the
  Objects of the charity may produce complaints and lead to the Charity
  Commission asking for its removal from the site.
- All links from the charity's website to other websites should be to those
  broadly supportive of the charity's Objects and main purpose.
- The charity must not promote anything which may be illegal, offensive,
  embarrassing or discriminatory.
- The charity is ultimately responsible for all emails that are sent out from its
  server. If the charity allows the staff to have personal use of the email

facility, then a policy should be in place to define the purposes for which it can be used.

• The charity needs to ensure that the server is reasonably protected by a suitable firewall from those who would try to get access to the charity's records or database.

It is important for a charity to back up all work regularly on the system and to ensure backed-up copies are stored off site and can be used to recreate the appropriate records and database in the event of damage or destruction.

Policy on the use of information technology

Charities are well advised to set out a policy that is binding upon their employees/volunteers concerning the use of the charity's IT systems. This would include telephones, computers, fax machines and any other electronic telecommunication equipment. Compliance with the policy could be linked to the staff member's employment contract to ensure the appropriate disciplinary procedures are applied in the event of a breach.

The main contents of such a policy would include:

• Security of the system – ensuring that passwords are not disclosed to third parties and outside persons who do not have use of the IT system.
• Inappropriate use of the IT system – to preclude the equipment being used to receive, browse, download or store material that may be illegal, offensive or embarrassing. Furthermore, to ensure that all personal use is consistent with the charity's rules, policies and procedures.
• Monitoring – the charity formally reserving the right to monitor emails, voicemails and other data held on the IT system.
• Emails – reminding staff that what is disclosed in emails can give rise to personal or charity liability. Given the possibility that emails may be read by unintended recipients, great care should be taken on the contents of each email.
• The worldwide web – ensuring that the charity's IT system is not used to access any sites that could be regarded as illegal, offensive, in bad taste or immoral.

SECTION 15 INTELLECTUAL PROPERTY

Intellectual Property is the collective name given to describe the ownership of the rights to intangible items that are nevertheless assets of a charity, for example a name, a logo, a publication or a recording. Although initially the worth of those rights may be difficult to calculate, nevertheless they have a certain value to an organization and can be worth protecting. Such protection can come in the following ways.

Copyright

It is not an idea that is copyrighted, but the way in which that idea is expressed. Copyright can cover written, artistic, musical and dramatic works. For example, once a book has been written or a song composed, then providing it is an original work, it is capable of being copyrighted.

Generally speaking, copyright lasts for the life of the author of the work plus an additional seventy years. The copyright owner has the right to prevent another person from copying or publishing that work. In fact, it is not necessary for the copyright itself to be registered formally, although the person entitled to the copyright would usually affix a legend ('copyright © Paul Martin 2007') on any works they wish to protect. This action both establishes their claim to the copyright and warns the public at large not to infringe it.

Charities involved in publishing and/or the production of music and dramatic works should take care to research the issue of copyright carefully and understand how it applies to the charity's activities. For further information on this important subject, the reader should take specialist advice.

Trademark

A trademark is a sign (usually shown as 'TM') which distinguishes the goods and services of one organization from another, for example a logo or a brand name.

If a charity wishes to register a trademark, the registration will give the owner the exclusive right to use that mark for the particular goods or services for which it has been registered. Clearly, before a mark can be registered, it has to be distinguishable from any other registered marks.

Patent

Patents cover new inventions that have the potential for a commercial application. Once granted, a patent gives the inventor an exclusive period (currently twenty years in the UK), during which he can stop others using the invention. Patents are often granted for new drug compounds or methods of manufacture. They are granted by the UK Patent Office and before one is granted the invention is carefully examined. The process can take several years and may be very expensive.

The main areas in which charities may be concerned about intellectual property rights include:

Publications
The charity, or those employed by it, may write manuals, books and other documentation that may have some commercial value at the time they are written. In such circumstances, the charity would be wise to affix the © to the works they have produced. However, before doing so the issue of ownership may need to clarified. Take for an example the instance where the pastor of a church writes a book that is subsequently marketed. Who can rightfully claim the copyright in the authorship? The church may claim the authorship of the work on the basis that the pastor is employed by the church full time and that he wrote the book during the period of his employment. Alternatively, the pastor may claim the copyright and authorship on the basis that he wrote the book in his spare time.

It is suggested that, to save such a dispute arising, the pastor's contract of employment should make clear the issue of ownership in any works (written or musical) that the pastor may produce during his employment. If it is not made clear, then the strong presumption is that the copyright and the ownership rests with the church as the employer. If the pastor wishes to be able to claim the copyright (and therefore receive the royalties), his employment contract should make that point clear at the outset.

Recordings

Copyright in any new music or songs written by a member of the church or charity will belong to them, and if the church wishes to use the songs on a regular basis, they will need to come to an appropriate arrangement.

If there is to be a live music performance in the church, then ordinarily the consent of the owner of the copyright in the music (provided the music is still in copyright) will be required. This is often dealt with by paying a licence fee to the Performing Rights Society. However, there is an exception to this rule where music is played in a church or other worship service.

If the performance is to be of pre-recorded music, then ordinarily consent is required from both the Performing Rights Society (copyright) and the Phonographic Performance Ltd (Public Performance). However, again there is an exception where the playing of the sound recording is heard in public as part of the activities of, or for the benefit of, a charity. In this example, if the public are charged an admission price for the performance, then the exception can be claimed only if the admission charge is applied exclusively for the benefit of the charity itself.

Churches and Christian organizations seeking to reproduce songs for public worship and include them in their song book or service sheet, or project them, are advised to take advantage of the copyright scheme administered by Christian Copyright Licensing International. For a small annual subscription it allows most hymns and worship songs to be reproduced for public worship, provided that the appropriate acknowledgment is included at the end of each song, quoting the 'CCL' and the licence holder's number.

Websites

Any written material or music included in a charity's website is legal only when permission has been obtained in writing from the copyright owner.

Name

A charity's name may become increasingly valuable over a period of time, particularly if the charity has become well known for innovative and unique work. To successfully defend a charity's name against any party seeking to use it or a name that is remarkably close to it would require the charity to show that is has built up good will or reputation in that name over many years.

Protection

A charity can consider protecting its intellectual property in one of the following ways:

1. Passing off

A passing off action can protect good will, a name, copyright and even the product itself. To succeed in an action for passing off, the charity will need to show that the third party whose action is adopting the name, style or appearance of the organization is likely to confuse the public and lead them to believe that the organization's goods and services and the third party's are one and the same. However, it is also necessary to show that the charity is likely to suffer damage to its reputation and/or lose out financially. Passing off actions are usually very expensive, mainly because they are difficult to prove.

2. Trademark action

If the charity has a registered trademark, then action can be commenced based on that trademark against any third party that is infringing the same.

3. Confidentiality

Before disclosing any information owned by the charity which could cause the charity damage if such information was supplied to a third party (confidential information), then consider the use of a Confidentiality and Non-disclosure Agreement. Such an agreement puts the third party to whom this information is disclosed (for example, a marketing company who may be retained by the charity to advise on the marketing and promotion of a particular issue) on notice that, if they allow the confidential information to be communicated to the public at large, or to a competitor, then they could be liable in damages to the charity.

4. Assignment

If the charity has ordered and paid for a unique piece of work, for example a design or a particular piece of music to be written for it, then they should consider obliging the originator of the work to assign its copyright specifically to the charity. This would then allow the charity to utilize that design and exploit it commercially, although the originator may ask for royalties in return for either assigning or licensing the use of the work.

For further information on this important subject, please look at the Patent Office website at www.ipo.gov.uk and the Christian Copyright Licensing International website at www.ccli.co.uk.

SECTION 16 EMPLOYMENT AND DISCRIMINATION ISSUES

One of the most noticeable areas of growth in regulation in recent years has been in the area of the employment and management of staff.

With the growing trend towards the protection of and provision for employees' and workers' rights in the United Kingdom, there is now much at stake for all employers. The number of tribunal claims grows year on year, and this has become a key consideration in any charity's approach to risk management. In addition, wave after wave of legislation has tightened the regulation upon all organizations in respect of how they deal with their staff, how they handle disputes, and how they recruit and select potential employees or workers.

Following the declining influence of trade unions in the United Kingdom, the area of employment relations is now dominated by legal regulation and strict procedures with which employers must comply.

Establishing employment status

It is important to establish the status of those individuals who are working for an organization. It is vital to question into which category each individual working for the charity should rightfully be placed. They may be an employee, a worker, an agency worker, a self-employed contractor, or, as in the case of many charities, a volunteer. It is essential to be clear at the outset, as the status of each individual can have serious consequences for both the organization and the individual.

Individuals may have status as one of the following.

Employees

There are several criteria that need to be assessed for such status to be conferred, as the definition is not apparent from legislation. The Employment Rights Act 1996 defines an employee as 'an individual who has entered into work under a contract of employment'. In the same statute, a contract of employment is defined as a contract of service or apprenticeship, whether express or implied.

The important point to note with regard to these definitions is that the employment contract may be express, or implied. Therefore, if a certain working relationship and criteria can be established, a contract of employment may be found to exist (even in the absence of a signed, written contract), and the individual will be an employee of the organization for whom they work.

There are three criteria that are applied to help decide whether or not an individual is an employee:

1. Mutuality of obligation: This is often known as the 'work/wage bargain'. That is, the employer will provide work for the employee to do and will pay the employee to undertake that work. The employee will satisfy their side of this 'bargain' by undertaking that work in the appropriate manner.
2. Control: As the word suggests, this points to the employer having a sufficient degree of control over the employee, to the extent that they may provide orders and tasks for the employee, and indeed discipline them, should that prove necessary.
3. Personal performance: This point requires that the employee personally undertakes the work given by the employer, and they cannot substitute another to do so in their place. This does not affect the employee's power to delegate; rather that they themselves are generally responsible for the work they are given.

(NB: These criteria have been the subject of a great deal of case law, and interpretations may differ as further cases unfold.)

The presence of such criteria will not automatically mean that an employment relationship exists. However, where they are present, there is a significant prospect that the individual will be deemed to have an employment contract with the organization for whom they work, save for specific exceptions.

What is clear, however, is that significant legal rights will be conferred upon any individual who is correctly deemed to be an employee in UK law.

It is crucial that any organization is clear as to the rights that an employee has before it undertakes any disciplinary action or amendment to the employment contract, or considers any requests by the employee to exercise any of the rights that they have.

Workers

This grouping generally includes all employees working under a contract of employment, and those who work pursuant to other contracts, such as a contract for service. Those who are deemed to be workers will also include individuals who are provided by an agency to work with an organization. These can include temporary staff or seasonal staff.

It is important to note that agency workers are now also covered by employment legislation and have significant statutory rights, as do most types of workers. This category does not include those who are self-employed and provide services as part of their own enterprise. These are dealt with below.

Volunteers

Many charities rely heavily on the provision of help by volunteers, who undertake work for the charity but are not remunerated.

It is vital that charities are very clear as to the status of individuals who wish to work as volunteers. There have been cases where charities have been required by HMRC to pay out large sums in backdated salaries to individuals they later decided were employees rather than volunteers.

The key criteria to consider in such circumstances are those set out above regarding mutuality of obligation, control, and personal performance.

In addition, it is important to ensure that volunteers have no formal working practice (other than that agreed informally), are not remunerated in any way (other than reimbursement of limited expenses), nor are they subject to the disciplinary procedures of the charity.

In essence, the volunteer must have almost no formal tie with the charity, and all working arrangements must be informal, albeit that in some circumstances they may be long-standing and well established.

Self-employed

This area covers those individuals who are personally in business to provide services to organizations for a specific purpose. This would include a business consultant or accountant who provides services to various different companies or charities.

They are self-employed and are not covered by any form of employment legislation in respect of their relationship with the organizations for whom they provide their services.

A self-employed individual may provide services to a number of different organizations at any one time. However, in the event that they provide their services solely to one charity, it is possible that HMRC will regard them as an employee of that charity. In these circumstances, any charity should look at the services provided by any self-employed consultant or contractor, to see whether they provide such services to other organizations. If they do not, the charity should take professional accountancy advice.

If HMRC deem them to be an employee for taxation purposes, then the charity could be made liable for the tax and National Insurance to date, notwithstanding the consultant being 'self-employed' for the period of the consultancy.

Recruitment and selection

If a charity is seeking to recruit a new employee or a worker (perhaps through an agency), careful attention must be paid to how this procedure is applied. This is an area in which potential claims for discrimination may arise.

Advertising the role and interviewing candidates

Before undertaking any advertising, the organization should prepare a full job description, considering the qualities, qualifications and experience required for the role. Deciding the remuneration and benefits for the role is also important.

It is also helpful to look at existing staff in the charity to see if anyone should be considered for internal promotion.

Once these initial tasks have been undertaken, it may be decided to advertise externally for the right candidate. At this stage, a number of documents should be prepared in advance of any shortlisting of candidates or interviews. These will include the advert for the role, an application form (these are preferable to CVs), a job description, and a contract of employment.

The advertisement itself must comply with employment legislation and regulations and, in particular, the law relating to discrimination.

It is not permitted for any group of individuals to be excluded from applying for a particular role based on grounds of gender, race, disability, age, religion or belief, or sexual orientation. Neither is it lawful to exclude individuals (as listed above) from applying, nor should there be any suggestion that a certain category of individual is preferred. (There are, of course, exceptions to this rule, and these are examined later in this section.)

The advert should give some detail regarding the type of work to be undertaken, if possible the remuneration package, and a profile of the candidate required.

When shortlisting and interviewing possible candidates, it is important to be aware of the laws regarding discrimination, as selection must be made purely on terms of merit and ability.

Claims have been brought in the employment tribunal against organizations whose candidates assert they have discriminated against them for not offering them the position, or not shortlisting them for an interview.

It is not always easy to ascertain from an application form and an interview whether a candidate is suitable for the organization, and indeed able to perform the role to the required level. It is thought advisable for at least two individuals to interview prospective candidates, and for correct notes to be taken during the interviews. (On the issue of taking notes, organizations should be aware that candidates are permitted to request copies of any notes taken during the interviews. It is important to ensure that full and appropriate notes are made by those conducting the interview.)

Candidates should be given full opportunity to answer all questions put to them (within reason), and should also have a chance to ask questions not only about the role itself, but also more broadly about the organization.

Selecting and appointing the right candidate

Following the conclusion of the interview process, all candidates should be given consideration, and if possible, a clear objective set of criteria established to properly assess their suitability. Subjective 'gut feel' decisions can leave organizations open to criticism, and perhaps even a challenge by an aggrieved candidate in the employment tribunal.

Having undertaken that process, the successful candidate will then be offered the position. Even at this stage, there are important issues to consider.

First, the work of many charities can be of a sensitive or very specific nature. Therefore, it may be necessary to seek not only standard references, but also those such as proof of right to live and work in the UK, a medical, or indeed a Criminal Records Bureau check (see Appendix 1, paragraph 2). Other checks may also be necessary depending on the type of activities undertaken by the charity.

Any offer to the successful candidate should be made subject to successful satisfaction of all relevant and necessary references. Provided these areas are satisfied, and the candidate accepts the job offer, a start date can be set, and an appropriate contract of employment provided to the new employee, subject to successful completion of any probationary period. At the point of offering the position, and appointing the new member of staff, it should be made clear that the contract of employment is subject to successful completion of a probationary period.

Commencing and continuing employment

Upon appointment of a new employee, the charity and the employee will now owe each other a duty under the terms of the contract of employment, and statutory and contractual rights will apply to both parties.

Induction and probation
It is worthwhile giving thought to an induction programme for the new member of staff. How brief or comprehensive this is will depend upon the nature of their work, and perhaps the seniority of the position.

Some form of training, where appropriate, and clear introductions to other members of staff and the organization generally, are an important part of giving a new recruit every opportunity to succeed in their position.

An induction programme is helpful not only to orientate the member of staff to the organization, but also for purposes of future work performance and the new member's own morale.

The usual probationary period is three months, although this can be extended or reduced depending upon the nature and seniority of the position. Clearly, probationary periods would not ordinarily apply where appointments are made for temporary or seasonal staff, or perhaps where the appointment is made pursuant to a fixed-term contract.

Beyond the induction and probationary stage, it should also be made clear that employees should be subject to at least one review per annum through-out their period of employment. This should take the form of a performance appraisal by their line manager, and should deal with both the quality of the work undertaken by the employee, and their general conduct within the organization.

The employment contract
On the basis that the new employee successfully completes their probationary period, they should be notified in writing, and should have already received an employment contract or at the very least written particulars of employment.

The contract between an employer and employee must clearly state and explain a number of formal and legally binding express terms. These include, but are not limited to:

- the names and addresses of the employer and employee;
- the commencement date of the employment;
- the place where the employee will be required to work, and their hours of work;
- the tasks that they will be required to perform and the title of their position;
- details regarding their manager, remuneration, benefits, annual leave, notice period, and so on.

Reference should also be made to the organization's grievance and disciplinary procedures, and, if appropriate, the staff handbook generally.

It should be noted, at this point, that all employment contracts (written or oral) are deemed to contain an implied term of what has become known as mutual trust and confidence between the parties. This means that the employee must have trust and confidence in their employer to act in accordance with the terms of the contract, and treat them fairly as an employee.

Similarly, an employer must have that same trust and confidence in the employee to perform their tasks properly, honestly and conduct themselves in accordance with the requirements of their contract.

Many of the claims in the employment tribunal over the years have arisen out of an alleged breach of this implied term of the employment contract, following a breakdown in the employment relationship.

As indicated above, the employment contract should be provided to the new member of staff as soon as possible after they have commenced employment. The employee should be given sufficient time to consider the terms of the contract, to consult where they have queries regarding its content, and then to agree and sign the contract.

The terms of the contract are legally binding on both parties, and it should be reiterated that they immediately give rise to considerable rights for the employee, which then increase during their period of employment.

Staff handbook, policies and procedures

In addition to the contract of employment, all members of staff must be made aware of the organization's grievance and disciplinary procedures. Also, any specific details regarding, among others, annual leave, sickness absence, and general health and safety policies should be made available for their review.

It is now common practice for many charities to contain these details, and others, within their staff handbook. The handbook contains some policies that are legally binding (such as the statutory grievance and disciplinary procedure), and some that are company policy, such as the procedure to be adopted when away from work with sickness. The handbook may also contain some background information about the charity, its history, charitable objectives, and so on.

If a staff handbook has been prepared, it should be made available to the new employee for their review as soon as possible and preferably at the same time as the employment contract.

It is worth remembering the need to update the handbook on an ongoing basis. Depending on the size of the organization, this may be a regular occurrence, or something that can be undertaken perhaps once or twice a year. Where the handbook contains statutory policies and procedures, these must be updated as soon as any changes in the relevant regulations or legislation are made.

The benefit of such a handbook is that it enables all the organization's policies and procedures to be contained within one document, and provides easy access for all members of staff.

It is essential that all organizations give sufficient thought to the types of policies and procedures that they will need in order to comply with current employment legislation. Incorporating such policies and putting them into practice can often act as the first and crucial line of defence against any potential claim by an aggrieved employee in the employment tribunal.

Terminating employment

Where the employment relationship is to come to an end, for whatever reason, this must be done in accordance with the terms of the employment contract. This will be the case whether the contract is terminated by the employer, or by the employee.

There are three main ways in which a contract of employment can be terminated: by the employee (resignation), by the employer (dismissal), or by mutual agreement between the parties.

Resignation
This is perhaps the most common form of termination of an employment contract, and is effected when the employee tenders their resignation to the organization.

This will involve a written resignation with the employee working their notice period, where required. The written resignation is acknowledged by the employer, and references are provided when requested by any new employer.

In some circumstances, the notice period may involve 'garden leave', with the employee restricted from working for the organization, or indeed any other organization, for the period of their notice. This tends to apply to senior employees, or those in more sensitive circumstances.

Dismissal

An employer may terminate a contract of employment by a dismissal. Considerable case law has built up over the years around this area, and many cases have resulted in victories for employees when they have been deemed to have been unfairly dismissed.

An employer, therefore, must handle any dismissals carefully and sensitively. All members of staff (including most categories of workers), irrespective of their position within the organization, are legally entitled to be dismissed for fair reasons only, and in a manner that does not breach their contract with the employer.

Two of the most common forms of claim in the employment tribunal now relate to dismissals that are deemed to be unfair (including constructive dismissal) or wrongful dismissal.

Unfair dismissal

Generally, and before an employee can bring a claim for unfair dismissal, they must satisfy the eligibility criteria, namely that they have been with the organization continuously for at least one year.

There are some exceptions to this rule, and in some circumstances, employees will enjoy protection immediately depending upon the reason given for dismissal. Once the qualifying period has been completed, employees are afforded statutory protection from being dismissed unfairly.

Such a situation can arise where an employee is dismissed for an unfair or inadmissible reason. An obvious example would be where there is simply a clash of personalities and the less senior employee is dismissed, or where preferential treatment is given to a friend or relative over another member of staff, and they are dismissed.

A further situation where a dismissal will be deemed to be unfair would be where it can be established that it was discriminatory. For example, where the reason given for the dismissal was because of the employee being of a certain age, or having a specific disability.

The six potentially fair reasons for dismissal are: incapability, misconduct, redundancy, retirement, contravention of a duty or restriction; or some other substantial reason.

In addition, where the statutory dismissal procedure is not adhered to, the dismissal will be automatically deemed to be unfair. It is worth noting here that even if the reason for dismissal is fair, if the procedure is not properly adopted, the dismissal will nevertheless be automatically unfair.

Finally, an unfair dismissal claim may be brought by an aggrieved employee where they believe that they have been constructively dismissed. This situation arises when an employee resigns from their position on the grounds that they can no longer work under the pressure or in the environment that they are required to.

Employees must bring their grievance to the attention of their employer, and if it is not properly addressed, they may then resign and claim constructive dismissal. The essence of their claim will be that they had no option other than to resign, and were effectively dismissed. The employee may then pursue a claim for compensation for loss of earnings (including future earnings), and possibly a related personal injury claim, if there have been elements of stress in the workplace.

Wrongful dismissal

All employees are entitled to statutory protection from wrongful dismissal as soon as they commence employment. There is no qualifying period.

Wrongful dismissal can arise where an employee is dismissed for a fair reason, but they are dismissed instantly, and without notice. The breach of contract by the employer in these circumstances is not the decision to dismiss, but rather the failure to adhere to other elements of the contract, such as an entitlement to a notice period.

A good example of such a situation would be where an employee is not considered to have passed their probationary period, and are not retained. They are still entitled to a notice payment in accordance with the terms of their contract.

In some circumstances, a claim may be brought for wrongful dismissal where an offer of employment has been made and then withdrawn by an organization. A contract is deemed to exist at the point that the offer of employment is made and then accepted, and therefore, the employer would need to terminate that contract fairly and in accordance with the correct procedure, and indeed the terms of the contract. Failure to do so may, rightfully, result in a claim for wrongful dismissal.

Redundancy

This occurs, generally speaking, when an employee is deemed surplus to requirements by an organization. There are three main scenarios when redundancy can usually occur, as follows:

1. The organization is closing down.
2. The employee's workplace or division of the organization is closing down.

3. There is a reduced or reducing need for certain employees to carry out
    work of a particular kind.

Before commencing any action leading to decisions about redundancy of
any employees, an organization should think and plan very carefully about
how those decisions will be implemented. The law regarding redundancy
is considerable and complex, and professional advice is strongly recommended, given the potential pitfalls that exist, and indeed the potentially
enormous cost of failing to avoid those pitfalls.

Termination by consent

Finally, a contract of employment (as with any other contract) may be terminated by consent between the parties. There may be an amicable agreement
that there is no longer any need for a particular work to be undertaken or
indeed for the business itself to operate in the manner that it has done so to
date. This is relatively unusual, and usually occurs in a situation such as an
employee taking early retirement.

There must be written mutual agreement between the parties, and it
should be noted that this must be an entirely different procedure to a redundancy situation where an employee may be compelled or encouraged to leave
the organization for any of the three reasons mentioned above.

Equality and discrimination in the workplace

General principles

The Charity Commission encourages charities to consider diversity within
their organizations, and indeed among their trustees. This is an area which has
had, and continues to have, enormous impact upon the way employers deal not
only with their staff, but also with job applicants, workers, and even ex-workers.

Under current UK employment legislation, individuals are protected from
discrimination before, during, and after employment. Earlier in this section
we considered the job applicant and discrimination. It was stated that any
advertisement (and indeed application form) should not give rise to any
category of individual being excluded, or discriminated against.

There are, however, certain circumstances where such exclusion may lawfully occur, and that is usually when there is what is known as a genuine
occupational requirement for a certain category of individual to undertake a
certain role.

An obvious example would include a male actor for the part of a male
character in a film or play (although this would not have applied in the days

of Shakespeare!), or a Christian being required for the role of head teacher in a Christian school. In both cases, there would be no unlawful discrimination on the part of the organization advertising the post.

Employers should note that claims in discrimination are growing each year, and there is no limit to the amount of compensation that a tribunal may award to an aggrieved employee who feels that they have been discriminated against. It is essential that organizations comply with discrimination legislation, and deal with any such grievances by an employee in accordance with statutory guidelines.

Direct and indirect discrimination

Discrimination can occur either directly or indirectly. Direct discrimination occurs when there is 'less favourable treatment' of an individual, compared with the treatment of another person of the opposite sex, or different age. Indirect discrimination may occur where an individual is treated in a manner that appears fair and reasonable, and with good motive, but turns out to have a disproportionately adverse effect upon individuals in a certain category. Further, indirect discrimination may be deemed to have occurred even when it can be clearly demonstrated to have been unintentional.

Harassment and victimization

Employees will also be deemed to have been discriminated against if they have been harassed or victimized during the course of their employment.

Harassment will occur where an employee has been subject to conduct that is intimidatory, bullying, or where physical and/or verbal abuse have occurred on the basis of, for example, their sex or race.

Generally speaking, the degree to which an employee has been subject to such harassment will determine whether or not the actions would be sufficient to amount to a claim for discrimination.

In addition, an employee may suffer victimization in the workplace, and be deemed to have been discriminated against. Victimization is, in essence, less favourable treatment of an employee because they have previously pursued legal action for discrimination, or indeed raised a complaint of discrimination in their current workplace. Victimization is often considered to be a form of direct discrimination against an employee.

It should be noted that many general principles apply to most, but not all, of the grounds upon which an individual cannot be discriminated against.

There are essentially six main grounds upon which an employee may be deemed to have been discriminated against, namely: gender, race, disability, religion or belief, sexual orientation, and age. In addition, there are clear equality provisions in respect of equal pay. These are all considered below.

It is worth noting that the first three categories (gender, race, and disability) have been established for longer, and those categories of religion or belief, sexual orientation, and age have become protected categories more recently.

Gender

This is, broadly speaking, discrimination based on an individual's gender, namely whether they are male or female. The main legislation setting out the protection that individuals are afforded in this area is the Sex Discrimination Act 1975. This refers to less favourable treatment on grounds of the individual's own gender.

Therefore, if an employee is overlooked for promotion simply on grounds of their gender, or indeed may not be selected or recruited to a position due to their gender, where there is no justifiable or lawful reason for doing so, they will have been discriminated against on grounds of their gender.

In order for the action to be justifiable or lawful, however, there must be a genuine occupational requirement for taking certain action. Also, certain specific provisions must apply to certain roles that require there to be discrimination, for example, complying with another piece of legislation.

In addition, an individual may be discriminated against on grounds of gender, where less favourable treatment occurs due to pregnancy and childbirth and/or maternity and paternity leave.

One of the key areas where organizations are often in difficulty in this category is where a pregnant woman is treated unfairly simply because she is pregnant. She may be denied promotion, or indeed made redundant for this reason alone, and this will invariably give rise to an instance of clear discrimination on grounds of gender.

It should be noted that, save for the example of pregnancy, male and female workers are protected on the same terms.

Race

It is unlawful to discriminate on grounds of an individual's race. The key statute governing this form of discrimination is the Race Relations Act 1976 (RRA), although other directives and regulations have since broadened the law in this area.

Thus, racial grounds (within the RRA) include not only an individual's race, but also their colour, nationality, or ethnic or national origins. Clearly, these are wide-ranging categories, and organizations are well advised to be very aware of the need to comply with the law in this area.

It is possible for an employer to be liable for racial discrimination, even when an employee does not belong to the racial group that the employer believed them to.

Therefore, it is the employer's perception of their race or ethnic origin, etc., that is also important. It can be sufficient if an employer believed that an employee was of a certain race and thus discriminated against them, for it to be unlawful, and for liability to arise.

It should further be noted that, as with other forms of discrimination, protection afforded to employees is not limited to the employee's own racial group. This means that an employee can bring a claim for racial discrimination if they do not agree with work or instructions given by their employer to discriminate against a particular racial group. The employee need not be part of that racial group to bring an action for discrimination.

The law regarding discrimination on grounds of race (and gender or disability) is well established, and yet organizations continue to find themselves in difficulty in this area. This appears to be because there are not sufficient systems and procedures in place within the organization that prevent instances of discrimination occurring.

Disability

The Disability Discrimination Act 1995 (DDA) makes it unlawful for an employer to discriminate against a disabled person in respect of their employment with that organization. The DDA has since been amended and the law broadened further to provide increased protection for employees with disabilities.

The central issue facing any employer in this area is what constitutes a disability for the purposes of the DDA, and indeed any other legislation in this area, regarding discrimination on grounds of disability.

The DDA states that an individual has a disability if they have a physical or mental impairment which has a substantial and long-term adverse effect on their ability to carry out normal day-to-day activities. Unsurprisingly, this definition has given rise to a vast number of cases in employment tribunals, and legal and medical practitioners continue to wrestle with what may or may not constitute a disability.

Indeed, there have been instances where a medical practitioner has provided a written report and sworn evidence to the effect that an individual is disabled, but a tribunal has found that the individual is nevertheless not disabled, from the perspective of the statutory legal definition.

It is clearly necessary for any employer to be aware of any individuals in their organization who may be disabled for the purposes of the DDA, and take appropriate steps to ensure that their status in respect of their disability is established medically and legally.

Subsequently, they must ensure that there are no procedures in place in the workplace that discriminate against them on grounds of their disability, or indeed that they are treated less favourably for the same reason. This may include making reasonable adjustments to the workplace (including physical adjustments) to provide that discrimination does not occur.

Please note that, dissimilar to other areas of discrimination law, the law relating to disability discrimination does not protect an employee who is treated unfairly because they are wrongly perceived to be disabled, or because they feel that they have been discriminated against on the grounds of someone else's disability.

Religion or belief

Since 2003, it has become unlawful to discriminate against an individual (for employment purposes) on grounds of their religion or belief. The regulations governing this area, issued in 2003, define religion or belief as any religion, religious belief, or similar philosophical belief. The definition within the regulations does allow for protection to be afforded to individuals where they lack a particular religion or belief, which may be held by an employer.

In determining whether or not an employee's religion or belief would be included in the definition, a number of criteria should be considered. These would incorporate, among others, evidence of collective worship, a clear belief system, and a profound belief affecting their way of life or view of the world.

Given the recent advent of these regulations, there is not considerable case law assisting with the way in which tribunals will interpret them, and only time will permit a clear understanding of what types of religion or belief will be included within the definition given above.

However, it is safe to say that any claims in this area (and other newer areas of discrimination, outlined below) will receive the same degree of attention and importance as the more established areas.

Sexual orientation

Protection from discrimination on grounds of sexual orientation was also established in 2003, following the introduction of the Employment Equality (Sexual Orientation) Regulations 2003 ('the regulations').

Sexual orientation is defined within the regulations as a sexual orientation towards persons of the same sex, the opposite sex, or the same sex and the opposite sex. In other words, towards anyone!

The intention, although not necessarily clear, is to protect all people within these regulations, and not just those whose sexual orientation may be deemed to put them in a minority and perhaps, therefore, more vulnerable to discrimination.

Again, perception of someone's sexual orientation (even if it is not correct) may give rise to liability for discrimination if the employee is treated less favourably as a result. Clearly, there are likely to be claims for this reason on the basis that another individual's sexual orientation is not always apparent, and is essentially a private matter. Similarly, it is worth noting that, as with some other forms of discrimination, an employee or worker may claim under this heading if the discrimination is on grounds of someone else's sexual orientation.

An email or comment insulting a certain group on grounds of sexual orientation may be discrimination against any employee if they object to what has been said or done. Another example may be an employee who is treated less favourably than another employee because they have a son or a friend who is of a particular sexual orientation.

The Sexual Orientation Regulations

In addition to the types of discrimination outlined above, the latest regulations that are likely to affect Christian charities are those set out within the Sexual Orientation Regulations (SORs). These regulations will apply *in addition to* the legislation regarding discrimination on grounds of sexual orientation outlined above.

The SORs were brought into force by the Equality Act 2006, wherein it has now been made illegal for anyone (whether an individual or an organization) who provides 'goods, services, facilities, premises, education, or public functions' to discriminate against that person on the grounds of their sexual orientation.

This is intended to cover anyone who provides goods, services, facilities, premises, or any school or public authority. This is an extremely broad application and certainly will include numerous charities.

Indeed, Christian charities are not exempt from these regulations, unless, for example, they exist solely for the purpose of serving either homosexuals or heterosexuals. These would be covered by Regulation 18 of the SORs, but this would cover a very small number of such organizations.

Regulation 14 of the SORs provides a further exemption (the 'religions exemption') for certain organizations. However, this will only include those which have 'as their main purpose' one or more of the following:

- to practise a religion or belief;
- to advance a religion or belief;
- to teach the practice or principles of a religion or belief; or
- to enable any persons of a religion or belief to receive any benefit, or to engage in any activity within the framework of that religion or belief.

Clearly, the breadth and application of this exemption are difficult to define at this stage, and will become more apparent as specific cases and circumstances are established.

In particular, it is important to note that even if an organization is deemed to fall within the religious exemption (above), if it provides goods, services, facilities or exercises public functions on behalf of a public authority under a contract, they will *not* be exempted from the regulations.

Therefore, whilst churches and many organizations may be exempt from the regulations, there will be many Christian charities that are not. It is essential, therefore, to establish whether or not the activities of a charity are likely to be included within the regulations, and what actions, if any, might need to be taken as a result.

In considering the implications of this matter, up-to-date information is available on the websites of organizations such as the Lawyers Christian Fellowship (www.lawcf.org) and the Christian Institute (www.christian.org.uk).

Once again, as with the religion or belief regulations, it will be necessary to see how the employment tribunals and courts determine what does or does not constitute discrimination in this area.

Age

The most recent category of workers and employees to come under the auspices of discrimination legislation are those who may be deemed to be less favourably treated because of their age.

The law in this area has been introduced under the Employment Equality (Age) Regulations 2006 ('the regulations'), and came into force on 1 October 2006. Both the Department for Trade and Industry and ACAS have issued helpful guidance notes in dealing with this new legislation.

When addressing this issue, the obvious conclusion may be that this law is designed to cover employees who are older than others, and perhaps therefore less favourably treated than younger members of staff. This would be a mistake, however, because this deals with employees at every stage in life and indeed in their career, and clearly focuses very much on younger employees as well as those who are more mature and experienced.

These regulations are likely to have a considerable impact upon how organizations deal with, and indeed recruit and dismiss, their staff. In addition, issues regarding an employee's retirement age, redundancy, and occupational pension schemes will need to be taken into account as a result of this new legislation.

It is clear that an individual may bring a claim for discrimination in this area even if the discrimination was not intentional, or it was based on an incorrect perception of their age. However, there are some instances where such discrimination may be justified. Indeed, the law does offer greater flexibility in this area of discrimination than in others.

For example, an employer can establish that discrimination on grounds of age can be justified if the treatment constitutes a proportionate means of achieving a legitimate aim. Justification for discrimination on grounds of an individual's age may also apply where, as with other forms of discrimination, there is a genuine occupational requirement for the individual to be of a certain age group.

In addition, a particularly important justification for an employer's conduct in this area will apply on the issue of dismissal. If an employee is dismissed due to retirement, namely reaching the normal retirement age, this will not be unlawful and will not constitute discrimination, or indeed, unfair dismissal.

One note of caution here, however, is that specific statutory procedures will apply if an employee seeks permission to remain working beyond the normal retirement age.

Equal pay

Having considered some of the more recent legislation and regulations regarding discrimination law, it is worth noting that the law regarding equality in the workplace arguably began to evolve in light of the Equal Pay Act 1970 (EPA).

This legislation dealt primarily with a disparity in remuneration, principally between male and female workers and employees. The EPA entitles an individual to receive the same contractual remuneration and benefits in the same employment. The key phrase here is 'same employment', and there are three criteria establishing this, at least one of which must be satisfied for 'same employment' to be deemed to apply.

These include:

Like work (this is the most straightforward and deals with work that is almost identical or sufficiently similar in comparison).
Work rated as equivalent (this would be less straightforward, and would be work that may be equivalent when evaluated and assessed by a job evaluation scoring system).
Work proven to be of equal value (an evaluation on this basis can be extremely complex and would involve the input of independent expert evidence, and job evaluation studies based on worth and impact in the organization).

This third item was introduced many years after the EPA and has given rise to a significant impact on how organizations address the issue of remuneration and reward programmes for their staff.

Summary

It is apparent that this particular area of employment law has grown almost inexorably over the past thirty years, and increasingly so more recently. What is also apparent is that employers can take measures to protect their staff and their organizations from difficult and damaging situations arising, and discrimination claims being brought against them.

On the basis that prevention is better than cure, employers should look long and hard at the policies, systems and procedures that they have in place for running their organization. Serious questions need to be asked, in light of this area of law, as to whether or not they are putting themselves and their employees at risk of discrimination by the way they conduct not only themselves individually, but also the organization as a whole.

Specifically, employers would do well to heed the errors that have been made in the past by other organizations in this area, and seek to incorporate an equal opportunities policy within their staff handbook, and ensure that all members of staff adhere to it.

There is little doubt that discrimination legislation is here to stay, and is likely to increase in the future. This may be achieved by adding further protection to those categories already protected, or indeed by adding further categories. The former is more likely at this stage.

In any event, this is an important issue for charities in particular, given the potential personal liability that the custodians of the charity may face when dealing with such a claim.

Further, it is incumbent upon the custodians to ensure that the charity does not fall foul of the law in this area. Nor should they contravene the guidelines of the Charity Commission with regard to seeking to establish a diverse workforce carrying out the activities of the charity.

Employment practice and procedure

Introduction

These topics deal with the various obligations that employers face when managing staff on a day-by-day basis, and how to deal with some of the more specific and challenging matters that arise during the history of any organization.

There are, of course, many other important areas to consider, and it is always advisable for managers of charities and trustees to seek professional advice when addressing some of the more difficult, time-consuming and indeed risky issues that will present themselves from time to time.

Managing sickness absence

One of the most important, but perhaps less obvious, considerations for any employer is the health of any new employees that they recruit. It is reasonable to presume that a new employee (or indeed an existing employee) is in good health, and there is no expectation that they will suffer long-term or short-term absence from work due to ill-health.

However, most, if not all, employers in the UK will testify that sickness absence is one of the greatest problems facing them today, and is the cause of a great deal of financial loss and disruption. The number of working days lost in the UK each year due to sickness is rising year after year. The estimated financial effect on the economy through days lost to sickness runs to billions of pounds, and the impact of sickness absence cannot be discounted. This applies as much to charities as it does to profit-making organizations, as the disruption caused can have a financial as well as a logistical impact. Stress, in particular, is a growing concern and appears to be particularly prevalent among the UK workforce.

If a member of staff is either away from work on long-term sickness absence, or is persistently away on short-term sickness (i.e. for one or two days at a time), the effect on any organization can be significant. This may involve hiring short-term temporary replacements at extra cost and disruption, and also investing time and money training the temporary replacements during the period of absence.

Throughout this time, the employee who is absent retains their rights under the contract of employment, together with their statutory employment rights. These are likely to include contractual sick pay, and will certainly include statutory sick pay.

It is wise for employers to consider any strategies or procedures they can adopt that may serve to limit or reduce risk in this area for their organization. Organizations may wish to consider the wealth of information that is available to assist in this area. One document, in particular, that provides considerable guidance is the Confederation of British Industry report entitled 'Focus on absence'.

A strategy for sickness absence

Whatever the size of the charity, it is advisable to operate a formal sickness absence policy. This should deal with matters such as how sickness is reported and recorded, and what level of sickness will trigger an investigation and possible action by the organization.

The sickness absence policy is for internal use, and certain elements will remain strictly confidential to those responsible for running the organization, or the human resources department, if applicable.

Furthermore, it is essential that the policy (or the relevant parts of the policy) are communicated throughout the organization. Staff must be aware of how they are to report their absence due to sickness, and of their responsibilities in respect of evidencing their sickness. A doctor's certificate or self-certifying document will usually apply for short-term sickness.

In addition, the organization must give very serious thought to the strategy that they will adopt in the event that an employee is signed off work on long-term sickness, or repeatedly takes one or two days sickness at a time.

Charities must be bold, as well as sensitive and diligent, in dealing with such matters. Clearly, there are numerous issues to consider when dealing with staff who have a poor sickness record, and organizations must not immediately seek to dismiss such employees, or make them redundant. Should they do so, they may face a strong claim in the employment tribunal.

However, where employees are off sick in the long-term, the organization will wish to seek medical evidence, and this would extend to a medical report over and above a simple certificate. This will give a clearer indication as to the likelihood of the employee returning to work in the short to medium term. On the basis of the evidence, and the anticipated impact on the organization, the employer can then decide how best to deal with the situation, and this may include retirement on grounds of ill-health.

With regard to employees with poor short-term sickness records, the situation is sometimes more straightforward. There is evidence to suggest that much short-term absence that is attributed formally to sickness is nothing of the sort. Employers understandably feel at a loss when faced with a doctor's certificate or self-certifying document. However, organizations should have a clear strategy for dealing with those individuals who are regularly or habitually absent for one or two days at a time.

The reason this is so important is not only the disruption that it causes to the organization, but also the potentially damaging impact it may have on morale with other employees, who may even seek to 'take advantage of the system' in a similar fashion.

Family-friendly policies

Alongside the considerable growth in discrimination legislation in recent years, there has also been a similar extension to the rights for employees under what have become known as 'family-friendly' rights.

These include rights regarding maternity and paternity leave, rights regarding leave for adoption and care for dependants, and other policies regarding flexible working and, indeed, working parents.

What is immediately apparent from the steady flow of new and increased family-friendly rights is that the law seems to seek to improve the work-life balance of parents, but provides little for those who are not in that situation. Some of the family-friendly rights are set out below.

Maternity leave

Although the UK has provided statutory maternity rights to mothers since 1974, it is only recently that these rights have been substantially extended. Indeed, it is possible that these rights will be extended yet further in the future. The recent legislation dealing with maternity rights is the Employment Rights Act 1996 and the Maternity and Parental Leave Regulations 1999.

Due to the recent legislation, there are now three specific types of maternity leave, namely: ordinary maternity leave, compulsory maternity leave, and additional maternity leave.

Ordinary leave entitles female employees who are pregnant to twenty-six weeks' leave, at any stage of their employment. Interestingly, but somewhat confusingly, members of the armed forces, the police and share fisherwomen are excluded!

Compulsory leave is comprised simply of the first two weeks following the birth of the baby. The mother is not allowed to return to work during that period, and it is worth noting that the onus is on the employer – not the employee – to ensure that no work is undertaken during this period.

Finally, additional leave is an entitlement for certain female employees who have satisfied a qualifying period and seek extended maternity leave. This allows for a further twenty-six weeks' leave, and provides for an absence from the workplace for a full year should a mother wish to make use of this entitlement.

However, not all contractual terms and conditions apply during the second twenty-six weeks, and employees and employers should establish a clear plan as soon as possible, as to if and when the employee will return to work.

Paternity leave

Similarly, a father is entitled to take a period of time away from work for the birth of his child. This will be a period after the birth of the child, and has been introduced to allow him to be able to provide support and care for the mother and his child during this time. This right was introduced by the Employment Act 2002, and is set out in detail in the Paternity and Adoption Leave Regulations 2002.

The allowance under the 2002 Act is for two weeks' paid leave (statutory or contractual) following the birth of the child, and the father must satisfy certain criteria before he is entitled to payment during this period of leave.

Adoption leave

This is the right for employees to take leave following the recent placing of an adopted child with them. It was introduced under the same legislation and regulations as paternity leave in 2002.

It should be noted that this applies specifically to the new placement of a child with an employee, and not step-family adoption, or adoption by a child's current foster carers.

As with paternity leave, qualifying criteria apply, and only one of the adoptive parents may take adoption leave. The other parent may seek paternity leave (if applicable), subject to qualifying criteria.

Dependant care leave

Provided for in the Employment Rights Act 1996, this right entitles an employee to take time off work to care for, or to arrange care for, a dependant when that dependant is ill, injured, gives birth, or dies.

For the purposes of qualifying for such leave, a dependant will be defined as a spouse, child, parent, or person living in the same household as the employee.

This right is generally strictly applied, however, and it is usually to be taken as unpaid leave, with the emphasis on arranging care for the dependant, rather than actually undertaking the care over a prolonged period.

Health and safety

The law relating to health and safety in the workplace is one that all charities would do well to consider, and apply, in detail. Not only does non-compliance give rise to possible financial compensation for any employee who is injured or becomes unwell, but also may incur potential criminal sanctions.

The essence of health and safety law in the workplace is to seek to protect employees (and others) from either becoming ill or being injured whilst at work.

It may be helpful at this juncture to establish that those employees who work from home also fall within this category, and the responsibility rests with the employer to comply with health and safety legislation.

Once again, employer's obligations in this area are wide-ranging and extend beyond simply ensuring the building and equipment are safe. They include the conduct and behaviour of other employees, and the manner in which employees are expected to undertake their work.

There are three main sources from which health and safety obligations arise for employers. These are:

• duty of care owed by employers to their employees;
• the Health and Safety at Work Act 1974;

- contractual obligations (including contracts of employment) which incorporate health and safety obligations.

In accordance with their general duty of care, employers are responsible not only for the health and safety of their employees, but also that of their workers, contractors, visitors to the premises, and indeed, members of the general public.

Broadly speaking, employers must consistently and correctly discharge, among others, the following obligations:

- provide safe premises (including the equipment used by all staff);
- provide a safe mode or method of work;
- ensure they employ and retain safe and competent fellow workers;
- provide for the health, safety and welfare of employees at work (as far as reasonably practicable);
- conduct their operation in such a manner as to ensure that individuals other than employees are not exposed to a health and safety risk.

Such responsibilities cannot be delegated, and must be the sole responsibility of the employer in the on-going conduct of their work.

There are helpful approved codes of practice, issued by the Health and Safety Executive, which assist employers in addressing these issues. However, given the broad nature of the obligations placed upon the employer, it is important, once again, that professional advice is sought. In addition, ongoing assessments should be conducted, with senior management being kept up to date with any current or developing issues.

TUPE regulations

The TUPE regulations refer to the Transfer of Undertakings (Protection of Employment) Regulations 1974, those regulations up-dated in 2006, and a series of related regulations and directives.

Essentially TUPE legislation provides for the protection of employees' rights when their employment is transferred by their employer to another.

This can occur when a charity 'merges' or is taken over by another. The effect of this is that their employment status and terms are transferred to their new employer, and the TUPE regulations provide for the protection of employees' rights in these circumstances.

When an employee is transferred to a new organization, certain rights, obligations and liabilities must, by law, transfer with them. Establishing what sort of transfer qualifies in these circumstances, and what rights pass across, are two of the key questions that must be addressed.

An employer is advised to begin to build up such knowledge before any such transfers are even considered, due to the nature and scope of the subject and its ramifications.

Handling employment tribunal claims

The costs of dealing with employment claims are generally measured in financial terms, but can also involve management and charity time, and indeed possible adverse publicity in local or even national media. Even when an organization successfully defends any such claim, their legal costs are not usually required to be reimbursed by the individual bringing the claim.

This fact inevitably results in many organizations reaching uneasy settlements and compromises at the mid-way point or early on in the life of the claim, and employees are increasingly aware of this.

For these, and various other reasons, it is advisable to seek to avoid such claims wherever possible.

Types of claim

There is much in the preceding paragraphs that has established some of the circumstances under which an employer may be faced with a claim by a disgruntled employee or former employee.

Claims for unfair dismissal, wrongful dismissal, various forms of discrimination, and so on are extremely common in the employment tribunal. There are many other types of claim that can also be brought. In addition, employees often include more than one type of allegation or head of claim within their overall claim.

Practice and procedure

A tribunal claim must be instigated by an individual issuing a form ET1, which must be served upon the employer. This form (and any attached particulars of the claim) must properly set out the nature of the claim, and the basis upon which the claim is being brought.

At this stage, all evidence relating to the claim does not need to be brought before the tribunal or served on the respective parties. This will follow later, when the tribunal will give directions as to how the case must progress, together with timescales for the full hearing, if one proves to be necessary.

The employer will be required to respond to the claim form (ET1) with their defence or response, contained within a form ET3. This sets out the employer's response, also indicating if any aspect of the claim is accepted.

Following the exchange of the claim and the response, the tribunal will, depending on the size and complexity of the case, set out how the matter should then proceed. This will usually involve either written directions, or in more complex and substantial matters, a case management conference (known as a CMC).

The CMC will enable the parties to discuss any significant issues upon which they require guidance from the tribunal, and indeed provide for the disclosure of any evidence or other documentary details that each party has sight or possession of.

If settlement is not forthcoming between the parties, the case will then proceed to a final hearing. The length of such a hearing will be dependent upon the requirements of the case, and the weight and size of evidence involved.

This whole process can take anything from two or three months to a year or more. Again, the timetable that the case follows will depend, in the main, on the nature and complexity of the case itself, and the evidence related to it.

How to avoid employment claims

Whilst there is no magic wand that an employer can wave to avoid any such claims, there are some key actions that can be taken at various stages of an individual's employment.

1. At the recruitment stage, it is essential that it is not only the skills and experience of a candidate that are considered. A discerning assessment (albeit brief) of their character at the interview stage should assist in recruiting the right person for the organization. For example, where departures from previous organizations cannot be properly or honestly explained, it should be a clear warning sign for any prospective employer. Indeed, it is essential that the character of the individual seeking employment with the firm is one that will not bring difficulties and strife, culminating in an employment claim.
2. During the course of an individual's employment they should, from the outset, be fully conversant with the policies and procedures of the organization. These should cover all the duties and obligations of the employer towards the employee, and also the required conduct of the employee within the workplace. Such policies should be applied clearly and consistently to all employees, and any changes or amendments should be communicated to all members of staff.
3. Fair and equitable treatment of all staff must sit happily and consistently alongside any written intention to provide a fair and dignified workplace. The application of the policies and mission of an organization can sometimes be overlooked in the rush to achieve the charity's objectives. It

is certainly worth reiterating the point to those responsible for the welfare and performance of members of staff.

4. The point when an employee is dismissed, or a grievance is raised, can often be the point when an employer puts themselves in the position of giving the employee no option other than to bring a claim. This can often be the case when an employee is dismissed for good and fair reason, but the procedure is not handled properly, and the employer falls foul of their statutory obligations. Such instances are not uncommon. Similarly, an employee may correctly exercise their right to raise a grievance with their employer, and this again, may be badly, or indeed unlawfully, dealt with, or even ignored.

The key point here is that employers do have an obligation to their employees – and indeed to themselves – to follow the right procedures when necessary, and when required by law. Failure to do so leaves the employer wide open to a possible claim, and indeed criticism and punitive action by the employment tribunal in the event that the claim reaches a final hearing. Indeed, any employer that takes all grievances seriously (however minor they may seem), and follows correct disciplinary and dismissal procedures, will significantly reduce the prospects of facing, and indeed losing, a tribunal claim.

Wise recruitment, together with clear and sensitive management of staff and difficult employee situations, will be a very strong foundation for the running of any organization. It should also help significantly reduce the risk of costly, time-consuming, and potentially damaging employment claims. However, if and when claims arise, the charity should take prompt and expert legal advice, before any battle lines are drawn.

SECTION 17 PENSIONS, INSURANCE AND INVESTMENTS

James Swanson, Wellserve Financial Ltd

Forward planning is a hallmark of a well-run organization. Often in the charitable sector, however, the majority of the time can just be spent maintaining the status quo, but a charity neglects forward planning at its peril.

Specific examples of where forward planning can benefit a charity are illustrated as follows:

- Charity workers will be motivated and reassured by an organization that makes a pension provision for them.
- The effects of the loss of a key worker can be mitigated by the receipt of a payment from a key man insurance policy.
- The employees of a charity can be provided for during an extended period of illness with an income protection policy.
- The wise investment of a lump sum gift or a cash surplus can assist the long-term cash flow of a charity.

In summary, good financial planning can enhance the charitable organization and assist it to face future challenges robustly.

Pensions

The law states that employers must offer their employees access to a stakeholder pension scheme. This involves the employer formally choosing a stakeholder pension scheme and ensuring that employees can participate in it.

As with all rules there are exceptions, and these are as follows:

1. If the organization has fewer than five employees, then there is no requirement to offer the employees access to a stakeholder pension scheme (all of the employees are counted for this purpose, including paid trustees, but not self-employed people).
2. If the organization offers an occupational pension scheme that all the staff can join within a year of starting work.
3. If the organization offers its employees access to a personal pension scheme under which:
    3.1 It is open to all employees (although it is possible to offer an occupational pension scheme to some staff and a personal pension scheme to the remainder).
    3.2 The employer contributes an amount of at least 3% of the employee's basic pay to this scheme.
    3.3 It has no penalties for members who want to cease contributions or who want to transfer their pension.
    3.4 The employer agrees to pay the employee's contribution by way of deduction from their salary.

There are various options available when it comes to providing pensions for employees. As a rule, a company pension scheme would not be an appropriate way for a charity to provide for its employees. This is due to the expense, ongoing financial and administrative liability, together with the significant regulatory burden imposed on such schemes.

The following schemes are likely to be the most appropriate for consideration by charities:

Stakeholder pensions

Stakeholder pensions were created by legislation in 1999, and whilst they work in a similar way to a personal pension, there are distinguishing features imposed on the schemes so that a Pensions Regulator can register them specifically as a 'stakeholder' pension.

Management charges in each year must not amount to more than a specific limit. For people who join a scheme on or after 6 April 2005, 1.5% per annum is the maximum that they can be charged for the first ten years of membership. If the member stays in the scheme for more than ten years, the management charge will reduce to 1% thereafter.

In addition to management charges, stakeholder pension providers are permitted to recover costs and charges, for example, Stamp Duty or other charges for buying and selling investments.

The stakeholder pension contract must not impose charges for members who transfer in or transfer out of the scheme. The only charge that a provider is permitted to make is a 'dilution levy' (or, in the case of a with-profits fund, a 'market value adjustment'). This levy is to protect the members who stay in the scheme and whose funds could otherwise be disadvantaged by the monies being taken out. All stakeholder schemes must accept contributions from as little as £20. Stakeholder schemes must be able to accept transfers in from, or out to, other schemes.

To ensure that all stakeholder pension schemes are run in the interests of their members, the schemes are administered either by trustees or by scheme managers who are authorized by the Financial Services Authority (FSA). In some cases, the trustees will also be authorized by the FSA.

The whole rationale for stakeholder pensions was to encourage people to provide for their own retirement and to do this within the constraints of a safe, low charging product. Since their introduction, a number of personal pension providers have now adopted a similar charging structure for their products. However, those products offer a greater degree of flexibility than stakeholder pensions.

Personal pension plans

These plans involve contributions of a regular amount or a lump sum payment to the pension provider, who then invests it in one or more funds that the pension provider offers. Personal pension funds are usually administered by financial organizations, such as a building society, a bank, an insurance company or a unit trust company. Upon receipt of the contribution, the pension provider claims back basic rate tax on the contribution and this is used immediately to enhance the original payment.

The value of the personal pension fund (and a stakeholder pension) depends on:

- how much has been contributed to it;
- how well the fund's investments have performed;
- the nature and amount of the charges.

The pension provider imposes a charge for commencing the pension fund and for the ongoing administration. These charges are normally made annually and deducted from the fund.

At the selected retirement date, the monies in the personal pension fund are then applied to provide an income during retirement. At that stage, 25% of its value can be taken as a tax-free lump sum, and the remainder is usually invested in an annuity (not necessarily with the same pension company) in order to provide a regular income during retirement. It is often the case that companies that provide excellent growth rates during the period when contributions are being made do not necessarily offer the best annuity rates upon retirement.

The annuity at retirement can be paid out on the life of the policy owner or, if they have a spouse, the spouse can also be included in a way whereby he or she will receive a continuing payment (albeit at a lower rate) after the policy owner has died.

Advantages of a personal pension plan include:

- The pension assets are held by independent trustees and are therefore kept away from the policy owner's personal assets.
- The management of the scheme is undertaken by the pension provider using their expertise.
- Contributions are tax efficient.
- There is flexibility of fund choice, contribution and the dates when the benefits can be taken.

Disadvantages of a personal pension plan are that there is no guarantee on the returns from a personal pension scheme (the value can go down as well as up). Once the monies have been put in to the scheme, the policy owner cannot have the use of that money until retirement. Even then it can only be accessed in the way prescribed by HMRC. Currently a maximum of 25% of the fund value can be taken as a tax-free cash lump sum. The rest of the fund must be used to provide an income. One can take pension benefits from the ages of fifty to seventy-five years. This is to change to a minimum age of fifty-five in 2010.

If the holder of a personal pension dies before the selected retirement age, the value of the personal pension will form part of their estate. It is wise to consider holding a personal pension in trust, which means that its value falls outside the person's estate for inheritance tax purposes. Furthermore, the value of the fund is likely to be paid out to the deceased beneficiaries more quickly, as there is no need to obtain a grant of probate or letters of administration before the value can be paid out.

Group personal pension scheme
Such a scheme uses either a personal pension or a stakeholder pension and groups them together for the benefit of employees of an organization.

In practice, the scheme is set up for the employees and is managed by an external trustee. The employer's responsibility is primarily limited to ensuring the contributions are made from the organization's payroll to the pension provider. These schemes are attractive to charitable organizations and offer advantages over the more traditional occupational pension scheme.

A group personal pension scheme also offers flexibility in the choice of the particular funds that the monies will be invested in. Overall, the costs of a group personal pension scheme are likely to be less than the costs involved with individual personal pension schemes. However, organizations should ensure that cost is not the only factor that is considered. Ultimately it is what is best for the staff's long-term welfare that should be the paramount consideration.

Tax

Contributions made to a pension scheme by an employer are a tax efficient way of remunerating staff. Primarily there are two ways in which these can be made.

A contribution made by an employee to a pension scheme is made net of tax and then grossed up. For example, an employee making a contribution of £100 into a pension scheme will ultimately result in the pension company investing £128 on their behalf (assuming current income tax rates). The extra £28 comes from HMRC and is applied to the pension fund by the pension company. There is no administrative burden upon the individual to collect the tax.

An alternative way in which the tax benefit can be applied is known as a 'salary sacrifice'. Here the employee not only benefits from the tax effectiveness but also from savings from National Insurance contributions.

An illustration as to the application of these two principles is given in the following example (overleaf). For the purpose of this illustration, the charity worker receives an annual gross income of £20,000 and makes a gross pension contribution of £200 a month. Such a contribution would cost the worker £156 a month net (the difference between the figures is the tax that is rebated back to the pension company).

From the example overleaf, it can be seen how the employer pays the same amount of money and the employee has the same amount of disposable income after the pension contributions have been made. However, the contribution into the pension fund is significantly increased from £156 per month (net) to £262.63 per month using the 'salary sacrifice' method.

In the example of salary sacrifice, however, it could be that making contributions under that methodology would have the effect of reducing National Insurance contributions towards the State Pension which may in the long term reduce the benefits that might be paid. Many commentators feel that in

Standard pension deduction

A	Gross earnings	£20,000.00
	Employer's pension contribution	Nil
B	Personal tax allowance (2006/7)	£5,225.00
C	Taxable income	£14,775.00
D	Income tax (22% basic)	£2,982.90
E	Class 1 National Insurance contributions	£1,628.00
F	Total of tax and National Insurance contributions (D+E)	£4,610.90
G	Gross earnings less tax and National Insurance (A–F)	£15,389.10
H	Employee's pension payment (£156 × 12)	£1,872.00
I	Net disposable income (G–H)	£13,517.10
J	Employer's National Insurance contributions	£1,894.40
	Total cost to employer (A + J)	£21,894.40

Salary sacrifice

A	Gross earnings	£17,205.99
B	Employer's pension contribution	£3,151.56
C	Personal Tax Allowance (2006/7)	£5,225.00
D	Taxable Income	£11,980.99
E	Income tax (22% basic)	£2,368.22
F	Class 1 National Insurance Contributions	£1,320.66
G	Total of tax and National Insurance contributions (E + F)	£3,688.88
H	Gross earnings less tax and National Insurance (A–G)	£13,517.11
I	Employee's pension payment	–
J	Net disposable income (H)	£13,517.11
K	Employer's National Insurance contributions	£1,539.77
	Total cost to employer (A + B + K)	£21,897.32

future years the State Pension will become less valuable, and the emphasis will be far more on private pension provision.

Third-party contributions

Under current legislation, it is possible to make a contribution into a third-party's pension fund.

If a church is making full use of a pastor's tax allowance and pension contributions and wants to further reward the pastor, it might be possible for them to make a contribution towards the pastor's wife's pension. Providing this conforms to HMRC limits, it could mean a significant sum could be paid into the pastor's household by way of a contribution to his spouse as his pension for no extra tax or National Insurance costs.

Making money go further is the art of good stewardship in any environment and there may be opportunities to make the charity's money go further in regard to how a charity pays its staff.

HMRC offer guidance on legitimate ways of passing on tax-free benefits. The following guidance books are produced by them.

CWG2   Employer's Further Guidance to PAYE and NICS
480   Expenses and Benefits
490   Employee Travel

Copies are available from:

HMRC Website: www.hmrc.gov.uk
HMRC Order Line: Tel: 0845 7646646
Facts: Tel: 0870 2406406

In conjunction with these documents, it is vital to seek professional advice from a tax adviser.

Protecting the charity

There are insurance policies for almost every eventuality. Ultimately, the trustees of a charity have to make a decision on what is appropriate for their particular charity, but the benefits of having appropriate insurance policies in place can enable a charity to cope with many of the difficulties that it may encounter.

The following are some of the policies that are applicable to charitable organizations.

Key man insurance

It is likely that in most charities there are people who are key to the ongoing work. They may be the visionary, a major fund-raiser, a technical expert or, indeed, the leader.

Key man insurance helps mitigate the financial cost that would result from the loss of a key person in the event of death, critical illness or long-term sickness. The proceeds of such insurance would enable the charity to recruit a replacement person(s) and perhaps avoid having to cease a particular activity or otherwise suffer financial loss.

Critical illness insurance

As its name implies, such a policy provides an indemnity in the event that a key worker suffers a critical illness. These policies are based on the specific definition of 'critical illness' contained therein. If the illness suffered is included in the list, then the policy will pay out. However, it is vital to ensure that the charity understands exactly the nature of the cover that they are purchasing. It is not about getting the cheapest policy, but rather about getting the one that meets the particular needs of the charity and its employees.

Income protection

If a charity has a member of staff who is suffering from a long-term illness, then the charity can have a moral dilemma. On the one hand, the charity wants to look after its staff member, but on the other hand it may not have sufficient resources to continue paying the salary, particularly if another person has been recruited to continue the work.

Income protection allows the charity to function in the knowledge that after a deferred period (usually six months) the individual salary will continue to be paid. If the employee's work is of an administrative nature, then premiums for this type of policy are quite competitive.

If the policy is purchased by the charity, there is no tax liability on the individual in connection with its existence. If a claim is made under the policy, the benefit is paid by the insurance company to the charity and then to the employee by way of the charity's payroll.

Income protection can be set up on an individual basis or a group basis.

Trustee indemnity insurance (see section 25)

Kidnap, ransom and extortion (see section 20)

Buildings and contents insurance

Charities that own buildings need to ensure that they are properly covered for the full reinstatement value. This obligation includes contents and third-party risks. If the charity occupies leasehold property, there may still be an obligation upon the charity to effect part of the insurance cover, and regard should be had to the lease itself to determine this responsibility.

Failure by the charity to insure its buildings properly could, in the event of a loss, render the trustees liable personally.

Miscellaneous policies

If the charity is involved in projects in the community or is not completely confined to its building in providing its services, then additional insurance may be necessary to cover public liability, third-party risks, negligence, etc. It is wise to consult a professional insurance broker to ensure that all aspects of the charity's activity are covered by the appropriate insurance. The Charity

Commission have produced a useful guide called 'Charities and Insurance', which can be obtained from their website.

Investment of charitable funds

Where a charity has more funds than are needed for its immediate needs, then these funds need to be invested wisely. The Charities Act 1993, The Trustee Act 2000 and the Financial Services Market Act 2000 set out the principles concerning investment by charities. Due to the nature of investments, this can be a complex area and this section of the *Handbook* is a general overview of the subject. For more detailed information, the reader is referred to the websites of the Charity Commission and the Ethical and Investment Research Services.

Trustees' duties

Trustees can invest a charity's money only within the constraints of the charity's governing document and of the powers of investment otherwise available to them. The trustees can be liable for losses that result from any disregard of this principle.

Trustees have a general duty of care which is set out in the Trustee Act 2000. This duty is to exercise such skill as is reasonable in the circumstances, paying particular attention with regard to (a) any special knowledge or experience that the trustee has or holds himself out as having; and (b) situations where a trustee acts in the course of business or a profession.

The specific duties of charity trustees with regard to investments can be summarized as follows:

1. To have regard to the suitability to the charity of any investments made.
2. To have regard to the need for diversification of investments for the charity.
3. From time to time to review the investments of the charity with regard to the suitability and diversification ('from time to time' depends on the nature and size of the charity's investment portfolio).
4. Before exercising any power of investment, trustees must obtain and consider proper advice (if the amount of the funds to be invested is small and the obtaining of investment advice would not be cost effective, then in such circumstances independent advice need not be obtained).
5. When reviewing the investment of the charity's monies, the trustees must obtain and consider proper advice concerning the suitability and diversification of the investment.

Consideration will also need to be taken with regard to: (a) the proportion of funds that will be allocated to different classes of investment (asset allocation) and the overall level of risk; and (b) the merits of individual investments within each asset class (stock selection), not only in terms of their economic prospect, but also in terms of their individual contribution to the overall management of risk.

Where a charity has an ethical or socially responsible investment policy, the trustees will want to recognize the need for consistency with that policy.

With regard to 'proper advice', the trustees should be quite sure that the person providing this advice is suitably qualified, and that their ability has been demonstrated in practical experience and qualification. It is possible for the adviser to be one of the charity's trustees (provided one or more of the trustees can satisfy the others that they have the necessary financial ability and experience). The trustee giving the advice may, like any other adviser, incur a liability to the charity if losses result from advice that has been given negligently. It may be that the trustee so advising does not possess the necessary professional indemnity insurance cover that an external professional adviser would have. This is a valid consideration to bear in mind when trustees make a decision as to whether to use one of their number or an outside professional adviser.

The Trustee Act does not make any distinction between a regulated adviser who can provide advice based on the whole range of investment products and an adviser who can provide advice only in relation to a particular company or a particular company's products. It can hardly be in the charity's best interests for it to restrict investment to a narrow group of funds recommended by one company, just because the adviser is employed by that company. Rather, it would seem to be best practice for charities to use an independent adviser who can give advice based on the whole range of investments available in the marketplace.

Investment risk

As investment requires the active consideration of risk, it is important to outline what is meant by risk in this circumstance. Essentially there are two aspects: counterparty risk and investment risk.

Counterparty risk is the risk that one of the companies with which the charity carries out its investment business (bank, stockbroker, investment manager, Independent Financial Adviser) will default on its contractual obligations. Perhaps this risk is quite low in a climate where financial services are closely regulated and where a compensation scheme is in place. However, regulation does not cover the whole of the investment marketplace, and trustees should be careful as to which companies they use and what counterparty risk they are being exposed to. It is considered important for charity trustees to choose regulated companies and individuals as opposed to non-regulated ones.

Investment risk is inherent in any investment and is based on the failure or the under-performance of a particular investment. However, this risk can obviously be mitigated by having a suitably diverse portfolio.

A bank account has a low investment risk (and a low return). At the other end of the spectrum, investments such as futures and options could give a great return one day and a loss the next.

Investment risk is managed by having a diverse portfolio and by looking at the different asset classes. One of the most important aspects of managing risk is ensuring the correct asset allocation in a portfolio. The main asset classes are listed below in increasing order of risk.

Bank deposits
Government gilts
Corporate bonds
Property
Global bond funds
Managed UK equity funds
UK equity
Managed global equity funds
European equity
US equity
Managed specialist funds
Far East equity
Emerging markets equity
Futures and options

Government gilts and corporate bonds are often referred to as fixed interest, but there is a distinction between the two from a risk point of view. Gilts are government backed and tend to attract a lower volatility and lower risk ratings, whereas corporate bonds are issued by companies which can be big international ones or alternatively small 'start-ups'. There can be quite a spread of risk between these types. The investment risk of gilts and corporate bonds can be reduced by holding them until maturity.

Not only is diversity important with asset allocation, but also within stock allocation. This means that once the asset allocation has been decided on, then the underlying investment within that allocation should be spread. For example, if UK equity makes up part of the portfolio, then not all of the UK equity should be in one particular share or with one particular fund manager. Obviously this level of diversification is limited by the funds, and the greater the funds the greater the opportunity to diversify and spread risk.

Ethical investments

Increasingly, ethical and socially responsible investments are a very important part of a charity's investment strategy. Ethical investment is a wide phrase used to convey many different approaches to investment.

Usually the investor will apply their own ethical principles as to how they choose (or how they get their manager to choose) their investments. This can be done in two ways, by using negative criteria or positive criteria.

The negative criteria will give a list of activities that the investor does not feel that it is appropriate to invest in. Many Christian charities would feel that gambling, armaments or pornography are not appropriate areas to invest in and would therefore clearly state their funds should not be in companies involved with those activities. Sometimes the negative criteria list can be quite long and therefore the opportunity to diversify a portfolio is diminished.

The positive criteria look at providing a list of activities that the investor would like to be involved in. For example, investors wishing to invest in an environmentally friendly way might look to companies involved in renewable energy and showing good governance and equal opportunities to their workforce. The governing document of a charity might impose ethical restrictions on the trustees' power of investment. Even if the governing document is silent on this point, increasingly trustees of Christian organizations are deciding to adopt an ethical investment policy. In doing so, however, the trustees must remember that their power of investment should be used to obtain the maximum return that is consistent with commercial prudence, in order to further the purposes of the trust. In the case of Harris (Bishop of Oxford) v. Church Commissioners (1993), commonly known as the Bishop of Oxford case, the judge stated, 'Most charities need money and the more of it there is available the more the trustees can seek to accomplish'. If the ethical criteria are so tight that it results in very little growth or income, then this will have an impact on the charity.

In recent years, the marketplace with regard to ethical investment products has grown considerably. There are discretionary managers who have great experience in the whole area of ethical investment, and there are also fund managers offering socially responsible and ethical funds. Many of those funds have performed particularly well historically and the reason for this could be that the sectors in which they are investing are areas where there is a lot of potential growth.

The trustees may consider the question as to how far they can allow their investment strategy to be governed by considerations other than the level of investment return. The Bishop of Oxford case highlights three possible scenarios:

1. There may be instances (albeit rare) where investment in a particular type of business would conflict with the aims of a charity (e.g. a temperance charity investing in the shares of a brewery).
2. The trustees may need to consider carefully the likely effect of holding particular investments that could alienate supporters or beneficiaries and therefore hamper the charity's work.
3. The governing document of the charity may require trustees to take into account non-financial criteria.

In 1 and 2 above, the trustees would need to balance the difficulties they would encounter or the likely financial loss the charity would sustain if it were to hold those particular investments against the risk of financial detriment to the charity, if those investments were excluded from the portfolio. The greater the risk of financial detriment, the more certain the trustees should be of the difficulty/loss to the charity before they incur that risk.

The judge in the Bishop of Oxford case summarized the position as follows:

> Trustees must act prudently. They must not use property held by them for investment purposes as a means of making moral statements at the expense of the charity of which they are trustees. Those who wish may do so with their own property, but that is not a proper function of trustees with trust assets held as investment.
>
> ... in most cases the best interests of the charity require that the trustees choice of investments should be made solely on the basis of well-established investment criteria having taken expert advice where appropriate having due regard to such matters as the need to diversify, the need to balance income against capital growth, and the need to blance risk against return.

EIRIS (Ethical Investment Research Services) have produced some comprehensive independent guides to ethical investments in general and for charities in particular. These can be found on their website (www.eiris.org).

Investment policy
It may seem hard to make this judgment, but the trustees should decide their investment policy based on their own charity's needs and circumstances rather than trying to conform to 'public opinion'. The Charity Commission consider that trustees should:

1. Consider the aims and objectives of the charity.
2. Keep in mind the fundamental principle of maximizing the term.
3. If an ethical policy is adopted, it should be set out in writing and should be clear both on positive aims and any exclusions.
4. If companies or sectors are excluded, the reason for exclusion should be clearly thought through. The more restrictive a policy (in terms of exclusion), the greater the risk there may be to returns.
5. The trustees need to evaluate the effect that any proposed policy may have on potential investment returns, and this will usually require expert advice.
6. If the proposed policy increases the risk of lower returns, this must be balanced against the risk of alienating supporters and damaging reputation.
7. The trustees are unlikely to be criticized for adopting a particular policy if they have considered the correct issues, taken appropriate advice and reached a rational result.

Forming an investment policy

Before obtaining advice on specific investments, the Charity Commission suggest that the trustees decide on an investment strategy for their charity. It should be recorded clearly in writing and agreed by all the trustees. The policy should then be kept under regular review.

For charities that use an investment manager, the Trustee Act requires trustees to have an investment policy. This enables them to hold the invest-ment manager accountable to that policy. The trustees would include reference to this policy in their Annual Report as contained within the audited accounts.

An investment policy should address the following considerations:

1. The creation of sufficient financial return to enable the charity (together with its non-investment resources) to carry out its purposes effectively and without interruption.
2. The time period wherein the charity sets out to provide the service or length of time that the capital can be invested.
3. The maintenance and, if possible, the enhancement of the value of the invested funds while they are retained.
4. The management of risk.
5. The charity's stand on ethical investments.

Taxation and charity investments

Charities in the UK are exempt from tax on most income and gains from investments, estates, land and property, so long as that income/gain is used for charitable purposes.

A charity can arrange to have income received from some of these sources paid to it before UK tax is deducted. They include:

- Bank interest
- Income from land and furnished property
- Royalties

The above statement said 'exempt from tax on *most* income and gains from investments'. This means that there are some investments that are not tax efficient in regard to a charity. That is why it is important for a charity to have the right type of investments so that the tax is not taken away from them at source, or, if it is taken away, it can be reclaimed.

The trustees need to be careful before selecting a form of investment in which there is either no tax relief in respect of the investment returns, or for which no such relief is necessary because the investment returns are generally non-taxable. Charity trustees are not prohibited from making such investments, but the inability to use the charity's tax advantage may mean that the investment is intrinsically disadvantageous as compared with one where the returns are relieved from tax in the case of a charity. This would question the suitability of the investments for the charity.

This is an area where a professional adviser can add real value, enabling a charity to make the most of their investments and receive the greatest benefit back from HMRC. It is often when a financial adviser works in conjunction with an accountant that the most advantages are made and the charity's funds are best managed.

SECTION 18 VULNERABLE PERSONS

David Pearson, CCPAS

Over the past few decades, great advances have been made in recognizing and understanding the nature and effects of child abuse – physical, sexual and emotional – and the consequences of neglect.

More recently, it has been recognized that similar issues arise amongst other vulnerable groups of people. For example, adults with disabilities can be equally vulnerable to abuse and neglect, as well as those with mental health problems and conditions such as dementia.

Most abuse of children and adults occurs within the family. However, both children and adults are abused by those in positions of 'trust' – for example, church leaders, children's workers, music teachers, counsellors, etc. Places of worship differ from many organizations in that they open their doors to all. It follows, therefore, that people who pose risks to children and other vulnerable groups may be attending or may even (unknown to the church) be involved in activities within the church, organization or group.

It is essential, therefore, that charities have formal policies in place to safeguard children and vulnerable adults. The trustees are responsible for ensuring that such policies are adopted in accordance with government and other expectations or requirements (e.g. of the insurance company and Charity Commission), and that such policies are reviewed regularly. This is important so that the highest standards can be maintained in preventing and responding to abuse for both those in receipt of the services provided by the charity, and those with whom the charity comes into contact.

Safeguarding and a duty of care

'Safeguarding' is a term that describes the responsibility of charities and other agencies working with children/young people, vulnerable adults and their families. It involves them in taking reasonable measures to minimize the risk of harm, and acting appropriately when concerns of possible abuse arise.

Charity trustees, their workers and representatives have a duty of care towards children and other vulnerable people with whom they have contact. Effective safeguarding policies and good practice guidelines within an organization are not only essential in safeguarding and promoting the welfare of children and others, but are also necessary in addressing the charity's responsibilities towards staff and volunteers, parents and carers, statutory and other agencies, as well as the general public.

As far as the law is concerned, a 'child' is someone under the age of eighteen years. As far as vulnerable adults are concerned, there is no single definition. However, for most practical purposes a vulnerable adult could be defined as a person aged eighteen or over, whose ability to protect him/herself from violence, abuse or neglect is significantly impaired through a physical or mental disability or illness, through old age or otherwise.

Legislation and statutory guidance

1. Children

Current government guidance on safeguarding in England is set out in the statutory guidance, 'Working Together to Safeguard Children: A guide to inter-agency working to safeguard and promote the welfare of children' (2006) (www.everychildmatters.co.uk). This guidance has been issued in accordance with the requirements of the Children Act 1989, which provides a comprehensive framework for care and protection of children, and the Children Act 2004, which underpins the 'Every Child Matters: Change for Children' programme. It also reflects the principles contained in the United Nations Convention on the Rights of the Child, ratified by the UK government in 1991, and takes into account the European Convention of Human Rights.

'Working Together' sets out how organizations (including places of worship and other charities and individuals) should work together to safeguard and promote the welfare of children. Section 2.153 states that 'churches, other places of worship and faith-based organizations need to have appropriate arrangements in place for safeguarding and promoting the welfare of children', and in particular, that there should be 'appropriate codes of practice for staff, particularly those working with children, such as those issued by the Churches' Child Protection Advisory Service (CCPAS)'.

The Home Office produced a code of practice, 'Safe from Harm (1993)', for voluntary organizations. This stressed the need to treat all would-be paid staff and volunteers as job applicants for any position involving contact with children (see *3. Appointing leaders and workers*, below).

Although the issues and expectations concerning safeguarding children are broadly similar throughout all four nations in the UK, there are some procedural and legal differences in Wales, Scotland and Northern Ireland. Further information can be obtained from any local authority (in England, Wales and Scotland), Social Services and Health Board (Northern Ireland) or from the Churches' Child Protection Advisory Service (CCPAS).

As part of the Charity Commission's registration process (England and Wales), organizations working with vulnerable beneficiaries (children and adults) will be asked for (a) information about policies and procedures that they have in place for keeping children safe and (b) confirmation that Criminal Records Bureau (CRB) Disclosure certificates (where applicable) have been obtained in respect of all trustees.

2. Vulnerable adults

In March 2000, the Department of Health and the Home Office published statutory guidance, 'No Secrets', which gives guidance to local authorities that have a responsibility to investigate and take action when a vulnerable adult is believed to be suffering abuse. Adult Social Care has lead responsibility for investigating all allegations or suspicions of abuse. Where there is evidence that a criminal act may have been committed, then the police also become involved.

In England and Wales, a vulnerable adult is a person aged eighteen or over 'who is or may be in need of community care services by reason of mental or other disability, age or illness, and who is or may be unable to take care of him or herself; or unable to protect him/herself against significant harm or exploitation' (Who Decides, Lord Chancellor's Department [1977], quoted in 'No Secrets').

For CRB purposes, the term 'vulnerable adult' has specific meaning under the Care Standards Act 2000. It is important to understand the term correctly as its interpretation affects whether or not a charity can obtain a CRB Disclosure for trustees.

If a person is aged eighteen or over and has a condition of the following type, then they are considered to be a 'vulnerable adult' for the purposes of the Care Standards Act 2000:

- a learning or physical disability;
- a physical or mental illness, chronic or otherwise, including an addiction to alcohol or drugs;
- a reduction in physical or mental capacity.

A charity that is concerned with the provision of care or advocacy services to vulnerable adults, and where the trustee position enables a trustee to have access to vulnerable adults in receipt of such services in the course of their normal duties, is entitled to a CRB Disclosure for its trustees.

A 'care' position is defined by the Care Standards Act 2000 as:

- a position which is such as to enable him/her to have regular contact in the course of his/her duties with adults to whom accommodation is provided in a care home;
- a position which is concerned with the provision of personal care in their own homes for persons who by reasons of illness, infirmity or disability are unable to provide it for themselves without assistance.

An Enhanced CRB Disclosure applies where the vulnerable adults receive any of the following care services:

- accommodation and nursing or personal care in a care home;
- personal care or support to live independently in his or her own home;
- any services provided by an independent hospital, independent clinic, independent medical agency or National Health Service body;
- social care services;
- any services provided in an establishment catering for a person with learning difficulties, and in consequence of a condition, including:
  a. a learning or physical disability; or
  b. a physical or mental illness, chronic or otherwise, including an addiction to alcohol or drugs; or
  c. a reduction in physical or mental capacity;
- or if they have disabilities, including any of:
  a dependency upon others in the performance of, or a requirement for assistance in the performance of, basic physical functions;
  severe impairment in the ability to communicate with others; or
  impairment in a person's ability to protect him or herself from assault, abuse or neglect.

If the trustee's duties mean that they are eligible to apply for a CRB Disclosure, they should do so (see also section 9).

Some of the essentials

This may all sound rather daunting, but the main denominations will have their own policies that local churches would be expected to adhere to. The same may be true of other umbrella organizations. For others it isn't a question of having to reinvent the wheel! Model policies and safe practice guidelines for work with both children and vulnerable adults are available from CCPAS. The material is available as part of a comprehensive manual, but is also supplied on computer disk so that policies and other useful documents can be easily adapted and produced for any organization. CCPAS also have a 24-hour helpline, which will be able to provide professional advice on policy issues or in regard to individual cases.

There is no fail-safe system that can rule out the appointment of someone who is intent on abusing children, but in adopting recommended procedures and practice, trustees will minimize the risks of this happening. In addition, failure to follow such procedures might prove crucial to the outcome of a negligence claim against a church or an organization where there has been an incident of abuse. Church specialist insurance companies have advised that failure to follow appropriate policies may invalidate any insurance cover.

We have already said that most child abuse takes place in the home. More often than not, therefore, workers having to deal with these issues will be responding to concerns and suspicions that relate to circumstances outside the place of worship or organization. Workers have no less a responsibility towards children in these circumstances, as illustrated in the case of Victoria Climbié, who died as a result of injuries inflicted by her carers. In the statutory inquiry into her death, three churches were severely criticized for not taking appropriate action in bringing her situation to the attention of the authorities.

The most important areas which will need to be considered are:

1. *The policies*
Safeguarding policies for both children and vulnerable adults need to contain the following:

- How to respond if there are concerns/suspicions of abuse, including allegations/concerns in regard to employees (paid or voluntary).
- A named contact (and deputy) in the charity to co-ordinate concerns and to take action. Separate child/adult/protection/safeguarding co-ordinators could be appointed in respect of children and vulnerable adults, or the same individuals could fulfil both roles.
- Safe recruitment procedures for both paid and volunteer workers.

- Guidelines for running the charity's activities for children and vulnerable adults.
- Actions and procedures necessary where someone who is a known risk is involved with a group (e.g. a sex offender is a member of the church congregation).

2. *Responding to concerns or allegations*

Where safeguarding concerns arise, workers should immediately record in writing what they have seen or heard that has worried them and/or what they have been told by someone else.

In the case of suspected abuse or deliberate injury, if there are concerns for a child's safety or if the child is afraid to return home, the local authority Children's Social Care or the police Child Protection Unit should be contacted. In circumstances where there are concerns regarding a vulnerable adult, the Adult Social Care or the police should be contacted.

CCPAS have issued the following guidelines for any worker or individual responding to a child or vulnerable adult who may have been abused:

- Do not ask leading questions.
- Do not make promises you may not be able to keep, e.g. not telling anyone else.
- Accept what you hear without passing judgment.
- Tell the child/young person/vulnerable adult what you are going to do.
- Make careful notes (the circumstances, what the child/vulnerable adult said, what you said, etc.) as soon as possible, preferably within an hour. Include dates and times of the incident, record and keep the notes safely. Do not question or investigate.
- Contact the person responsible for child/vulnerable person protection concerns or, in their absence, take action yourself without delay.
- The child/vulnerable person protection co-ordinator/safeguarding officer should contact the appropriate Social Care Department in the local authority, the police, or CCPAS for further advice.

The government has issued guidance to organizations in a publication, 'What to do if you are worried a child is being abused' (2003). This says that everyone working with children and families should:

- Be familiar with and follow your organization's procedures and protocols for promoting and safeguarding the welfare of children and know who to contact in your organization to express concerns about a child's welfare.

- Remember that an allegation of child abuse or neglect may lead to a criminal investigation, so don't do anything that may jeopardize a police investigation, such as asking a child leading questions or attempting to investigate the allegations of abuse.
- Refer any concerns about child abuse or neglect to Children's Social Care or the police. If you are responsible for making referrals, know who to contact.
- Seek to discuss your concerns with the child, as appropriate to their age and understanding, and with their parents, and seek agreement to making a referral to Children's Social Care *unless* you consider such a discussion would place the child at risk of significant harm.
- When you make a referral, agree with the recipient of the referral what the child or parents will be told, by whom, and when.
- If you make a referral by telephone, confirm it in writing within forty-eight hours. Children's Social Care should acknowledge your written referral within one working day of receiving it, so if you have not heard back within three working days, contact Children's Social Care again.

3. Appointing leaders and workers

In order to meet the statutory guidance already mentioned, it is important that the organization has written job descriptions for all leaders and those working with children and young people or vulnerable adults. This should apply to all, whether pastor or crèche worker, paid member of staff or volunteer. All workers should be chosen with care; no one has a right to work with children and young people, or vulnerable adults. With a shortage of workers, the temptation to appoint all who volunteer must be avoided. The following recruitment process should be followed:

1. All would-be applicants should be advised of the recruitment process and that, if successful, it will be necessary to undergo a Criminal Records Bureau check.
2. A detailed application form should be completed, which would include a declaration as to whether the applicant has been the subject of criminal or civil court cases, and whether they have caused harm to any child or put them at risk. This includes 'spent' convictions under the Rehabilitation of Offenders Act 1974. Applicants should be asked to declare all convictions and cautions, however old, and given the opportunity of voluntarily disclosing any relevant information. This will avoid having to go through a full appointment process if clearly someone is not going to be suitable for the position. It is also a test of their honesty, as information subsequently revealed by a criminal records

check could be checked against information that has been supplied, and again may prove useful in determining suitability.

3. At least two references should be taken up. The charity should reserve the right to make any character checks they deem necessary.

4. The applicant should be interviewed, and if it is decided to make an appointment, a criminal records check at enhanced level should then be undertaken.

5. Those with responsibility for recruiting workers (paid or voluntary) should be satisfied that the applicant is suitable for the job.

6. The position should be offered subject to satisfactorily completing a probationary period.

7. All workers should be made aware of the need to challenge behaviour when there are concerns, and advised of the organization's child/adult protection policies.

4. Abuse of trust

Although as already stated most child abuse takes place within a family context, we need to recognize that those intent on abusing children will seek contact through employment (paid or voluntary). It is therefore essential to recruit safely (see *3. Appointing leaders and workers*).

Churches and places of worship are unique in working with vulnerable beneficiaries, and in providing pastoral care within a context where people are in positions of power and authority, e.g. church minister and member of the congregation. It is therefore essential that churches follow abuse of trust guidelines, 'Caring for Young People and the Vulnerable: Guidance for preventing abuse of trust' (Home Office, 1999). This guidance can be accessed via the CCPAS website.

5. Guidelines for the day-to-day running of activities

There are some general principles that should be followed. These include:

Treating everyone with respect

Respecting personal privacy

Being available, but also being ready to refer a situation or problem to someone more experienced to deal with it

Being sensitive to needs, likes and dislikes

Avoiding questionable activity, e.g. rough/sexually provocative games and inappropriate language

Following accepted guidelines relating to physical contact

Challenging unacceptable behaviour

Reporting all allegations/suspicions of abuse

Other matters

Practice guidelines should be prepared in relation to each activity, and need to include:

- procedures for recruitment, training and supporting of workers;
- guidelines specific to each group activity (see below);
- a statement that:
  a. the interests of the child/vulnerable adult are paramount at all times;
  b. if necessary to depart from general guidelines (in particular circumstances and in the interests of the individual concerned), this will only be done with the knowledge of the worker's supervisor or in an emergency reported in writing after the event.

The sort of issues that need to be considered, depending on the activities, include the following:

Essential practice guidelines
Definitions of abuse
Recognizing possible signs of abuse
How to respond to a child/adult when there are concerns
Action following disclosure
Handling of CRB disclosure information and associated guidance
Discipline policy (for children)
Leader to child ratios
Guidelines on physical contact
Safety of premises
First aid and medication
Taking children off the premises

Practice guidelines as applicable
Home visits
Children attending the group without a parent's knowledge
Babysitting arrangements
Peer group activities
Working with disruptive children
Appointing workers from abroad
Transporting children
Children with special needs
Swimming trips
Use of the internet and safety issues
Videos and photography

Drop-in centres
Working overseas

Within the context of this chapter, it is impossible to cover all these aspects, but detailed information is available from specialist organizations such as CCPAS.

6. Safe supervision of known offenders
Another essential area in safeguarding children, young people and vulnerable adults is how the leadership responds if someone who has committed sex offences attends a church. They must never be allowed to work with children or vulnerable adults, or be left alone with them at any time. Indeed, if an individual has been banned from working with children, the church could be committing a criminal offence if they allow this to happen, in any capacity.

Sexual offending can be extremely addictive. For this reason, however repentant an offender may appear to be, there are no cast-iron guarantees that they will not re-offend. Even if the offender has undergone treatment or received prayer ministry, it should not be assumed they are safe. The follow-on from repentance is to 'go and sin no more' so, apart from the safeguarding considerations, it would be irresponsible to place someone in a position of vulnerability where they might be tempted to re-offend. Sex offending needs to be approached in the same way as any other addictive behaviour.

When an offender starts to attend a place of worship, or leaders first become aware of a situation, it will be important, in consultation with agencies such as the police and/or probation service, to carry out some sort of risk assessment. In some situations, it would not be appropriate even to try to work with an offender – for example, in circumstances where the building is small and overflowing with children. There may be other churches without children attending who are better placed to help.

In circumstances where it is judged possible to supervise an offender safely, behavioural boundaries need to be put in place. These should help the offender feel secure and less at risk of false accusations. More importantly, these boundaries will serve to protect children and vulnerable adults attending activities. Such boundaries need to be personal to the individual involved and should be reviewed regularly. The following would need to be considered:

- An offender should not be permitted to get close to children (either physically or emotionally).
- An offender should never be allowed to work with children and young people.

- An offender should not sit in the vicinity of children at church or attend house/cell group meetings where there are children.
- Offenders should not hold positions of leadership or responsibility where they are seen by children within the church, even in a role such as handing out hymn/song books. This is because a child is likely to regard them as someone they can trust. The additional stress that leadership brings could also increase the temptation to re-offend.

NB: these principles are equally applicable for vulnerable adults.

Such a contract would need to be reviewed on a regular basis and would be on-going. Risk is not related to the period someone might spend on a sex-offenders' register and therefore would need to continue even though statutory involvement might come to an end.

Where there are reasonable grounds for concern, the church will still need to respond, even if an allegation is denied (or someone is not convicted) and, in particular, by applying appropriate boundaries. Failure to do so could place children at risk. It is also in the interests of someone who feels they have been falsely accused to work within given boundaries in order to minimize the risk of further allegations.

The help and pastoral support available in the church needs to run alongside the monitoring of an individual by police and probation. Multi-Agency Public Protection Arrangements (MAPPA) exist in all areas of England and Wales. MAPPA places a duty on the police, the probation service and the prison authorities to assess and manage risks posed by offenders with whom they are working. Similar arrangements apply elsewhere in the UK.

Helpful organizations

Churches' Child Protection Advisory Service – child protection support, training and policy/practice issues including work with sex offenders.
Tel: 0845 120 4550
email: info@ccpas.co.uk
web: www.ccpas.co.uk

Lucy Faithfull Foundation – a national child protection agency working with adult male and female perpetrators of child sexual abuse. Lucy Faithfull Foundation runs Circles of Support (see also below).
Tel: 01527 591 922
web: www.lucyfaithfull.co.uk

Circles of Support and Accountability – a community support system for sex offenders.
Tel: 0870 774 6354
email: helen@quaker.org.uk
web: www.ccjf.org/what/circles.htm1

Stop It Now! – a national campaign that aims to prevent child abuse by encouraging offenders to seek help. It also provides adults with information to help protect adults.
Helpline: 0808 1000 900
email: help@stopitnow.org.uk
web: www.stopitnow.org.uk

NSPCC – a national child protection charity
Helpline: 0808 800 5000
email: help@nspcc.org.uk
web: www.nspcc.org.uk

Sanctuary – training and support to help churches working with child sexual abusers
Tel: 0870 991 1876
email: info@sanctuaryuk.com
web: www.sanctuaryuk.com

SECTION 19 RESOLVING DISPUTES

It is almost inevitable that disputes will arise from time to time in a charitable organization – not that a charitable organization is any better or worse than any other organization. It is perhaps a reflection on human nature that where two or more people work together in close proximity for a period of time, stresses and strains can develop into full-blown disputes.

At the time of writing this section, the latest statistics from the Charity Commission show that 56% of all disputes referred to them are taking place in faith-based charities.

For a charity, the critical issue is not the existence of the dispute itself, but rather how the charity will manage or respond to that dispute. There are insufficient pages in this book to set out all the circumstances that could give rise to a dispute, although there are three main areas that seem to germinate more than their fair share of difficulties:

1. Personality
2. Programmes
3. Pressure

When disputes arise, it is likely that the parties themselves, as well as the charity, are looking for appropriate intervention to enable the dispute to be resolved. People working in any organization look for a forum to raise concerns, expect to be listened to positively, and require a response.

The cost of a dispute to a charity is not insubstantial. The aggregate of the cost of people's time, the damage to the goodwill and image of the organization, the effect on its financial support and fund-raising potential, as well the negative effect on the remainder of the staff, all need to be considered.

In addition, if the dispute goes to either litigation or mediation, the charity needs to consider the effect of: (1) the delay, (2) damage to relationship and morale, (3) stress, (4) the limiting of the work of the organization, and possibly (5) legal fees.

Larger charities may well have a dispute resolution procedure in place. Denominational churches can often appeal to regional or national bodies to assist in times of dispute. Fundamentally, however, when a dispute arises it is important:

- To identify and recognize the existence of the dispute.
- To agree a forum whereby the nature of this dispute can be understood and the parties can be encouraged to try to work towards a resolution. A third-party facilitator can be significant at this juncture.
- To recognize that if the parties will not commit to try to work the issue through, then steps may have to be taken to isolate the parties concerned from the day-to-day running of the organization whilst the issue continues to be addressed.
- To ensure that steps are taken to minimize the fallout on the remainder of the charity and its work.

Spotting the dangers

Taking the three areas of possible dispute mentioned above, we should look at them in a little more detail.

Personality
Character – dominant leader/bully/independent spirit
Ambition – plotter/manipulator/controller
Frustration – inadequate leadership/blocked goals

Programmes
Too much activity/inadequate rest
Too much exposure to a crisis situation
Inadequacy of programmes towards perceived need
Lack of finance
Resistance to change

Pressure
Hostile environment
Political or board 'interference'
Lack of adequate staff
Temptation
No one to talk to/no accountability

Options for dispute resolution

If the dispute cannot be resolved 'in house', then the options include:

Mediation
Mediation is fast becoming the preferred methodology for resolving disputes, particularly when the subject matter of the dispute is between personalities, or concerns issues such as doctrine.

The main characteristic of mediation is that it is the parties themselves, with the help of the professional mediator, who work out a mutually acceptable solution. In this respect, it differs from litigation or arbitration where the solution is imposed.

In mediation, each party outlines their position before the mediator, and thereafter each party meets in confidential sessions with the mediator. The mediator then 'shuttles' between the parties, analysing and isolating the main areas of disagreement and exploring ways in which difficulties can be overcome. The parties can be legally represented during the process and, if the mediation reaches an agreement, the settlement itself is written down and signed by the parties and the mediator.

The success rate in mediation is quite high and, given that it is the parties themselves who ultimately come to an agreement, they 'own' the settlement and the settlement tends to become binding in the vast majority of cases.

Other advantages of mediation include its cost effectiveness, the fact that it is private (court hearings are very often reported publicly), and almost 80% of mediations are settled within one day.

The mediator can be either a trained professional or one endorsed by a regulatory organization such the Centre for Dispute Resolution (CEDR).

Litigation
In certain circumstances, it may be right for a charity to go to court, either to protect an asset or establish a right. Generally speaking, charities require consent from the Charity Commission before commencing an action in court. Litigation is expensive and the outcome uncertain. Therefore, unless

all other options have been exhausted and/or the charity has been professionally advised that they have a strong case, then litigation should be avoided if at all possible.

The Charity Commission

The Charity Commission's powers of intervention in a charity dispute are limited. They will assess whether their intervention is a proper use of public resources and whether it will protect the charity's assets from risk or loss.

Areas of dispute where the Charity Commission consider getting involved include:

* disputes in the way a charity is being run, which puts assets or funds at risk (bad financial management or dishonesty);
* where the charity's income is not being used for its stated purpose;
* where the trustees of the charity are acting in a way that is contrary to the governing document or charity law;
* situations where there is a danger of the name of the charity being brought into disrepute;
* where the administration of the charity has broken down and the charity is not working effectively.

The Charity Commission will not intervene in disputes where:

* there are disagreements between trustees or between the trustees and members, for example, over policy or doctrine;
* where the dispute is between a charity and third party concerning property rights or a breach of contract with the charity;
* the charity changes part of its operation – for example, closing a residential care home.

If the Charity Commission intervene in a dispute, the options they have include:

* appointing additional trustees to break a deadlock between the existing trustees;
* suspending a trustee or an officer of the charity for a period of up to twelve months pending consideration as to whether or not that person should be removed;
* vesting property of the company in the Official Custodian for Charities;
* preventing a person who holds property on behalf of a charity from disposing of that property without the consent of the Charity Commission;

- appointing an Interim Manager in respect of the property and affairs of the charity.

The above powers may be exercised by the Charity Commission, providing they are satisfied that there has been misconduct or mismanagement in the affairs of the charity, or that it is necessary to act in such a way as to protect the property of the charity.

In addition, the Charity Commission have powers to impose a permanent resolution by:

- removing any trustee or employee of the charity who the Commission believe by their conduct has contributed or facilitated misconduct or mismanagement; and
- making a Scheme for the administration of the charity.

However, before one of these permanent solutions can be imposed, the Charity Commission must first institute a formal inquiry into the charity and be satisfied that the proposed course of action is necessary to protect the property of the charity, and that notice to this effect had been given to each of the charity's trustees.

Given the wide powers that a charity's governing document usually gives to the trustees, the Charity Commission are of the opinion that disputes concerning the management and administration of the charity are initially a matter for the charity trustees themselves to resolve. The Charity Commission cannot overrule a charity's decision that has been validly taken within the powers that the trustees have. It is for those trustees to decide policy for the charity and this may include:

- resolving differences over spiritual or doctrinal matters within faith-based charities;
- deciding how community facilities (schools, community centres) are used;
- deciding applications to admit or remove from membership, and whether proper procedures have been complied with;
- deciding how to consult support groups about decisions and policies of the charity they use or support;
- the terms and conditions of occupancy of any land owned or administered by the charity;
- issues relating to employment or claims for unfair dismissal;
- disputes between charities and people or organizations who have entered into contracts with the charity – including landlord and tenant disputes;

- issues connected with a planning application or enforcement of planning law.

In summary, if there is no evidence of wrongdoing, or the issues themselves are not sufficiently serious, then the Charity Commission are unlikely to get involved. Certainly they cannot act on unsubstantiated allegations, rumour or opinion.

In cases of faith-based organizations, the Charity Commission are committed to improving standards of governance and accountability in those organizations. Given the statistic quoted at the beginning of this section, there is clearly still a great deal more to be done in this area.

SECTION 20 CHARITIES WORKING OVERSEAS

UK registered charities working either wholly or partly overseas often find that the mixture of culture, environment and local laws present a challenge over and above the charitable purposes that the organization seeks to undertake in that country.

There is a challenge, too, for the charity's UK-based trustees who need to ensure that the assets of the charity are expended exclusively in the furtherance of the Objects of the charity in the overseas country (or countries) in which it is working. Not only does this require good systems of governance and management, but the trustees must also be prepared for the 'What if?' scenario.

The principles contained in this section are applicable only to organizations that are governed by the laws of England and Wales or, in the case of a charitable company, one that is incorporated in England and Wales.

An important first step for any charity considering working overseas is to ensure that its charitable activities are actually lawful in the particular country in which it intends to work.

Local subsidiaries

Charities intending to work in overseas countries are advised to ascertain whether they are required to register in the particular country in which they intend to work. Even if they are not required to register, there may be benefits for the charity in voluntarily registering in that country.

Registering in a foreign country (a local registration) usually involves: a certified copy of the charity's governing document; its Certificate of Incorporation (in the case of the charitable company); and a Power of Attorney appointing a local resident as its contact point in that country, being legalized by the UK foreign office before being tendered for stamping by the particular country's embassy in London (see www.fco.gov.uk/legalisation), and then produced for registration in the particular country. It may also be necessary to ensure that the documents are translated into the local language by an accredited translation firm.

The requirement for a Power of Attorney is to ensure that at least one person who is ordinarily resident in the particular country can transact business in that country on behalf of the charity. Care should be taken in the appointment of that person, as they will have considerable freedom to enter into contracts and obligations on behalf of the charity. Sometimes this person can be a senior member of the UK charity, but some countries require a national to operate in that role.

Benefits of local registration can include:

- in some cases certain tax benefits in the particular country;
- the possibility of closer cooperation with other NGO's governments and other locally based entities;
- the ability to hire staff locally;
- simplified procedure for obtaining visas or work permits for expatriate staff.

The possible drawbacks to local registration include:

- the necessity to comply with additional local laws in that country;
- the need to have a local audit of finances in that country;
- the possibility of influence or control from the government of that country.

Issues relating to the audit arrangements for local subsidiaries can complicate the UK charity's audit, as the local figures must be audited in the subsidiary's country and presented to the UK Auditor in an acceptable way. The UK-based charity trustees are ultimately responsible for ensuring that the locally registered subsidiary fully mirrors the charitable purposes for which the UK charity has been set up.

Many UK charities working overseas testify to the fact that time spent in building good local contacts, particularly with the various ministries of the government who supervise charitable activity in that country, is time well spent. It is wise, too, to ensure that the British or EU Embassies in the country are aware of the activities of the UK charity, as they may offer guidance, advice and support in appropriate cases.

Fundamentally, it is essential that the UK charity trustees have control over how its monies will be used, and have influence over the selection of beneficiaries or projects that will be supported. It is not sufficient that the UK charity is merely a conduit to pass funds through to the entity in another country in circumstances where it has no say in how those funds are to be used.

Charity trustees based in the UK may nevertheless feel detached and therefore uncomfortable when a sizeable proportion of the charity's resources are sent overseas to support its charitable activities in other countries, even if those trustees have a considerable say in how those funds are to be used. Trustees who are concerned to ensure the proper discharge of their governance responsibilities may choose to adopt one or more of the following steps:

1. If the charity has a Chief Executive or general director who travels overseas regularly to supervise the charity's work in various countries, the board may consider inviting him/her to become a member of the board (provided that the charity's governing document allows that person to be salaried as a board member). As that person travels overseas he or she will be representing the other members of the board and making decisions as a board member as well as a paid member of staff. In other words, he/she will be their ears and eyes from a governance position as well as an executive one.

2. The trustees may consider it advisable for one or more of them to travel overseas from time to time to personally view and appraise the nature and effectiveness of the work in those countries. Their reasonable travelling expenses may well be a legitimate expense of the charity, provided that the expense is in proportion to the total income and expenditure of the charity, and that it is properly agreed that one or more of the trustees should actually travel (of course, if they are paying their own expenses, they are free to travel whenever they wish!).

3. Charities working overseas often prefer to employ local people rather than to second staff from the UK. This can be beneficial to the charity in enabling the charity to more readily understand local laws and customs, and it also provides additional benefits to the community in which they work. It is important, therefore, that charities fully understand the employment laws. Money spent on good quality local legal advice will often prove to be a wise investment in such matters. If the UK charity has not effected a local registration in the particular country, then the staff hired are effectively hired

by the UK charity, although it is by no means certain that, in the event of a grievance, that person would choose to pursue their claim in the UK courts.

Compliance with local laws

For charities working overseas, there is no substitute for gaining a good understanding of the local laws and customs that could affect the charity's work. In addition to the law of the land, in some countries tribal or religious laws or cultural obligations may be just as significant. To breach any of these can have serious implications on the reputation and standing of the charity in that country. Good intentions count for little, if the local cultural, tribal or religious laws are broken.

(On a visit to a Central Asian country on behalf of a client charity, I recall being regaled by an official of that country with a true story of how a foreign worker had been in ignorance of the cultural sensitivities concerning a matter and as a result had felt threatened by the reaction of the nationals and had summoned his Embassy for help. The Embassy had dispatched a helicopter to winch the person concerned out of the charity's compound and take him to a place of safety at the Embassy – much to the amusement of the local people!)

Some charities working overseas have entered into agreements with national governments in order to pursue a common purpose. Invariably such agreements are written under the laws of that particular country. Some of those that I have seen enable the government, in the case of the failure of the particular project, to call on the assets of the parent charity in the UK.

Charities working overseas may be offered the opportunity of working together with the national government in an arrangement akin to a joint venture. Often the documentation involved can expose the charity to financial liability in the event that the project is not successful. Whilst the charity may feel that such a joint venture gives it an excellent opportunity to develop its work in that country, the trustees need to weigh carefully the risk against the potential benefit. In such circumstances it may preferable for the charity to consider setting up a wholly owned subsidiary (probably a company limited by guarantee but without charitable status) to enter into the joint venture. Providing that the objects for that company limited by guarantee are in line with the charity's own objects and the company precludes the distribution of any profits to its members, then the charity can properly advance monies to that subsidiary for it to enter into the joint venture project. In the event of financial or other failure, the funding from the charity would cease, and it is only the company limited by guarantee that is at risk, rather than the parent charity itself.

It is of fundamental importance for a UK charity working overseas to ensure that unfettered control of all its projects there remain with the trustees of the UK charity. In some cases, a charity may seek to delegate operational decisions to a field council or perhaps to a body that is an amalgamation of several charities working in a particular region. Again, the trustees of the charity need to be comfortable with the limit of authority that is given to the field council, as ultimately they remain responsible for what is carried on in the name of the charity and under their remit.

Calculating and managing risk

As has been stated elsewhere in this book, a charity faces many risks in undertaking its work. For those charities working overseas, there are some additional issues that may need to be dealt with:

Kidnap or abduction
War or political instability
Earthquake or other natural disaster
Disease
Terrorism
Serious accident or injury
Murder or accidental death
Missing persons
Imprisonment or expulsion
Entrapment

Charities and their trustees need to be aware of the potential risks and must ensure that the staff member, volunteer or worker who is to be sent overseas is fully aware of the situation to which they are being exposed. In instances where the charity is working in countries where there is a higher than average risk, the charity should take the following steps:

- Consult with appropriate organizations such as the Foreign and Commonwealth Office in London (www.fco.gov.uk), The Hospital for Tropical Diseases (www.thehtd.org), and possibly the embassy of the particular country, to get the most up-to-date and complete picture in order that the charity's workers can be fully briefed before travelling.
- Ensure the charity has in place adequate procedures for dealing with emergency evacuation (with an appropriate method of communication

between the worker and the charity). NB: This procedure should be communicated to the staff workers' next of kin in the UK as well.

- Possibly require the staff worker to sign a declaration before they travel, promising to abide by the charity's emergency evacuation policy and acknowledging that in default of compliance the charity has no further responsibility.
- A policy that clearly sets out the charity's procedures in the event of kidnap or abduction (including whether or not ransoms would be paid).
- The setting up of a crisis management team in the UK or in the particular country that is empowered to make decisions and implement pre-agreed policy in response to the particular challenge that has arisen.
- The setting aside of emergency funds that can be utilized quickly to enable the crisis management team to respond purposefully to the challenge.

In the particular country in which the crisis has arisen, the charity and its staff will need to be sensitive to the authorities and how they may wish to respond to the incident, as the authorities may be minded to exclude the charity from direct involvement and try to resolve the issue themselves.

Crises will arise from time to time, and it is how the charity and its trustees respond to those crises that is important. Time spent in agreeing appropriate policies and procedures in advance is considered time well spent.

In cases where the charity is sending workers overseas who perhaps have been seconded to the UK charity from other countries, then the UK charity must bear in mind that staff members, friends and families from the seconding country may well have a different interpretation as to how the charity should respond in an emergency. In the midst of a crisis situation, the charity will not wish to receive a claim from friends and family of the staff member who live in another country and who feel that the charity should be sued for exposing that person to unreasonable risk or having a less than efficient system of managing those risks overseas.

The charity Global Connections (www.globalconnections.co.uk) has some excellent guidelines in crisis management for charities working in high-risk areas overseas. They are available to be downloaded from their website.

Kidnap, ransom, extortion, child protection and health and safety issues

Charities working in certain high-risk areas may wish to consider the possibility of purchasing specialist indemnity insurance to cover the risks of kidnap, ransom and extortion. This can provide an indemnity against any ransom or extortion monies that may be demanded, together with related expenses.

Charities sending workers in to 'high-risk' areas: (1) need to register with the appropriate embassy; (2) should take advice from other major agencies working in those countries such as the United Nations; and (3) should ensure they receive basic security training.

By their very nature, many charities working overseas focus their work with the most disadvantaged and needy members of society, in circumstances which could be open to abuse. The trustees are responsible for ensuring that the beneficiaries of the charity's work are not harmed through their contact with the charity. For example, a charity working overseas with children should ensure that its UK child protection policy is fully binding on its staff and volunteers overseas.

It is considered that where charities are working with children or vulnerable persons overseas, the charity should ensure that all its workers and volunteers have the appropriate CRB Disclosure certificate before they travel overseas to work with the charity. For any staff or volunteers who are recruited locally in the country, it may be possible to take up references locally so that the charity is at least seen to be doing what it can to maintain minimum standards. The website of CCPAS has practical information on this important topic (www.ccpas.co.uk).

The health and safety of the charity's workers overseas is a paramount consideration. Prolonged exposure to relief work amongst people who have been affected by natural disasters, famine, disease, war and poverty can have a lasting impact on a person's health and mental well-being. The wise charity considers ways in which the needs of the staff members can be met, and these may include:

- access to appropriate medical support and advice;
- provision of counselling;
- specialist training, including personal security;
- appropriate support, encouragement and guidance from senior people working for the charity in the country or in the region;
- the provision of regular periods of rest and relaxation away from the main area of activity;
- a confidential medium of communication to senior leadership either in the region or in the UK;
- reassurance that the charity's work will not be abandoned.

Before allowing workers to travel overseas, many charities require the worker to complete a Power of Attorney appointing a near relative to handle their affairs in the UK, and to leave a valid will together with instructions for any funeral arrangements.

Working with other NGOs

Increasingly many charities now work closely with other charities or NGOs overseas in order to pool resources and reduce unnecessary management overheads. The benefits of charities working together often outweigh the disadvantages. Before deciding to work with another organization on a particular project, the charity must ensure that its objectives and those of the other party (or parties) are compatible. If the arrangement is likely to last for a period of, say, in excess of one month, then it is advisable that a formal agreement is signed by the parties setting out exactly what each party brings to the arrangement and what is the desired goal. Funding arrangements, accountability, decision-making, audit requirements, etc. are all valid issues that need to be considered.

Charities responding to natural disasters often decide to pool their resources for the common good. In practical terms, there may be a charity that has an established base or reliable contacts in the geographical area in question, and it makes sense for that charity to be the main coordinator of the response to the disaster. Other charities bring money, personnel and other resources.

The international community's response to large-scale disasters such as the 2004 tsunami have shown that there can actually be significant duplication of resources and efforts when charities come together. Trustees need to be convinced that working with other charities or NGOs is the most efficient way of utilizing resources to respond to the need in question.

Accounting and management issues

Charities working overseas will invariably need to set up banking facilities in the country in which they are working. Primarily the bank account should be operated in exactly the same way as the main account is operated by the charity in the UK. In areas where access to banks is somewhat restricted, there is often the temptation for charities to hold money in cash. In addition to the possible threat to the security of the staff members concerned, this is not considered to be a satisfactory way of working unless full receipts are obtained for all monies dispersed.

Monies spent overseas have to be accounted for either in the UK Audit of the charity or, in the cases of charities that are registered locally, in the local

Audit. It is quite permissible for charities working overseas to keep reserves in a currency other than the local currency (e.g., sterling or US dollars) and then convert it into the local currency on an 'as needed' basis. This can provide protection against violent currency fluctuations or possibly the collapse of the local banking system. Charities are reminded of the need to respect the local laws. In some cases these require all money transfers to be done within the country itself, and it may be illegal to bring large amounts of foreign currency in or take local money out, other than through the national banking system.

Some charities use specialist money transfer companies to move money into countries where there is not a reliable conventional banking system. Providing these money transfer companies are legitimate, and full records are kept of all monies paid to the company for transfer, this presents a valid alternative.

Charities anticipating transferring considerable sums of money overseas may decide to forward buy the foreign currency or enact other steps with the bank to take out foreign currency Futures or Options.

As intimated above, charities working overseas need to keep accurate records of all financial transactions so that accounts can be prepared:

a. In situations where the charity has registered in a particular country then accounts will need to be prepared in that country and audited to the appropriate Generally Accepted Accounting Principle (GAAP), so that they can be included in the Audit of the parent charity in the UK. Difficulties arise where it is not possible to find an Auditor locally who can undertake the work to GAAP.

b. In the event that the charity is not registered locally, all receipts and payments made in the country need to recorded in the books of the UK charity and included in its income and expenses, and therefore its Audit. UK Auditors are not impressed when vouchers are not available, and this can lead to the UK charity's Audit being qualified and its Audit fee significantly increased.

NB: Care needs to be exercised in the disclosure in a charity's accounts of the existence of a large grant, as this could prejudice the charity's operation in a particular country or indeed expose its key staff to increased personal danger in countries where there is civil unrest. The Charity Commission have a procedure that can be utilized in such cases to enable the grant to be excluded from the accounts.

Charities working overseas need to be aware that they could become a target for:

- money launderers, who wish to use the charity to move monies to and from the country in question;
- those who would use the charity's 'people focus' to smuggle people into countries illegally;
- those who would seek to use the money raised by charities in a particular country to fund terrorist organizations or drug deals;
- those who would use the charity's educational programmes as a base to recruit young people for military or terrorist activities or to spread propaganda;
- fraud.

Finally, charities working overseas need to review their risk management strategy (see section 25) to ensure that it includes the overseas activity.

SECTION 21 FINANCE

Tony Bennewith

Accounts presentation, Audit and Independent Examination

Every charity, of whatever size, is required to prepare accounts. Most charities are required to submit these accounts to the Charity Commissioners, but some are not required to do so. Accounts are normally prepared for a twelve-month period. The accounting year-end can be changed from time to time, but it is still normal for annual accounts to be prepared.

Each charity needs to decide what year-end it is going to use (the accounting reference date) and should stick to this from year to year. There may be factors that affect the year-end. If the charity is connected with another charity, then it would help if the year-end of both charities were the same. Charities involved in education may well wish to work to a year-end that coincides with the academic year (1 September to 31 August). Charities involved with local government may prefer 31 March as a year-end. As Gift Aid recoveries normally relate to a tax year, 6 April to 5 April (when the tax rate recovered on Gift Aid may change), then this may be another reason for adopting 31 March as year-end. A charity with seasonal activities related to Christmas may well adopt 31 December as a year-end. In any event, the first decision to be made is the accounting reference date to be adopted.

Charities with total income or total expenses under £10,000 are not required to submit their accounts to the Charity Commissioners. They are also excluded from the necessity of having an Independent Examination (see more below). Churches not registered as charities do not need to submit their accounts to the Charity Commissioners. However, they are still required to prepare accounts in statutory format (SORP) and these must be subjected to Independent Examination or Audit as appropriate (see more below).

Some churches may be required to submit accounts to their denominational body, but there may very well be a separate format required (for instance, the Church of England, where accounts have to be submitted to the Diocese in a format not too dissimilar from the SORP required by the Charity Commission).

Charities with total income or total expenses below £100,000 may prepare accounts on what is called the cash basis. This means that they only bring into their accounts such items as have actually been paid or received in the year. Any sums due to be paid or received after the end of the year are ignored but incorporated into the following year's accounts. Once an income or expenditure of £100,000 is reached, the charity is required to prepare accounts on an accrual basis. This means that any sums due to be paid at the end of the year or due to be received at the end of the year must be incorporated into that year's accounts. An example of this would be tax due back under Gift Aid from HMRC. If the charity has a year-end of, say, 31 March, then the tax recoverable up to that date will obviously not be received until April or even later. Under cash accounting, it is permissible to leave this sum out of the accounts for the year ended 31 March. Under the accrual's basis, a debtor will be brought into the accounts of the amount of tax that will eventually be repaid. A debtor is an amount of money owed to the charity at the end of the year.

Format of accounts

The actual format of the accounts is very different from that of a normal trading business. The format is laid down in the Statement Of Recommended Practice (SORP) issued by the Charity Commission following the passing of the Charities Acts. From time to time, the formats are amended, and charities will need to consult their accountant or the Charity Commission website to obtain the formats applicable to them at the time.

In very simple terms, the formats attempt to classify funds over certain headings. There are three fund types recognized by the SORP.

1. General funds of the charity: these can be used for any purpose.
2. Designated funds: these are sums of money that have been set aside (designated), sometimes by the charity itself, for a specific purpose. The

charity decides on the designation and then keeps the moneys in a separate fund.

3. Restricted funds: the donors normally restrict these themselves. If somebody donates money to a charity for a specific purpose, then the use of those funds is restricted to that purpose.

These funds must all be shown separately in the accounts. The accounts of a charity may extend over many pages and will include a trustees' report, a Statement of Financial Activities (SOFA), a balance sheet and Notes to the accounts.

The trustees' report

The trustees' report can be as long as the trustees wish. There are, however, some basic matters that must be included in every trustees' report. These include:

- reference and administrative details;
- structure, governance and management;
- objectives and activities;
- achievements and performance;
- financial review;
- plans for future periods.

The items required under each one are as follows:

Reference and administrative details

This used to be called legal and administrative details, which probably sums up more accurately what it must contain. It must contain the name of the Chief Executive or senior staff member, legal details of the charity such as charity number and list of trustees, and probably bankers, solicitors, auditors and the registered address of the charity.

Structure, governance and management

This will refer to the nature of the governing document. It may also give details of how trustees are recruited, appointed and trained. There may then follow details of the management structure of the charity and the decision-making process.

Also under this heading comes risk management. The trustees of each charity are required to assess the risks to the charity and what action has been taken to minimize or prepare for those risks. For instance, a charity may operate out of certain premises either leasehold or freehold. One major risk

FINANCE

would be the destruction of those premises by fire or other disaster. The trustees would obviously take out appropriate insurance, but should also consider in advance what action would be taken in the event of a catastrophe to enable the charity to continue its activities were it to lose those premises (see also section 25).

Objectives and activities
This is the trustees' opportunity to communicate their enthusiasm for the charity! This sets out the long- and short-term objectives of the charity, along with the role of volunteers.

Achievements and performance
Again, this is an opportunity for the trustees to show how the charity has achieved the objectives referred to above and how successful their performance has been in fulfilling the objectives. Charities seeking to raise funds from outside organizations will undoubtedly wish to expand on this and the previous section. Smaller charities will often only give minimal information in these last two sections. However, grant-making trusts will look at these sections in detail. Many charities will therefore expand these sections with graphs, pie charts, etc.

Financial review
One of the most important areas in the financial review is the reserves policy. Each charity needs to consider how much it needs in liquid reserves to meet any immediate eventualities. For instance, a charity may decide that it needs three months of average expenditure to be kept in reserve. Once having made that decision, the reserves should be examined at each trustees' meeting to ensure that the situation has not deteriorated below that level. If such is the case, then the trustees need to consider what action should be taken.

Plans for future periods
Under this heading will come the objectives referred to above, but this section will put a time-frame on those objectives. This and some other clauses are not statutory if the charity is not subject to an Audit. However, it is always good practice to include more information than the minimum required.

Statement of Financial Activities (SOFA)
In a commercial business, this would be described as the Profit and Loss Account or, if on a cash basis, the Receipts and Payments Account. It is really an assessment of the income and expenses of the charity during its financial year. However, the Charity Commissioners are not so much interested in

whether the charity has a surplus or deficit, as the use made of funds available. The general public will also be interested in this aspect. For this reason, the charity is required to list its expenditure under certain headings so that the Charity Commissioners and the public can assess the charity's use of the funds available to them. An example of the current layout of the Statement of Financial Activities is available on the Charity Commission's website.

Balance sheet

Whereas the SOFA is a statement of what has happened over a period of time, the balance sheet is a snapshot of the charity at its accounting reference date. It shows all the items owned by the charity, which are known as assets and all the amounts owed by the charity, which are known as liabilities. The assets may be fixed assets or current assets. Fixed assets are items used in the charity that will be retained and used for a period exceeding twelve months. Current assets, on the other hand, are likely to change their form over the next twelve months. The only current assets are stock (if relevant), debtors (amounts owed to the charity) and cash in its various forms. Normally, investments are current assets, but if treated as an endowment, they may be shown as fixed investment assets. Otherwise, fixed assets would be buildings, machinery, vehicles, office furniture, computers, etc.

Liabilities are divided into current liabilities, which again are likely to change their status within the next twelve months, and longer term liabilities. These are normally divided into Creditors (amounts owed by the charity) due to be paid within one year, two to five years and longer than five years. This does mean that a long-term mortgage, which is being repaid on a repayment basis, will probably appear in three different places on the charity's balance sheet. This makes the accounts of the charity somewhat difficult to interpret for a layman, but does show a clear picture of the overall position.

Notes to the accounts

Many items in the balance sheet are then broken down in the Notes to the accounts. These could actually be shown on the face of the accounts, but it would make the accounts very hard to read and interpret. The Notes will give a detailed breakdown, for instance, of debtors between tax recoverable, prepayments, other amounts due to the charity and short-term loans made by the charity, perhaps to staff members.

Audit and Independent Examination

Any charity with total income or total expenditure under £10,000 is not required to have any outside person or body look at their accounts. Neither are they required to submit their accounts to the Charity Commission.

Any charity with income between £10,000 and £250,000 is required to be subjected to Independent Examination. The Independent Examiner can be anybody competent to carry out the work and, by definition, independent of the charity. Therefore, the Independent Examination cannot be carried out by one of the trustees, or by someone associated with the charity in any way.

A charity with total income or total expenses between £250,000 and £500,000 is still only subject to Independent Examination, but the Independent Examiner must be an appropriately qualified accountant.

Once income exceeds £500,000, the charity is subject to an Audit. This work must be carried out by a registered auditor, who must also be totally independent of the charity. This does not mean that the Auditor cannot carry out other advisory work for the charity, as long as the relationship does not become so close that the independence of the Auditor is undermined. Contrary to popular belief, there is no legal requirement for a charity to change its Auditors every three, five or seven years. There is no reason why the same Auditor cannot carry on undertaking the Audit for a long period of time. In fact, many charities find the relationship with their Auditor so helpful that they would not want to change to another firm.

When accounts are submitted to the Charity Commission, they should be signed by the Independent Examiner or Auditor. It was formerly a requirement for a copy signed by the trustees to be submitted to the Charity Commission, but this has recently been changed because of the incidence of people copying signatures of charity trustees. There must be a copy of the accounts signed by the trustees held on file, but the copy submitted to the Charity Commission does not have to be a manually signed copy.

Taxation issues

As a rule, charities are not liable to taxation. Amounts donated to a charity are not liable to tax in the charity's hands, even though the charity may recover tax under Gift Aid, and the donor may even have saved higher-rate tax on their donation to the charity.

If charities receive bank interest, either this should be paid to them gross (before the deduction of tax) or they should apply to HMRC for a refund of any tax deducted by the bank or building society concerned.

If a charity receives a dividend that has had tax deducted, then the charity cannot recover the tax deducted (as was the case until 1997). This may appear to suggest that equity investments paying dividends are not such a good investment for the charity. However, this could be balanced by the prospect of growth in equity values.

If a charity makes a capital gain on the sale of an Asset this will not be subject to Capital Gains Tax.

The only time a charity could be liable to taxation is on trading activities. For example, a church may make a large amount of its income from the commercial hiring out of the church building. This income would be taxable, but expenses may be deducted from the income before the tax is assessed. These expenses would relate to some of the expenses of operating the premises.

Periodically, the Inland Revenue send charities a corporation tax return. The charity must complete that return or suffer a penalty of £100 if the return is not submitted within twelve months of the year-end. If a tax return is received, then advice should immediately be sought from the charity's Auditors or a *qualified* accountant.

Charities should always encourage donors who are taxpayers to give under the Gift Aid scheme. The effect of this is that the charity can recover tax on amounts donated to it, and the donor may even save higher-rate tax on the amount of the grossed-up donation. For example, let us assume that the standard rate of income tax is 20%, the higher rate of income tax is 40% and a donor gives £80 to a charity. The charity can recover £20 from the Inland Revenue because the £80 is deemed to be the net amount after the taxpayer has paid 20% tax. However, if the taxpayer is a higher-rate taxpayer, then he or she would be entitled to 40% tax relief on the £100 grossed-up amount (£80 gift and £20 tax) that is deemed to be given. This means that the donor's own personal tax liability would reduce by £20 so that, in effect, it has cost them only £60 to give £100 to the charity. Some donors avoid ever paying higher-rate tax by using Gift Aid!

Credit control/cash flow

Charities have as much of a responsibility as trading companies to control their cash flow. If there is any form of trading by the charity, then credit control will also come into the scenario. Each charity needs to ensure that there are sufficient funds available for their day-to-day expenses. As well as preparing year-end accounts, there should be a continuous monitoring of cash flow to ensure that adequate funds are available to meet expenses as they arise. For example, a church may be considering an extension to its building. The trustees will need to look at the resources available to the church, the total cost of the project to be undertaken and the availability of other funds that can be borrowed to pay the initial building costs. They will also need to consider the repayment of the resulting loan as regards both interest and capital. It would be negligent for the trustees to embark upon any project without first ensuring that adequate funds would be available.

If a charity is trading in any way, the trustees have a duty to ensure that those who owe the charity money pay the right amount at the right time.

Annual budgets and projections

Each charity should prepare an annual budget and cash flow projections. Whilst not specifically laid down in the Charities Acts, it would be unwise for trustees to embark on a year's activities without having some idea of the financial implications of the decisions made at their trustees' meetings. If the charity does not have the expertise to prepare annual budgets, then advice should be sought from a *qualified* accountant.

There are two distinct documents that should not be confused. The budget is an estimate of the income and expenses for the coming year. The format and figures can be based on previous years' accounts. Once prepared, the trustees can monitor actual results with budget at each trustees' meeting. This will enable appropriate action to be taken in good time.

The other document is the cash flow. Whereas the budget will usually cover the year on an accruals basis, the cash flow is usually a monthly estimate of cash in and out. This will make clear any months where an overdraft may need to be negotiated or loans raised. Again, when monitored against actual figures, any problems can be identified at an early stage.

Receiving and accounting for cash

Many charities have cash transactions. A good deal of their funds may actually be raised in cash from either collections or other means. The trustees of the charity have a responsibility to ensure that cash is correctly accounted for and that risks of fraud or error are minimized. For example, when church offerings are counted, this should be carried out by two people, neither of whom is the treasurer. The funds should then be banked, after a signed statement as to the amount involved has been prepared by those counting the offering. Obviously, this sort of arrangement may not always be practical, but it is the ideal.

Similarly, charities undertaking any form of street collection should ensure that the risks of fraud and error are reduced as far as possible. At the end of the day, there has to be an element of trust in these situations, but, as most charities are using volunteers, it would be unusual for those volunteers not to handle the finances of the charity appropriately. The underlying moral is to ensure that all volunteers recruited to the charity are appropriately checked and references taken. Systems should also be in place to minimize any risk to the charity.

Borrowing money

As long as the governing document of the charity permits, a charity may borrow funds. There are many sources of funds. Mortgages are dealt with in section 12 of this book. There may be a need for borrowing on a day-to-day basis. It may be inappropriate for trustees personally to give any guarantee against bank or other borrowing and/or allow any charge over their personal property to secure such a loan. Any borrowing by a charity should ideally be fully at arms length from all those involved in the charity. It may be that from time to time a charity has an offer of a loan from either an employee or trustee. If this is the case, then the minutes of the trustees' meeting must clearly state the terms on which the loan is made as regards interest, capital and repayment. Such a loan should obviously be on no more onerous terms than could be obtained on outside borrowing. Market rates should apply. Professional advice should be taken from the charity's lawyers or accountants.

Investments

From time to time charities may well find themselves in possession of excess funds, which need to be invested. Indeed, many charities have large capital funds available to them that have built up in past years. These should obviously be invested wisely and with a view to maximizing returns and capital growth for the charity. The Charities Aid Foundation operates bank accounts on behalf of charities, which will give a better rate of interest than is normally obtainable from high-street banks. Charities can also purchase units in various Charities Aid Foundation Investment Funds, which again generally give a better return than other similar investments available in the general marketplace. If considerable sums of money are going to be held for an indefinite period, then professional advice should be sought from advisers who are experienced in handling a portfolio of equity investments on behalf of the charity. This will ensure that any decision-making on investments is carried out by an independent third party who will advise the trustees as appropriate (see section 17).

Needless to say, there are investments available, which may offer a very attractive return, but where the ability to repay the capital is somewhat in doubt. It would not be in the trustees' interests to take risks with the capital sums owned by the charity in the hope of receiving a slightly enhanced income. Thus, any substantial sums that need to be invested should be invested with the advice of an independent third party.

SECTION 22 FUND-RAISING

Charities can achieve very little without adequate funding. Whilst charities exist to spend money rather than accumulate it, they have first to raise the income before it can be dispersed.

In today's increasingly competitive environment charities are exploring new and innovative way to raise funds – the 'sponsored walk' of the past has given way to the 'Himalaya trek' or 'sponsored sky-dive' of today. Indeed, very few of us can pass through the high streets of our towns without being approached on behalf of a charity anxious to solicit our funds and support.

Ultimately, the methodology for raising funds for a particular charity rests with the charity's trustees to decide. Churches and other faith-based organizations still rely heavily upon gifts from the congregation and other like-minded people or organizations who closely identify with the objectives of the charity. However, there is growing evidence that many charities are now beginning to explore other means of attracting income. I deal with some of these in this section, not in an attempt to highlight them as being more effective or desirable than other ways; rather, they are mentioned due to the particular legal ramifications that affect them.

Before a particular fund-raising activity is undertaken, it is essential for the charity's trustees to review the methodology and ask themselves whether its adoption by the charity would lead to disapproval by the charity's main constituency and could damage the charity in the medium-to-long term. Whilst the possibility of substantial one-off gifts are attractive to a charity, ultimately most charities are underpinned by the small regular gifts of a large number of donors, and the reduction or loss of those donors would be immeasurably more damaging to the charity in the long term.

Perhaps before undertaking any major fund-raising initiative, it is wise for the charity to work out a strategy and to assess the likely cost of the fund-raising exercise over and against the amount of money that can realistically be expected to be raised. Such a strategy should also set out the likely areas that the charity will explore to raise funds – for example, grant applications to companies or government, the hiring of a professional fund-raiser, or direct mail campaign.

This book highlights five ways in which charities can attract income. As mentioned above they are not the only ways and for a fuller discussion on the possible avenues open to charities wishing to raise funds the reader is directed to organizations such as The Institute of Fundraising, The National Council for Voluntary Organisations, and the Home Office Guide, 'Charitable Fund-Raising: Professional and Commercial Involvement'.

Irrespective of the type of fund-raising activity the charity decides to pursue, there are three specific issues that are relevant in each case:

1. The purpose of the fund-raising should be clearly stated. If the funds are for the general work of the charity, then that should be made clear and care should be taken not to mislead potential donors by implying that the gift will be used for a specific purpose when that is not the case.
2. If the fund-raising is for a specific project, then again that should be made clear to potential donors. Furthermore, the charity needs to say what will happen with any excess funds that have been raised. For example, if the fund-raising is to raise £30,000 to enable the charity to buy a Land Rover for its work in Africa, then what happens to the balance if the fund-raising actually brings in £40,000? Conversely, if the fund-raising only brings in £20,000, will the charity wish to return the money to the donors or to spend it on another project? Again, this needs to be made very clear in all communications concerning the fund-raising.
3. If the fund-raising project is for a specific purpose and more funds are raised than is required and the appeal did not specify what would happen to any surplus funds, then the Charity Commission will need to be consulted as to whether a Charity Commission Scheme will be required to enable the money to be used for other charitable purposes. If insufficient monies have been raised, then the charity has a duty to return any monies given by donors that can be identified. If the donors can be found and do not want their money back, then they need to sign a disclaimer. If the donors cannot be found, an advertisement may need to be made following which the Charity

Commission would need to be consulted on the possibility of them making a Scheme to enable the money to be used for other charitable purposes.

All income received as a result of the fund-raising needs to be paid directly to the charity and under the control of the charity trustees. In circumstances where the trustees appoint a fund-raising consultant or organization to lead the particular fund-raising project, then the trustees need to be certain that they have ultimate control over the monies that are received from public donations, and to ensure that they are paid into a bank account controlled by the trustees.

Five possible ways to attract income

1. Public collections
The provisions of the Charities Act 2006 will have considerable effect on the regulation of public charitable collections. They are not yet in force, but when they are, they will provide a unified system to cover all types of public charitable collections, and will extend to cover privately owned land to which the public has unrestricted access, for example shopping precincts.

Under this system charities proposing to undertake collections from the general public will be required:

- To apply for a Public Collection Certificate from the Charity Commission. This is applied for by the person or persons proposing to promote the public charitable collection, and lasts for no longer than five years. The Charity Commission will decide on whether an organization is fit to undertake public collections and may grant the certificate subject to such conditions as the Charity Commission think fit, or indeed may refuse the application.
- If the fund-raising is to be undertaken in a public place, then the persons proposing to promote or undertake the collection need to apply to the local authority for a permit to conduct that collection in a public place. The applicant must hold the Public Collection Certificate from the Charity Commission before an application to the local authority can be made. The only grounds on which the local authority can refuse that application is if it appears to them that the collection would cause undue inconvenience to members of the public.
- Door-to-door collectors will be required to inform the local authority that a collection is taking place, but they do not need a specific permit.
- Short-term local collections will not need either a Public Collection Certificate or a local authority permit. However, those organizing the

collection will need to let the local authority know about it in advance. This provision is designed to ensure that small-scale activities such as carol singing are not affected by the requirement for a certificate and permit as above.

- Face-to-face fund-raising (the methodology of direct debit solicitation that is favoured by some national charities who have their agents working in our high streets) is covered by the Charities Act 2006 and requires the use of badges by collectors, and certificates of authority.

It is worth noting that if the charitable company that is directing or undertaking the public collection commits any offence of the regulations in the 2006 Charities Act with regard to fund-raising and the offence can be attributed to any consent, connivance or neglect on the part of any director, manager, secretary or officer of the charitable company, then he/she, together with the company, is guilty of an offence.

The 2006 Act suggests a 'good practice requirement' on charities is for them to take all reasonable steps to ensure that their fund-raising is carried out in such way that:

- It does not unreasonably intrude on the privacy of those from whom funds are being solicited.
- It does not involve the making of unreasonably persistent approaches to persons to donate funds.
- It does not result in undue pressure being placed on persons to donate funds.
- It does not involve the making of any false or misleading representation as to the extent or urgency for any need for funds, the use to which the funds will be put, or the activities or achievements of the charity.
- Fund-raising via telephone solicitation or radio and TV adverts needs to be carefully controlled to ensure the public are clear as to the purposes for which the funds would be expended. The Institute of Fundraising has produced an excellent code of practice for telephone fund-raising, and the Broadcast Appeals Consortium issues a code of conduct for charities and broadcasters.

The charity's name is a valuable asset to the charity in fund-raising, and therefore potentially vulnerable to misuse during a high-profile fund-raising campaign. This is particularly the case if the charity is to undertake a promotional campaign in conjunction with a commercial entity, and the trustees need to ensure that in such cases:

- The relationship would not damage the charity or its good name and reputation.
- The name of the charity would not be exploited for non-charitable purposes.
- The arrangement is for the benefit of the charity.
- The charity can disengage from the process and prevent its name being used in future if it decides it is in its best interest not to continue the arrangement. The Charity Commission have produced helpful guidance on sponsorship, 'Fund-raising through partnerships with companies', which can be downloaded from their website.

Charities proposing to undertake a specific fund-raising event, such as a dinner, a performance or an exhibition, may consider that there could be a risk of loss to the charity if the fund-raising event was less than successful. The Charity Commission suggest that if a particular fund-raising event is projected to have a turnover that is likely to exceed 25% of the charity's annual income, it may well be preferable for the activity to be undertaken by a trading subsidiary rather than by the charity itself. Whilst a major concert or dinner may be an enticing way of raising substantial funds, it could be risky, and the charity's general funds should not be used as 'risk capital' to underpin such events. By undertaking them in a wholly-owned trading subsidiary, it may also be possible to obtain outside sponsorship that underpins the event itself, rather than risk the charity's own funds.

The Fundraising Standards Board has established a 'Fundraising Promise', which is a commitment made to the public by charitable fund-raisers in the UK, whereby they commit to the highest standards of practice and agree to ensure that all their activities are open and fair, honest and legal. Charities proposing to do public fund-raising may well benefit by agreeing to adhere to the Fundraising Promise in order to give the public comfort on this point.

2. Outside consultants
A professional fund-raiser is defined as 'any person (being separate from the charity itself) who carries on a fund-raising business for profit and who is engaged in soliciting money for charitable purposes'. A commercial participator is 'a person who, although not in a fund-raising business, nevertheless engages in a promotional venture during the course of which representations are made that contributions are to be given or applied for the benefit of a charity'.

Professional fund-raisers themselves are required to indicate the institutions that will benefit and the arrangements for the fund-raisers' remuneration.

Currently, professional fund-raisers and commercial participators must have a written agreement with the charity and must make a statement telling potential donors that they are getting paid when they request donations for the charity. This is so that potential donors can make an informed choice about giving.

The 2006 Act makes two changes to these statements:

1. It requires the professional fund-raiser or commercial participator to disclose the amount that they are being paid for undertaking the appeal. If the specific amount is not known, then a reasonably accurate estimate of what they will receive has to be given. Broadly similar statements will also have to be made by employees, officers and trustees of the charities who act as collectors. However, the above provisions do not apply to volunteers.
2. The aforementioned agreement between the charity and the professional fund-raiser or commercial participator should also cover the transfer of funds raised by the professional fund-raisers to the charity.

In some cases, a local charity may work to raise funds for another charity. In this case:

- Prospective donors must be clear as to which charity will benefit from the gift made.
- In law the gift belongs to the charity that is going to benefit, which means that the collecting charity can only recover its costs if 'fund-raising' is within that charity's Objects.
- The permission of the beneficiary charity needs to be obtained in writing beforehand, and separate financial records should be kept.

It is worthwhile checking that the beneficiary charity is actually registered with the Charity Commission, as under the Charities Act 1992 it is an offence to state that an institution for which a person is raising money is a registered charity unless the person making the statement has reasonable grounds for believing it to be the case (i.e. he or she had actually checked the register beforehand!).

3. Grants
The making of grants is considered a favoured way for businesses, large organizations and government agencies to fund charities, no doubt because it enables a degree of accountability and performance to be factored into the arrangement.

The grant-making process usually involves the charity writing a grant proposal and submitting it to the potential grant-making organizations. The grant proposal is akin to a business plan, as it will set out:

- the particular issues which the charity intends to address;
- the appropriate explanatory background;
- the charity's proposal for meeting the perceived need or responding to the challenge;
- the timetable and milestones involved in the programme;
- the details of staff and other key facilitators who will be responsible for carrying out the programme;
- a detailed breakdown of the cost involved in the project (in larger projects this may involve cash flow forecasts), the proposed start date and finish date for the project, and therefore the length of the term of the grant;
- the measurable outputs;
- the indicators or benchmarks that will indicate the end of the project;
- the indicators that will measure the success of the project.

Potential grant-making donors will expect the grant application to show that it will produce positive outcomes and that it represents good value for the sums that have been requested.

The grant-making applications will be assisted if the charity can also demonstrate sustainability and competence in the particular field, perhaps with evidence of good outcomes and results from previous charitable activity.

If the donor decides to award the grant, then effectively it becomes a contract between the donor and the charity. The charity needs to consider the contents of the grant (i.e. the promises and representations it has made) carefully. A breach of any of the terms or a failure to achieve the agreed benchmarks or timetables can require the charity to repay the grant (either in whole or in part), or allow the grantor to withhold subsequent payments. (Grants are seldom advanced in one lump sum and they are usually drip-fed over the period of the grant against the agreed timetables and milestones.)

Often the grant will require the charity to prepare a report at its conclusion disclosing the results of the activity. The grant-maker may require this information so that they can in turn advertise their generosity. However, from the charity's perspective there may be a significant conflict in them disclosing fully the results of the project. For example, if the charity is involved in work amongst the victims of abuse, the charity may well be bound by its duty of confidentiality not to disclose the sensitive information that it may well have received as a result of the activity for which the grant was made.

Yet this may be the precise information that the grant-maker wishes to publish.

Some charities themselves exist to make grants to other charities (grant-making trusts). As mentioned above, grant-making is an effective way for an organization to have a degree of influence on the charity that is proposing to expend the money through the award of the grant. Grant-making charities need to ensure the following:

- The purposes for which the granted monies are to be used are exclusively charitable.
- There is an appropriate reporting and accountability mechanism in the grant arrangement.
- In certain circumstances, a representative of the grant-making charity should be permitted to observe the programme that it has funded and to visit the proposed beneficiaries.
- If at any time they have reason to believe that the funds are not being expended for the purpose for which they were originally granted, then they should take steps to cease funding pending clarification, and conceivably request the return of the funds that may have been paid under a misapprehension. It is not sufficient for the grant-making charity to shrug their shoulders on the basis that 'it is all in a good cause'!

4. Legacies

The success of the nationally promoted 'Make A Will Week' by several charities shows the importance that charities are now giving to gifts that they may receive in people's wills. There are two types of gift that can come from this source:

Legacy – this is usually a specific amount or a specific object that is given in the will to the charity.

Share of residue – this refers to a specific share of whatever is left in a person's estate after legacies, tax, debts and funeral expenses have been paid. Often an exact amount will not be known until the estate has been finally administered.

Once a person has died, if they leave a will, that will is admitted to probate, at which point the will itself becomes a public document. There are organizations who read the wills that are admitted to probate each day and advise charities if they are mentioned in them. This enables the charity to liaise with either the executors or the firm of solicitors representing the estate, to ensure that there is ongoing dialogue during the administration period. This can be especially helpful in circumstances where, for example, the gift to the charity is a portfolio of shares. The charity may wish to sell those shares at an early stage, in order to be sure of the income they will receive. By liaison with the executors during the administration, that request can usually be accommodated. If the shares are 'appropriated' to the charity during the administration period, this will avoid the risk of Capital Gains Tax being payable on their sale.

The following points are relevant to charities who are recipients of a legacy or a share of residue:

- It is important to check whether or not the legacy or share of residue is given for the 'general purposes' of the charity or for a ' specific purpose'. If it is for a specific purpose then the charity can only use the gift for that purpose, and if that purpose is no longer attainable by the charity there may be some difficulty. It is suggested that in such circumstances the charity should immediately open discussions with the Charity Commission to see if a Scheme can be made to accommodate the change in purpose (see section 26).
- If the deceased person was domiciled in the UK and paying UK tax, it is likely that the gift to the charity will not suffer an Inheritance Tax deduction. The charity needs to take particular care in ensuring that it receives all of the monies that it is entitled to in those circumstances. For example, if the estate itself was of a size whereby Inheritance Tax would be payable, then that portion of the estate which is the gift to the charity must be deducted from the gross estate before the Inheritance Tax calculation is made, in order that the charity receives in full the amount of money or the share of the residue that has been given to it. The tax calculations in these circumstances are very complex and specialist advice should always be sought to ensure the charity receives the correct funds.
- The charity is entitled to interest on a legacy from a date twelve months after the date of death through to the date upon which the charity finally receives payment. If interest is paid to the charity net, then it should ask for a tax deduction certificate so that it can reclaim the income tax directly from HMRC. This provision also covers interest or dividends that may be payable on the assets themselves during administration, until such time as those assets are sold or realized and the money is paid to the charity. A share of the residue in an estate is paid together with interest earned during the period of administration.

The charity should always ask for a copy of the will. If the charity is receiving a share of the residue, it should also ask to see the finalized estate accounts and should scrutinize those before finally accepting the gift. Charities receiving a share of the residue are in effect the ultimate beneficiaries and should satisfy themselves that the charity has everything that it is entitled to under the will. The charity's own lawyers may need to be involved at this stage, in order to consider the final accounts and to ensure that the charity's best interests have been served.

Care should also be taken if the executors ask the charity to indemnify them when the final distribution is made. Some zealous solicitors acting for executors ask charities to sign forms of indemnity that are much too wide.

In some cases, a charity is given a residual gift in a will but that gift is subject to an intervening life interest. For example, the charity may be left a freehold or leasehold property subject to the occupancy of a surviving spouse for the remainder of his or her life. Normally the charity would bide its time until the life interest ceased, whereupon the charity would receive the property.

It is possible, however, for the charity to consider buying out the life tenant and in effect accelerating its gift. For example, the life tenant may wish to downsize or indeed may need to go into residential care and need money for that purpose. The charity, after taking specialist legal and actuarial advice, could well agree a figure to buy out the value of the life tenancy. However, it is a fairly complicated procedure and it is only applicable in certain circumstances, requiring great care, discretion and wisdom on the part of the charity.

5. Trading

Charities may wish to undertake trading activities as a way of raising money. This is called 'non-primary purpose trading', and charity law does not permit a charity to carry out non-primary purpose trading themselves on a substantial basis in order to raise funds. It may therefore be possible to undertake non-primary purpose trading by setting up a wholly owned trading subsidiary. There are special rules to assist charities that wish to carry out a very small amount of non-primary purpose trading in circumstances where all the profits from that trading are used by the charity in furtherance of its charitable objectives. Unless prohibited by its governing document, the charity can carry out small levels of non-primary purpose trading and be exempt from the tax on the profits, providing those profits are applied for the purposes of the charity.

For a further discussion on trading subsidiaries, see section 23.

SECTION 23 TRADING

The question that is often asked is 'Can a charity trade?' The short answer is 'Yes, but . . .!'

There are three kinds of trading that are permitted:

Primary purpose trading – this is a trade that is undertaken in the course of carrying out the primary purpose (Objects) of the charity, for example, the provision of education by a charitable school in return for course fees, or a trade in which the work is mainly carried out by the beneficiaries of the charity (e.g. where a school is set up for people who suffer from a disability and which sells goods or products made by the students).

Ancillary trading – where the charity carries out a trade that is ancillary to the primary purpose of the charity, for example, the sale of refreshments by a theatre charity to members of its audience.

Occasional trading – where a charity holds the occasional jumble sale or fête at which items are sold.

In circumstances where a charity is trading specifically to generate funds for the charity (as opposed to primary purpose trading), care must be taken to ensure the charity does not become involved in commercial activity that would put the assets of the charity at risk. If it does, then a trading subsidiary should be utilized for this purpose.

Furthermore, the trustees should ensure that, in all decisions made with regard to a trading subsidiary, the interests of the charity are paramount. This means that the interest of the trading subsidiary, its directors, creditors and employees must be secondary to those of the charity. If the charity's assets are put at risk for the benefit of the trading subsidiary, its directors, creditors or employees, then the trustees of the charity may be personally liable for any loss or reduction in the value of the charity's assets.

It is important to bear in mind that the exact definition of 'trading' for tax purposes is a matter for HMRC to decide, and the fact that the profits of the activity are to be used for a charitable purpose does not in itself prevent that activity from being classified as 'trading'.

'Trading' does not include the sale of goods that have been donated to a charity or the grant of a lease of land or a building by the charity. If the charity is to be involved in trading that fits one or more of the above categories, then there are three important considerations for the trustees to bear in mind:

1. The appropriate vehicle for the trading activity. Fundamentally, the trustees must consider whether or not the governing document prohibits trading. If it does not, then the trustees may decide that the trading activity can be safely undertaken within the terms of the governing document of the charity. In other words, the charity itself will be doing the trading. The trustees should consider whether the trading activity will put the other assets of the charity at risk, or whether the trading activity will undermine the charitable nature of the organization in any way.

   If the trustees determine that the trading activity will be best carried out in an organization that is distinct from the charity itself, then the trustees could either (1) consider contracting with an outside organization for them to undertake the commercial trade in return for a share of the profits coming back to the charity, or (2) set up a wholly owned trading subsidiary that would exist as a distinct entity from the charity, although ultimately controlled by it. Further consideration of trading subsidiaries is set out below.

2. Tax. In principle, the income or profit that a charity receives from a trading activity is exempt from either corporation tax or income tax, providing the trade is:

Primary purpose trading
Ancillary trading
Occasional trading

However, the exemption only exists where the profits are applied solely for the purposes of charity.

If a charity undertakes trading solely to raise funds, then such trading is not supporting the primary purpose of the charity, and such activity is contrary to charity law. Furthermore, any profits may well be taxed. (Small scale non-primary purpose trading in order that the profits will be used by the charity is permitted, provided that the amount of income or profit made is within certain limits – see the Charity Commission website for further details.)

Charities are subject to VAT on the sale of goods or services in exactly the same way as a commercial company, unless their trade is either zero-rated or other exemptions apply (see Appendix 1 paragraph 33).

3. Losses. Any losses that result from non-primary or non-ancillary purpose trading may not be covered from the assets of the charity. Such losses may be regarded as non-charitable expenditure, and indeed there could be a breach of trust (potentially exposing the directors/trustees to liability) if the loss was incurred irresponsibly.

Losses from primary purpose or ancillary purpose trading would normally be covered from the assets of the charity.

Trading subsidiaries

Where the charity wishes to trade to raise monies in order to undertake its charitable purposes generally, or where the trading activity involves an unacceptable level of risk, the charity may decide to set up a wholly owned subsidiary (a trading subsidiary) to undertake the trading activity.

The profits of the trading subsidiary can then be passed back to the charity under the Gift Aid scheme, thereby reducing or eliminating the tax liability of the trading subsidiary each year.

The benefits of using a trading subsidiary include risk management and the ability to separate the commercial activity and charitable work from both an accounting and management perspective.

The disadvantages, however, include the additional costs involved in two sets of administration and the possible loss of some charity benefit, such as exemption from Stamp Duty Land Tax on any property acquired by the subsidiary.

Before a trading subsidiary is set up, the trustees of the charity need to consider (and take professional advice where applicable) to ensure:

• that, based upon their business plan/forecast, they consider there is a realistic likelihood that the trading activity will be successful;
• that the governing document of the charity allows for it to make an investment in a trading subsidiary.

Whilst the 'investment' may initially involve the costs of setting up the trading subsidiary and subscribing for the share capital, nevertheless the charity may also have to fund initial working capital until the trading activity is such that the company can be self-reliant. In such cases, the charity must ensure that its own investment powers allow it to make such an investment. Fundamentally, any monies advanced by the charity to the company must be justifiable as a proper investment of the charity's resources. The trustees will need to consider whether:

- this is a fair investment for the charity when compared with other forms of investment that could be selected;
- they are satisfied as to the financial viability of the trading subsidiary and its business prospects.

NB: The charity's assets must not be exposed to any kind of guarantee for the liabilities of the trading subsidiary, for example, to guarantee any overdraft or bank loan made to the subsidiary.

The trustees have a duty to review periodically such an investment to ensure it continues to be in the charity's best interests for the investment to remain in place. In the event that the charity is required to advance working capital to the trading subsidiary then the following should be borne in mind:

- The trustees must minimize any loss to the charity that would result from the trading subsidiary failing. For example if new working capital is required to go in to a company that is operating at a loss, then it is unlikely that the trustees could properly advance the working capital.
- Any monies advanced should normally be on the basis of a secured loan on market terms, and for an agreed length of time (it is important that the charity's assets are not otherwise tied up in long-term investments in a trading subsidiary).
- It is unwise for a charity to advance monies unsecured or interest-free to a trading subsidiary. If they do and the subsidiary company fails, the trustees may be personally liable for any loss to the charity's funds.

There are important tax considerations where monies are invested by a charity in a trading subsidiary, and further taxation advice needs to be taken in each circumstance.

Charities can normally make grants or loans to non-charities (including their wholly owned trading subsidiaries), providing that the grants are made for purposes that further the charity's own Objects. For example, a church charity may set up a wholly owned trading subsidiary to undertake a building programme to provide a new church building. Providing that the trading company exists for that purpose, and the appropriate safeguards are in place, the church charity could make a grant or a loan to the trading subsidiary in certain circumstances.

Although it is usual for the profits of the trading subsidiary to be passed back to the charity, either by way of a share dividend or Gift Aid payment, care should be exercised in circumstances where if the whole of the profit is passed back to the charity, that would leave the trading subsidiary with no funds for internal investment. If cash flow difficulties involve the charity needing to lend more monies to the trading subsidiary because the trading subsidiary has little or no substance (as it has Gift Aided its profits to the charity), then such an investment cannot be made under charity law. It may be important therefore for the trading subsidiary to retain some profits and accept the liability to pay tax on them.

Other practical considerations include:

- If the trading subsidiary is to use all or part of the charity's land or property, there should be formal lease or licence to cover such use at a commercial rent (Charity Commission consent may be required for this, given that the trading subsidiary and the charity are 'connected persons').
- If staff are to be used in common between the trading subsidiary and the charity, their expense should be costed against the two entities in proportion to the time spent with each.
- It is probably inadvisable to have the same persons serving as trustees of the charity and directors of the trading subsidiary. In such circumstances, it is difficult for them to make decisions objectively from either standpoint. Whilst it may be helpful to have some who are both trustees and directors, this should probably be no more than 60% of the board for either organization.
- The trustees of the charity should on an annual basis review the relationship between the trading subsidiary and the charity, to ensure that the continued investment is still in the charity's best interests and that the trading subsidiary is actually delivering real benefit to the charity.
- It is important to make the distinction to the general public that the charity and trading subsidiary are two separate entities, perhaps with different names.
- Care should be taken if any of the directors of the trading subsidiary are to be remunerated by the company. If these people are also trustees of the charity, then it is likely they will be precluded from being paid by the company. Unless specific consent is obtained from the Charity Commission, a 'related party' note will be included in the accounts of the charity.

- The charity's assets should not be used to settle the debts of the trading subsidiary.

Under no circumstances should a charity lend money to, or otherwise invest in, a trading company (notwithstanding that it is set up to raise money for the charity and actually Gift Aids its profits back to the charity), if the shareholders of that trading company form all or the majority of the trustees of the charity. The benefit that the trustees get by virtue of their shareholding in the trading company would be interpreted as an indirect benefit that they are receiving from the charity itself. Indeed, in extreme circumstances this activity could result in the charity losing its charitable status.

Fundamentally, the charity should bear in mind that the activities of the trading subsidiary should not in any way be allowed to damage the reputation and standing of the charity itself. Furthermore, the trustees should ensure that, in all decisions made with regard to a trading subsidiary, the interests of the charity are paramount. This means that the interest of the trading subsidiary, its directors, creditors and employees must be secondary to those of the charity. If the charity's assets are put at risk for the benefit of the trading subsidiary, its directors, creditors or employees, then the trustees of the charity may be personally liable for any loss or reduction in the value of the charity's assets. It is for the trustees to set the appropriate guidelines within which the wholly owned subsidiary should operate.

Charity shops

It seems that these are represented on most high streets today, and it is not only the large national charities that are operating them. In many cases, local charities may set up a shop in their particular area.

Whether the charity sets up shop in its own name or through a wholly owned trading subsidiary, there are important issues to bear in mind:

1. If the shop itself is to be taken on lease, then the lease will impose obligations on the charity as the tenant and probably on the trustees of the charity, who could be asked to join in as guarantors. This means that if the shop does not prove to be successful in its trading operation, it may be impossible to close it down without an ongoing liability under the lease until the lease can be sold on.
2. A robust business plan will need to be prepared by the charity before the venture is undertaken. Many such shops rely upon goods being donated

by members of the public, and also on voluntary labour to staff the shop. If the shop is to trade successfully, the charity will need to be satisfied that they can rely both on the supply of goods and labour.

3. Research will need to be undertaken on the catchment area around the shop, the competition from other charity shops, the availability of parking, etc.

Given that the charity's reputation is borne by the shop, the charity would wish to ensure that a reasonable level of profitability is returned by the shop to the charity. The charity should be able to demonstrate that a sizeable proportion of the gross takings of the shop are actually passed through to the charity itself. Notwithstanding that the goods and labour may be contributed at nil cost, the effort and risk involved in running a shop is scarcely worth it, if the actual contribution that the shop is making to the charity is only a small proportion of the charity's income each year.

The landlord of the shop (if it is rented) together with surrounding shop-keepers are unlikely to be well disposed to the charity if its shop bears all the appearance of a high-street version of a jumble sale! The shop needs to be well run and its products imaginatively displayed, if it is both to attract customers and not to have a negative effect on the retail values of the surrounding shops.

SECTION 24 WHAT CAN GO WRONG?

Charities are quite an attractive target for those seeking to take advantage of the wholesome trusting image of an organization that is reliant on volunteer labour for much of its activity.

Fraud and money laundering

The risk is not only from those outside; a fraud can be perpetrated just as easily by those who are working within the charity. Neither is it a risk that only affects large charities. Examples of fraud have included:

- outright theft of cash or assets from the charity;
- fraudulent investment advice;
- advanced fee fraud;
- falsification of records;
- bribes and other 'payments'.

In addition, charities are now the target of potential money launderers who would seek to use the good name and reputation of the charity to 'wash' dirty money and legitimize it. Such monies can be the proceeds of crime, terrorism or drug dealing. I have come across the following examples:

- A Christian charity being offered a donation of $1.5 million from a donor via a firm of 'lawyers' overseas, provided that the charity signed an agreement and remitted 'costs' of £39,000 to them.
- A UK church being offered a large sum of money towards its redevelopment programme from a source overseas, if it agreed to pass a proportion of that gift on to a named person based in another country.
- A charity being advised by a firm of 'solicitors' that it was the recipient of a legacy which would be paid to it in conjunction with a branch of a well-known church. Enquiries showed that the 'solicitors' did not exist, and that the church had had its database plagiarized and its name was being used to 'legitimize' certain activity.
- The Foundation for New Era Philanthropy in the United States collapsed in 1995 owing some $135 million. It had raised some $500 million from 1,100 donors promising to double their initial investment within three months by matching each donation with contributions from secret donors, thereby doubling the amount of the gift that could then be given to the charitable work. The programme was exposed to be a sham. Approximately 180 Christian groups, colleges and seminaries invested in New Era and lost considerable sums of money.

Remember the old adage: 'If a gift looks too good to be true – it probably is!'

In the light of this risk and in order that a charity is not the victim of fraud or another form of deception, its internal systems need to be robust to ensure it has established basic systems of control which will identify unusual gifts or activity, in particluar:

- The charity should not accept an individual cash gift of more than £1,000 unless a senior member of the charity can identify and personally vouch for the donor.
- The charity should not disclose its bank details or pass blank letterheads to any outside party unknown to it who requests that information for the purpose of making a gift. The real purpose of a fraudster is often to get the bank details (to empty the account) or to get letterheads (in order to commit further frauds).
- A gift from an unknown source that is conditional upon a portion of those monies being paid on to a third party should not be accepted.
- If a party wishes to make a gift to the charity that is out of all proportion to the charity's normal income levels, steps should be taken to verify the authenticity of the 'donor' before the gift is accepted.

- If possible, a member of the board of trustees (preferably with a legal or accounting background) should be the final arbiter or whether or not an 'unusual' gift is accepted.
- The charity should not put over-reliance on any one member of the charity in matters concerning finance. Any newly recruited staff who will be handling money should be subject to proper reference checks before they are hired.
- The trustees should receive adequate management information. Regular management accounts that are supported with copies of bank statements should be provided.
- If the charity has an investment portfolio, the internal monitoring of that portfolio (even if it is managed by outside professional managers) needs to be the responsibility of two senior people in the charity.
- Staff should be adequately trained and the systems within the charity should develop and grow in line with the growth of the charity itself.
- The charity should have appropriate controls on its IT system to prevent cyber crime.
- There should be appropriate safeguards relating to the hiring of agency or temporary staff.

In addition, when the charity is working overseas, monies sent overseas and administered there will heighten the potential risk of fraud. Care needs to be exercised in the dispersal of funds to ensure that 'partners' with whom the charity operates are not themselves operating as a front for illegal activity.

Remember that the charity operates under the laws of England and Wales, and the trustees are ultimately answerable in this country. In some regions of the world the attitude to fraud and deception may be a little more relaxed than UK charities and their officers may be anticipating.

The Charity Commission details some of the methods whereby criminal groups would seek to use charities to further their objectives. These include:

- using charities to smuggle people into countries illegally;
- using residential schools as possible recruitment and training centres;
- using charities that provide facilities for young people as areas in which they can organize and recruit volunteers;
- using charities as a base to spread propaganda.

An offer of a donation (in cash or otherwise), whereby the charity can receive the interest on the capital on condition that it returns the capital to the donor at the end of a specified period, should be very carefully analysed before being accepted. (Sometimes the donation may be in foreign currency with the condition that the capital is returned in sterling.)

Finally if charity trustees or their senior management have suspicions as to the true intentions of a potential donor (i.e. they think that they may be involved in criminal activity of any kind) then they should pass on full details to their local police station and to the Charity Commission.

Lack of governance

In section 6 we defined governance and explained the need for it. It therefore follows that if the charity does not have good governance, then it is likely to suffer, be it from a lack of direction, policy, long-term strategy or shared vision. If the key staff and volunteers of the charity are to be empowered and motivated to carry out their assigned role in an environment where the charity suffers from lack of good governance, it is likely that the staff and volunteers will become a group of individualists who are each doing 'their thing' with little or no organization, teamwork or a shared goal.

Many of the issues that cause damage and disunity in a charity can be traced back to lack of governance, and, although in faith-based organizations many staff and volunteers will claim they are working for a 'higher reward', the charity is unlikely to be sustainable in the long term without the critical issues of governance being addressed.

Depending on whether you are a trustee or a worker in a charity you may care to ask yourself the following questions: (If you are a trustee) 'Would I be satisfied in committing my long-term career in working for this organization?' or (if you are a worker) 'If I were a trustee would I be comfortable in governing this organization?'

There is a consensus that better governance results in better delivery of service and therefore improved accountability to beneficiaries, donors and other stakeholders.

Private benefit

It is a fundamental rule that charity trustees should not personally benefit from their position as a trustee. There are of course exceptions to this rule, but they are closely controlled. For example:

- If the governing document permits it, a trustee (e.g. a pastor or Chief Executive, and maybe more than one) may, if it is in the best interest of the charity, be employed by the charity, or remunerated for a service provided for the charity.

- A professional person who is also a trustee (e.g. a solicitor or an accountant) may charge professional fees for specific work done at the charity's request.
- A charity trustee may rent a property to the charity, but the terms and rental must be agreed between the trustee and the remainder of the board, and supported by professional valuation advice.

The Charities Act 2006 underlines the fact that charities must exist for the public benefit. There have been occasions where the Charity Commission have closed down a charity and removed it from the register on the basis that the level of public benefit (as opposed to the private benefit of the trustees and members) is insignificant. (NB: this would not apply to a small church with a small membership, provided that the church keeps its doors open to the general public.) Fundamentally, it is a question of degree and the test is 'does the organization exist primarily for the advantage of its members, or is the membership an administrative convenience or merely an effective way of delivering charitable benefits?'

The question is sometimes asked as to whether a church can legitimately provide social activities that may be enjoyed free of charge by those attending the church. For example, can a church provide a harvest supper free of charge to its members or are they getting personal benefit? Given that social activities are a necessary by-product of the main purpose of the church (the advancement of religion), then normally such social activities are merely ancillary to the main religious activity, and provided that the private benefit is not the main purpose of the charity then it is unlikely to be a problem.

Charity trustees should bear in mind that where one or more trustees are benefiting in some financial way from the charity, there arises the possibility for a conflict of interest. Where a conflict of interest exists, there is a danger that decisions may not be made on the basis of what is in the best interests of the charity, but rather what may or may not benefit one or more of the trustees. It is advised that if a potential conflict of interest arises, the trustees should develop a protocol for the disclosure of potential conflicts of interest so that the trustee affected can stand down on certain discussions and decisions.

The charity's board of trustees are advised to consider adopting a code of conduct which covers the trustees' behaviour and relationship towards the charity. The NCVO produce a model contract for charity trustees.

Fundamentally, directors and trustees owe a fiduciary duty of care and skill towards the charity, and they must also act in what they honestly believe to be the best interest of the charity. Failure to observe this fiduciary duty can result in directors/trustees incurring serious personal liability.

A director of a charitable company should disclose any personal interest he or she may have in a transaction with the charitable company to the board itself (usually at a board meeting), and a note of this should be included in the minutes of the board. This is important because if the transaction itself is subsequently challenged, then the minutes will need to be produced to rebut any allegation of a conflict of interest.

In the event that the director/trustee is involved in a property transaction with the charity, then special provisions apply and the charity must take legal advice at the first possible opportunity. This governs not only a transaction between a trustee and the charity, but also one between the spouse, child, associated company or partner or other connected person (of the trustee) and the company.

Lack of independence

For an organization to be a registered charity, it must be independent (i.e. it exists to carry out its stated charitable purposes and not for the purpose of advancing any decisions, guidance or proposals for any other person or organization). Furthermore, charity trustees must have an unfettered discretion to reach decisions that they believe (on the basis of professional advice where necessary) are exclusively in the best interests of the charity.

It follows that any attempt by an outside party to control or overly influence the decision-making process of the charity must be resisted. This principle can cause conflict in cases where the policy for an individual church or mission agency may be coming from another 'branch' of the organization that is registered in the UK or overseas.

A review of the reports of the Charity Commission Inquiries (i.e. where they have investigated charities) shows that the Commission take a firm line when they have found evidence that a UK charity has been 'controlled' by an outside organization, notwithstanding that the outside organization may have similar purposes or contribute towards the UK charity, or have been set up by a common founder.

Ways in which UK and overseas organizations may 'partner' towards a common objective are set out in section 11. However, the fundamental principle is that the trustees of a UK charity must not be fettered in any way in reaching their decisions.

In cases where an outside body seeks to appoint one or more of the trustees, then that trustee must not exist to represent or promote the interests of the body appointing them. A funding body cannot insist upon appointing a trustee in order to protect its interest and as a condition of providing the funding.

Funding failure

Given that most charities' income can be dependent upon many factors outside their control, it follows that many charities will at some point or other face financial uncertainty. If a charity finds itself in financial difficulties, it is important that the trustees take prompt and careful action before the risk of insolvency and potential personal liability becomes unavoidable.

A charity can be deemed insolvent when either (1) it is unable to pay its debts as they fall due; and/or (2) where the value of its assets is less than the amount of its liabilities (taking into account its possible and prospective liabilities).

In addition, directors of charitable companies are subject to the provisions of the Insolvency Acts 1986 and 2000. Those Acts do not specifically apply to unincorporated charities, but, for the purposes of this discussion, trustees of unincorporated charities should apply the same standards as if they were directors of a charitable company.

In principle, each trustee of a charity shares responsibility for a liability created on behalf of that charity, so long as the decision to incur the liability was taken at a properly convened meeting. In the normal course of events, trustees can expect to be reimbursed from the charity's assets in respect of those liabilities that have been properly incurred. In circumstances where a trustee has retired from the board, they can still expect to be indemnified from the assets of the charity unless the liability arises from a contract of employment. (Any claim against the trustees under a contract of employment is against the trustee body at the time the claim is made and not against the trustee body that existed when the contract started.) In the event there are insufficient assets in the charity to meet the liability, then the trustees may have to meet the debts and liabilities personally.

Each year when the charity's accounts are independently examined or audited (depending on the level of income), those undertaking the examination or Audit will apply a test for solvency and then state whether or not the charity has sufficient resources available to meet its immediate and short-term liabilities. If the Examiner/Auditor advises that the charity does not pass that simple test, then they may refuse to sign off the accounts until or unless steps are taken to address the issue. Please note, however, that as accounts are usually prepared in arrears (i.e. some months after the end of the financial year), the charity may have received a large gift or had good income during the months following the end of the financial year. The Auditor can insert a note to that effect (known as a 'Post Balance Sheet Event') in the accounts to explain why he considers that the charity is still solvent.

The charity may hold restricted funds (i.e. monies given for a specific purpose) and whilst these will boost the cash balance, they cannot be used for general expenditure and therefore, notwithstanding their existence on the balance sheet, the charity may still be insolvent, as it cannot pay its ordinary liabilities as they fall due.

Insolvency can arise over a period of time (in which case the trustees should have been alert to the tell-tale signs of falling income or rising expenditure), or it may happen suddenly where a major grant is withdrawn. The former may be preventable, the latter less so.

Ultimately, it is for the trustees constantly to monitor the overall financial performance of the charity, and to this end:

- Regular financial management reports (in an understandable format) should be provided to them.
- The preparation and agreement of an annual budget and cash flow projection at the beginning of each financial year should be undertaken. This projection should be monitored regularly throughout the year in question against the actual income received.
- If the charity is too heavily dependent on one or two funding sources, then urgent steps will need to be taken to create other funding streams so that the charity is not prejudiced if one or more of the main funding sources dries up.
- Any long-term contracts that the charity has should be reviewed, and if possible renegotiated, to ensure the charity can withdraw from them should the need arise. For example, if the trustees feel that the charity's financial performance is diminishing year on year, they may decide that new staff are hired on annual contracts rather than open-ended ones.
- Any long-term contracts that the charity is proposing to enter into (a lease on a property or a long-term loan) should be undertaken only once the charity has taken independent professional advice. In the case of a charity taking up a loan, it will usually be necessary for the trustees to receive independent advice from a person suitably qualified, and the advice will address the issues of the suitability of the funding source for the charity and its likely impact on the charity's cash flow etc.
- The charity needs to make proper provision for VAT, PAYE and National Insurance. These are statutory liabilities, and if the charity fails, the

trustees may be required personally to make good any shortfall. It is certainly not good practice for the charity to withhold payment of one or more of these statutory taxes in order to improve cash flow.

- The trustees should ensure that restricted funds are not spent on unrestricted matters. This can amount to a breach of trust and the trustees can be required personally to make good the shortfall.
- A prudent board of trustees would adopt a manageable reserves policy. This involves setting aside a sum of money that would be sufficient to fund the day-to-day operations of the charity for, say, a period of three or six months. By having this buffer, it means that if sources of funding cease, the charity will still have sufficient funds to achieve an orderly wind-down of its activities.

Specific steps that the charity can take to reduce the potential for financial exposure where income is consistently short of the required level include:

- reducing the charity's expenditure to a level below the sustainable income;
- launching an emergency appeal (donors would need to be made aware that new funds will be used to pay the charity's debts);
- attempting to renegotiate contracts and other commitments;
- transferring some of the activities of the charity to another like-minded charity;
- possibly a full merger of the charity with another charity;
- raising of interest-free loans from the charity's supporters;
- re-mortgaging the charity's main asset to release funds;
- seeking the Charity Commission's consent to borrow from any permanent endowment funds that the charity possesses;
- entering into an informal arrangement with the charity's creditors either to defer payment of a debt or to reduce the size of the claim. Such an arrangement needs to be made legally binding on the creditors, and therefore professional advice needs to be obtained.

If, notwithstanding the foregoing, the trustees are faced with an insolvency situation, i.e. the charity cannot pay its debts as they fall due and there is no reasonable prospect of the situation improving, then the following steps need to be taken:

1. Professional advice needs to be sought from the charity's accountant and from a Licensed Insolvency Practitioner. The advice received should be preserved in writing and any remedial steps strictly followed.

2. The trustees should take steps to minimize the potential loss by reducing or stopping some of the charity's activities.
3. The trustees may take the decision to wind up an unincorporated charity. Directors of a charitable company will need to place the company into liquidation (in conjunction with the Licensed Insolvency Practitioner).

In the case of a charitable company, it may be possible to enter into a voluntary agreement with the company's creditors for them to accept either a delayed payment or a reduced amount. Again, an Insolvency Practitioner or other professional needs to be involved.

By and large, the Charity Commission do not become involved in issues relating to restructuring or refinancing of charities. The Charity Commission will certainly take an interest as the charity regulator in order to find out the reasons for insolvency. Where there is a suspicion of mismanagement or maladministration, they may decide to open an Inquiry. They also have the power to appoint an Interim Manager (formerly a 'receiver and manager') where they feel the present trustees have not acted properly or where they perceive there to be a risk to the charity's property. The Interim Manager serves in the role of a trustee for the duration of their appointment, and ultimately this often ends in the appointment of new trustees who will take the charity forward.

In circumstances where the charity has launched a specific fund-raising project, for example, to buy a new building or undertake a particular activity in furtherance of the charity's objectives, and that fund-raising campaign does not raise sufficient money, then the issue of what happens to the monies raised is dealt with in section 22. However, notwithstanding the failure to raise the appropriate level of funding, the charity may be contractually obliged to fulfil a contract for which it no longer has the resources. For example, it may have exchanged contracts on the lease or purchase of a property, or it may have hired a large building and undertaken publicity in anticipation of a major project. The question, therefore, is how can this liability be settled?

If the charity has sufficient general funds, potentially they can be applied towards settling the liability. If the charity has insufficient funds, then its options would include:

- trying to raise a short-term loan or re-mortgage an asset;
- attempting to negotiate to withdraw from the contract – even if agreed damages are paid;
- issuing an appeals letter to its major donors.

If the potential liability is out of all proportion to the charity's assets then that in turn may result in an insolvency situation. It is recommended that professional advice, together with advice from the Charity Commission, be sought.

Malpractice

Whether the trustees know or suspect that the charity has been affected by malpractice (of whatever form), they should:

- Meet together and agree that there is an issue to investigate.
- Appoint an independent professional to investigate the matter (usually an accountant or lawyer). Such an investigation should include how the situation arose and the likely impact of it on the charity.
- Report the matter immediately to the Charity Commission (and forward them a copy of the investigator's findings).
- Consider whether the matter should also be reported to the police or other statutory bodies, e.g. HMRC.
- Proceed in the light of the advice received.
- Provided that the effects of the malpractice can be ring-fenced from the general activity of the charity, take any necessary steps to prevent a reoccurrence.

Failure to comply with legislation

This section should be read in conjunction with section 25, Risk management.

The trustees (whether the charity is an unincorporated charity or a charitable company) are liable for a breach of trust that results from the breaking of the law. Simply put, a breach of trust occurs when the trustees act in a way that is not authorized by the charity's governing document or permitted by charity law, for example, engaging in unlawful activity, spending charity monies on activities that are outside the charity's stated objective, or entering into contracts and liabilities against professional advice.

It is for the Charity Commission to decide whether or not to order a charity trustee to reimburse the charity for a loss that may have arisen as a result of a breach of trust. Under the Charities Act 2006, the Charity Commission have power to relieve a trustee or Auditor from liability for breach of trust, if they are satisfied that the trustee has acted honestly and reasonably and therefore ought fairly to be excused for the breach of trust.

However, that relief does not apply to any personal contractual liability of a charity trustee. So, for example, if the trustee joins in a finance agreement to purchase a vehicle in the name of and for the charity, yet the governing document did not allow for such an agreement to be entered into, then whilst the Charity Commission could excuse the trustee on the basis that he acted honestly and reasonably, he will still be personally liable as a signatory to the finance contract if the charity has insufficient funds to make the payments.

Trustees will also be personally liable for any payments that are due under legislation and for which the charity cannot pay (see section 24 with regard to PAYE, National Insurance, etc).

Fundamentally, it can be stated that if charities do not comply with current legislation, they risk not only the sanction that non-compliance will bring, but also the possibility of an injunction and claim for damages. These in turn attract the attention of the Charity Commission, which then leads to an Inquiry and the possibility of sanctions being imposed. All of which is extremely time consuming, costly and ultimately damaging to the charity, its reputation and the achievement of its charitable purposes.

Remember, ignorance of the law is no defence.

SECTION 25 RISK MANAGEMENT

Identification and management

Risk management has been defined as the process of measuring or assessing risk, and developing strategies to manage it.

Fundamentally, charities exist for the public benefit, and are often involved in innovative and practical objectives in order to facilitate change for the better in the desired area of activity. In the commercial world, companies and businesses are often constrained by the overriding need to make profit, whereas charities exist to expend their resources to achieve their charitable objectives.

Indeed, many of today's well-known charitable organizations, who have been, and are, so effective in making change, started off with the founders taking risks in order to address the issues on which they had decided to focus.

Risk, however, is not necessarily something be avoided (even in today's risk averse culture). Rather, charity trustees need to be encouraged to focus on the nature of the risk which its very mission requires it to face, if it is to be true to its charitable objectives.

Whilst all charities face risk (albeit to varying degrees), the trustees and key workers in the charity should engage in a process of Spotting the risk, Assessing the risk and then Solving the risk. In other words, SAS.

Spot it!

The following is a list of examples of possible areas of risk that affect charities today. Each charity will need to address those that are most relevant to its own situation. The list is not exhaustive.

Financial

A drop in income over a sustained period
Withdrawal of funding by a major grant maker
Lack of return on investments
Failure of a charitable project or a trading subsidiary
Fraud, corruption, or money laundering

Governance and management

Loss of the Chief Executive or other 'key' leader or manager
Dispute amongst board members or other failure by the board to give clear
  leadership and direction
Conflict of interest
Charity Commission Inquiry
Qualified Audit report
IT systems failure
A legal claim from a third party
Failure to adapt to the changing needs of the charity's beneficiaries

Staff Issues

Key members of staff in dispute or leaving
Employment tribunal claim brought by a staff member
Breach of health and safety/equal opportunities/data protection or other
  legislation
Employee/trustee theft

Miscellaneous

Exposure to foreign currency fluctuation
Underfunded pension commitments
Kidnap or ransom of overseas staff worker
Overseas government change of law or policy

Assess it!

Many charities undertake a simple SWOT analysis (strengths, weaknesses, opportunities and threats) for the charity as whole.

Fundamentally, it is important to assess the magnitude of the risk, in order to decide whether it can be managed, accepted, or needs to be avoided.

Part of the assessment process is to decide both the severity of the potential loss and also the probability that the loss will occur. For example, if a charity was attempting to assess the implication of losing a major grant, the potential severity of the loss would be fairly easy to ascertain, but the probability of it happening may be more difficult to project. In these circumstances, the charity should make a best educated guess in order to implement a risk management programme. It is important that the 'guess', and the reasons that were considered in arriving at that guess, are recorded in the charity's records, should they ever need to be referred to in the future.

It is considered best practice for charity boards to undertake a risk management assessment, and, given the diversity of most charities, this assessment is likely to result in the revealing of several areas of risk that will then need to be assessed. Once a definitive list has been produced, then that will need to be prioritized so that the charity does not spend all of its time in risk management to the detriment of its pursuit of its charitable objectives!

Solve it!
The solution to the risk, once it has been 'spotted' and 'assessed', can be broken down into four main categories.

1. Risk avoidance
Whilst avoidance may be the ultimate answer to all risks, it can also mean losing out on the potential gain to the charity that accepting the risk may have permitted. That said, however, there are some risks that the charity may decide are just too great for it to accept safely .

A review of the cases listed on the Charity Commission's website, where they have intervened in the affairs of a charity, will reveal some examples of instances where charities have accepted a risk that they would have been (albeit in hindsight) better advised to avoid.

It should be emphasized here that each charity is different (because each is made up of a unique combination of people, resources and opportunities). Therefore, the fact that one charity succeeds in a risky venture does not necessarily mean that another charity will be similarly successful if it replicates that charitable activity. Each charity must undertake and execute its own risk management strategy based on the particular circumstances that present themselves to it.

There are some occasions when the charity just cannot decide whether it should proceed with a level of risk or not. Short of deciding the matter by drawing lots, this is surely a situation where independent professional advice should be taken by the trustees, and that advice followed.

An example of risk avoidance could include a charity deciding not to work in a particular country in view of the risks to its personnel or from government interference, or of a church not proceeding with the acquisition of a property in circumstances where the church was concerned that the level of income needed to repay a large loan could be affected by a fluctuation in the church's attendance.

2. Reducing the risk

The charity may decide to accept a level of risk but put in place steps to reduce the level of risk or the likely implication of a loss. An example of this (using the above illustration) would be the church deciding to proceed with its property acquisition, having succeeded in securing a commercial tenant for part of the building that would bring in a guaranteed income for a set period to assist the charity to meet its mortgage repayments.

3. Retaining the risk

This involves the charity reaching a definite conclusion that it could accept the risk concerned, having calculated that even if the event itself took place, the organization would be able to survive notwithstanding.

Using the above example of the church property project, retaining the risk would be where the charity had decided that even if its income fell during the period of the loan, then it would have the resources (or perhaps the trustees and key workers would agree to ensure it had the resources) to make the loan repayments for a certain period of time. During this time, the trustees may decide whether the loan itself could be restructured over a longer period (thereby reducing the monthly payments), or whether it would be preferable to sell the building to clear the indebtedness.

4. Transferring the risk

This is where the risk itself is actually transferred to a third party. An obvious example is where the charity can take out insurance to offer a level of indemnity in the event of the risk materializing. In today's insurance market it is possible to insure a good many risks, including kidnap and ransom, theft of the charity's assets, indemnity for trustees against a claim, and legal expenses, as well as the standard policies that cover fire and damage to properties, public liability, etc. Banks offer a facility to 'hedge' likely exposure to currency fluctuations, which is an important issue for charities who move significant amounts of money overseas on a regular basis.

Once the charity has prepared a risk management programme, this needs to be reviewed on a regular basis, as some risks pass and are replaced by new ones.

Ultimately, it is considered part of the trustee board's role to ensure that an adequate risk assessment and management programme is in place. In medium to large charitable organizations, the trustees are unlikely to be involved in the day-to-day implementation of it, as this will be delegated down to senior management. In small to medium-sized charities, they may well have a more 'hands on' approach.

However, risk management is not something that is limited to the trustees and/or senior management. It is considered that everyone in the charity (even the volunteers) needs to be aware of these issues and to participate in the implementation of the risk management programme of the charity.

The current SORP requires the trustees of charities with a gross income of £250,000 per annum to report on risk management in their Annual Report, which forms part of the charity's audited accounts (trustees of smaller charities are encouraged to make a similar statement as a matter of best practice). The Charity Commission will be looking for such a report to clarify that:

- the trustees acknowledge that they are responsible for risk management;
- an overview of the risk identification process has been adopted;
- major risks that have been identified have been assessed;
- adequate systems have been established by the charity to address those risks (avoidance/reduction/retention/transfer).

The charity's Auditors are not required to formally audit the risk management statement in the accounts, although if they become aware (from the work done during the Audit) of some inconsistencies in what the trustees are saying in their Annual Report, they may need to qualify their Audit report if their reservations on the risk management statement cannot be resolved! (The Charity Commission provide some helpful examples of trustees' Annual Reports which are available via their website.)

Other steps in risk management

Other practical steps that charities can take to assist in the risk management process include:

A legal Audit – a review by a firm of lawyers experienced in representing charitable organizations will address areas within the charity that are not covered by the normal financial Audit. Many charities have found such a legal Audit of great assistance in clarifying the main areas of risk. The charity can then follow through with their own risk assessment and management.

Professional advice – independent professional advice is essential when charities are considering activities that are outside their normal day-to-day functions. A good example that faces many charities concerns a project perhaps to acquire or develop a property for the charity's use. Even if the charity board has representatives of the surveying, architectural, legal or accounting professions thereon, it is considered wise for the charity to bring in independent professional advice from outside on such matters. It is not unknown for there to be instances where, in the enthusiasm of the charity to acquire or develop a building for its use, decisions are made which are then substantially challenged by the independent advisers who are subsequently retained!

Trustee indemnity insurance – whilst not an absolute 'get out of jail free card', it is considered essential by many trustee boards to provide a level of indemnity for the trustees against the risk of personal liability arising from breach of trust together with the likely legal costs that would be involved in responding to a challenge. It should be noted, however, that such insurance does not protect charity trustees from all types of personal liability.

Trustee indemnity insurance

Before trustee indemnity insurance can be taken out, the following needs to take place:

1. The board needs to assess that there is a risk that the trustees could be held, albeit in extreme circumstances, to be personally liable and that, notwithstanding the implementation of a specific risk management programme for the charity, the risk remains.
2. The governing document must not prohibit the charity from taking out and paying the premiums on trustee indemnity insurance for its trustees. The Charities Act 2006 provides the trustees with legal authority to take out trustee indemnity insurance, provided that they are satisfied that it is in the best interests of the charity (not the trustees!) for it to be taken out. In other words, there must be a clear advantage to the charity, although there is nothing to stop the trustees taking out the indemnity themselves and splitting the costs of the premiums between them.

Trustee indemnity insurance will not normally cover liability in the following circumstances:

- Trustees of unincorporated charities from personal liability as a result of contracts that they have entered into on behalf of their charity. For example, if trustees of an unincorporated charity entered into a mortgage deed to assist in the acquisition of a property for the charity, then if the charity defaulted, it is possible the trustees would still be personally liable under the personal covenant they will have made in the mortgage deed itself.
- Any redundancy payments that may be payable to employees of the charity.
- Any liabilities under a lease that the charity has (for example, repair or maintenance of the building).
- Liability for fraud or dishonesty by employees of the charity.
- Fines that the trustees have to pay.
- The costs of an unsuccessful defence to a criminal prosecution arising out of fraud or dishonest or reckless misconduct of a trustee.
- The charity's liability arising from conduct that the trustee knew or should have known was not in the interests of the charity.

Currently there are some 900,000 charity trustees serving on the boards of approximately 190,000 charities that are registered with the UK Charity Commission. The aggregate annual income of these charities exceeds £36bn. Yet the instances whereby trustees are made personally liable are usually in single figures each year.

SECTION 26 CHARITY COMMISSION SCHEMES, ORDERS, CLASSIFICATIONS AND APPLICATIONS

On occasions, a charity may need to consider making changes to its governing document. Such changes may be to the charitable purposes (Objects) or to the administrative provisions given to the trustees to carry out those Objects (Powers).

An alteration to the charity's Objects will require the consent of the Charity Commission. The Commission has the power to change Objects by making a Scheme.

The charity's Powers can sometimes be altered by the trustees themselves, using provisions to that effect given to them by the governing document. If the trustees do not have the necessary provisions in the governing document, the Charity Commission can make an Order thereby empowering the trustees to amend the administrative provisions or indeed to confer additional powers that are not currently available in the governing document.

It is helpful to look at these in more detail.

Charity Commission Scheme

Essentially, a Scheme is a legal document made by the Charity Commission where they are satisfied that there is good reason for them to change the charitable purposes of the organization or make other significant constitutional arrangements. Examples of when a Scheme will be appropriate include:

1. Where the governing document of the charity is inadequate and needs to be replaced.
2. Where the Objects of the charity need to be changed. In this case, the Charity Commission can only make a Scheme in circumstances where the original Objects of the charity can no longer be carried out in a way laid down in the governing document, for example, when a group of people who were originally to benefit from the charity no longer exist.

Once the Charity Commission agree that a Scheme is appropriate, then after they have drafted the Scheme they will give the charity directions as to whether the draft Scheme needs to be advertised (to invite public comment) before it is finally sealed.

Once a Scheme has been made, a copy has to be displayed at the Charity Commission's office and, if the charity is a local one, at some convenient place in the locality of the charity.

Charity Commission Order

An Order made by the Charity Commission has the effect of conferring new powers on the charity's trustees. Examples of when an Order can be made include:

- Where there is a need to give the trustees a specific power of amendment in the governing document.
- Where the trustees need to be given powers that are additional to those contained in the governing document.
- To authorize charity trustees to transfer the assets and liabilities from one charity to another.
- To authorize a specific payment as being in the best interests of the charity.

Unlike a Scheme, an Order does not need to be advertised, unless it is one relating to the appointment, discharge, or removal of a trustee.

Excepted and exempt charities

An excepted charity is a charity that does not have to register with the Charity Commission, but otherwise falls within the Charity Commission's control. Examples of excepted charities include certain Baptist, Congregational,

Evangelical, Unitarian, Methodist, United Reformed, Quaker, Church of England and Church of Wales charities.

The Charities Act 2006 now requires some of these charities to register with the Charity Commission, providing that their income is in excess of £100,000 per year. Excepted charities with an income of under £100,000 will continue to come under the Charity Commission's jurisdiction, although they will not specifically need to register.

Exempt charities include organizations who previously had not been required to register with the Charity Commission because they were overseen by other public bodies, for example state schools, universities and some national museums. The Charities Act 2006 now requires that these charities be monitored to ensure their compliance with charity law.

Unregistered charities

The Charities Act 2006 defines 'charity' as an institution that is established for charitable purposes only, and is subject to the control of the High Court in the exercise of its jurisdiction.

The Act goes on to say that every charity must be registered with the Charity Commission unless:

- it continues to be an exempt charity;
- it continues to be an excepted charity, by the specific order of the Charity Commission, and whose gross income does not exceed £100,000 per year;
- it is a charity whose gross income does not exceed £5,000 per year;
- it is a place of worship that is formally registered under the Places of Worship Registration Act 1855.

Where a charity is required to be registered, it is the duty of the charity trustees to apply for that registration to be made.

Some very small churches have registered their buildings under the Places of Worship Act 1855, and such registration has been accepted by HMRC as being sufficient to allow the church to administer a Gift Aid scheme.

Cy-près applications

A significant number of the Schemes made by the Charity Commission relate to the expansion or updating of the Objects in a charity's Governing Document. The cy-près doctrine (French for 'near to') allows the Charity

Commission to make a Scheme in circumstances where the original Objects have either been fulfilled or are no longer possible. Subject to certain conditions being satisfied, the property of the charity can then be applied Cy-près.

Further application of cy-près can be illustrated where a charity undertakes a fund-raising campaign for a specific purpose and fails to get enough money to undertake that purpose, then the funds received can no longer be applied for that specific purpose. As a result, the charity is left holding a sum of money that it cannot expend and, unless it has taken the steps outlined in section 22 before raising the money, cannot return the money to the individual donors.

The Charities Act 2006 now permits a more liberal approach to be taken when a charity applies to either the Charity Commission or the High Court for guidance in how such monies can be used. The Charity Commission and the Court will take into account current social and economic circumstances, and also the spirit in which the original gift was made. This can include authorizing the charity to pass monies on to another charity with a duty imposed on the trustees of the recipient charity to ensure that the gift is applied as closely as possible to the original purposes for which the monies were raised.

SECTION 27 MERGER, COLLABORATION, TAKEOVER, CONVERSION AND CESSATION OF CHARITIES

Merger

Charity trustees, who are seeking to increase the influence of their work, reduce overheads and maximize efficiency, can view a possible merger with another like-minded charity as an attractive proposition.

Certainly, the Charity Commission encourage charities to consider whether they can achieve more for their beneficiaries through working closely with others. This can be achieved in two ways: (1) through a merger with another charity (effectively the combining of the assets and liabilities of two or more charities into one unit); or (2) by collaboration (where two or more charities work together on a common project, yet remain as separate organizations).

A merger can be achieved by:

1. Two or more charities transferring their assets and liabilities to a new charity that is established by them with similar charitable objectives. Charities proposing to do this should take professional advice to ensure:
   - The respective governing documents of the charities combining actually permit the merger.
   - Neither charity holds any Permanent Endowment (assets held by the charity on the basis that only the income and not the capital can be spent on the charitable purposes). However, the Charities Act 2006 may

offer a resolution to the issue of permanent endowment (see Appendix
1 paragraph 32).
- Any Restricted Funds can be passed over to the new charitable body.
- The employees of the charity are properly consulted and the
requirements of employment legislation are met (see section 16).
2. One charity transfers its assets and liabilities to another and then the
transferring charity closes down and is removed from the register.
3. One charity (or its trustees) actually become the trustees of another
charity.

The Charity Commission's consent is not needed for a merger. However,
they will become involved if one or other charity has insufficient powers to
effect the proposed merger. In such cases, they can be expected to work with
the charities to achieve the merger.

Special care needs to be taken by charities that have an active membership
structure. The governing document may require the members' consent
before a merger can be effected.

In addition to consulting professional advisers, it is strongly recommended
that any charity seeking to merge with another should go through a proper
due diligence exercise on that other charity in order to understand fully the
history, make-up and methods of operation of the other charity. Whilst in the
long term a merger can possibly save money, in the short term time and
money will need to be allocated to effect an integration of management information systems, accounting systems, contracts and administration generally.

Under the Charities Act 2006, the Charity Commission are required to
maintain a public Register of Mergers. Once the transfer of property
involved in the merger has taken place, then notification must be given to the
Charity Commission by the charity trustees clarifying the date the merger
took place and confirming that appropriate arrangements have been made
with regard to the payment of any liabilities of the transferring charity.

Collaboration

A collaboration or partnership is not limited to the charitable activity itself;
it may, for example, concern the combining of administration, working
together on a fund-raising project, sharing an asset, outsourcing specific
services or a specific joint venture.

Fundamentally, in collaborative relationships the trustees must always act
in the interest of the individual charities that are collaborating, as each
charity will be maintaining its independence throughout the relationship.

Whatever form the collaboration takes, the details should be properly recorded in a written document that is signed by a trustee from each charity participating. If the charity's governing document does not permit collaboration with another charitable organization, then the Charity Commission will need to be consulted. In certain circumstances, it may be wise for a more formal legal structure, for example a charitable company, to be put in place to facilitate the collaboration.

On a practical level, it will be important to ensure that there is an adequate mechanism for disengaging from the relationship should it not prove to be beneficial to both charities.

Takeover

When a larger charity takes over a smaller one, diplomatically it may be called a 'merger', but in reality it is a takeover!

Unlike a commercial organization, a charity has no shareholders or owners who would benefit from any premium paid. If the acquiring charity is to pay any money at all, it is usually to enable the other charity to discharge debts and liabilities in order that it may close with a zero balance sheet.

Professional advice needs to be taken on the terms of the proposed takeover to ensure, for both the acquirer and the other charity, that the transaction is in the best interests of each, and is on terms that are fair and reasonable in all the circumstances. (The comments made earlier in this section about Permanent Endowment funds and other Restricted Funds apply equally to a takeover.)

Conversion from one charitable entity to another

The trustees of an unincorporated charity may decide to incorporate and become a charitable company. The process involves the preparation of a Memorandum and Articles of Association. The Objects expressed in the Memorandum and Articles of Association should be identical to those in the governing document of the unincorporated charity. Otherwise, not all of the assets of the unincorporated charity can be transferred over. For example, if the unincorporated charity has as its charitable objects 'the advancement of religion', and the Memorandum and Articles of the new charitable company also include 'the relief of poverty' as a charitable object, then monies given to the unincorporated charity cannot be used for the 'relief of poverty' activity.

The company is then formed at Companies House and an application made for its registration with the Charity Commission. The trustees of the unincorporated charity can pass a resolution to transfer all the assets and liabilities of the charity (subject as above) over to the new charitable company (this includes any freehold or leasehold property, staff contracts, grant contracts, etc.).

Final accounts are prepared for the unincorporated charity, and once they are filed with the Charity Commission, that charity is removed from the register. It is usually possible to retain the name of the old charity and register that for the new charitable company.

If an unincorporated charity closes down and transfers its assets to a newly created charitable company, then such an action will also need to be notified to the Charity Commission for it to be included in the public Register of Mergers. When a merger has been registered, gifts and legacies that have been left to the charity that has closed down will as a result of the merger be automatically transferred to the new charitable entity that has replaced it.

The Charities Act 2006 allows for the creation of a new charitable organization known as a Charitable Incorporated Organisation (CIO). It is possible to convert either an unincorporated charity or a charitable company over to a CIO (see section 2).

Cessation

Trustees of small unincorporated charities (where the income in the last financial years does not exceed £10,000) have power to transfer the property of that charity to one or more other charities, or to amend the charitable objects and administrative powers of the charity. However, this provision does not apply to a small charity that holds designated land (e.g. a church hall), or is a charitable company.

The trustees, however, can only resolve to do this if they are satisfied that it is in the interests of furthering the purposes of the transferring charity and that the recipient charity has charitable purposes that are substantially similar. The resolution itself needs a majority of not less than two-thirds of the transferring charity's trustees.

Once the resolution has been passed, a copy is sent to the Charity Commission, together with a statement stating the trustees' reasons for passing it. The resolution itself then takes effect sixty days following receipt of a copy by the Charity Commission.

If the charity has Permanent Endowment then the Permanent Endowment can be transferred to the recipient charity (or charities), provided the recipient charity meets certain requirements with regard to its charitable purposes.

If the small unincorporated charity does not wish to pass its assets on to another charity, but finds that its existing charitable purposes are no longer valid, then providing it meets the tests as set out above, it may resolve that the charitable trusts of the charity should be modified, by replacing one or all of the purposes of the charitable objects of the charity with other objects specified in the resolution. The procedure for passing the resolution is the same as set out above and again a copy sent to the Charity Commission and, subject to the Charity Commission's response, it takes effect at the end of sixty days following receipt of the resolution by the Charity Commission.

Finally, the Charities Act 2006 also gives the trustees of an unincorporated charity the ability to resolve to modify any of the powers given to the trustees in the governing document or to regulate the procedure to be followed in connection with the charity's administration. Care needs to be taken that any alterations do not affect any clauses of the governing document, which are expressed to be unalterable without the consent of the Charity Commission. The Charity Commission publish a leaflet dealing with the cessation of small charities.

Finally, the procedure for closing down an unincorporated charity whose gross income is under £20,000 a year is assisted by the 'fast track' approach developed by the Charity Commission. Provided that the charity meets the necessary criteria, then the charity trustees can make the appropriate declaration, which is then filed with the Charity Commission. However, the procedure is more complicated if the charity owns land or other Permanent Endowment.

Once the charity has been closed down and removed from the Charity Commission register, then the accounting books and records must be preserved for at least six years following the date of cessation.

SECTION 28 EVALUATING EFFECTIVENESS

Many charities consider that their most pressing task is to raise enough money to enable the charity to function from year to year. However, in recent years the Charity Commission, perhaps picking up on public sentiment, are encouraging charities and their trustees to take time to measure how effective the charity is against its stated charitable purposes.

The accountability that charities have to their donors, potential partners and ultimate beneficiaries requires that the charity's effectiveness is both measured and monitored on an ongoing basis.

The trustees' report, contained in the annual accounts, is an excellent forum for charity trustees to demonstrate the measured effectiveness of the charity's work in the particular year that the accounts cover.

Steps to evaluate the effectiveness of a charity

Notwithstanding the fact that each charity is unique, in terms of size, make-up and activity, it should be possible to adapt the following check list of questions to help evaluate the effectiveness of most charities.

1. Are the stated Objects, activities and values of the charity clearly set out and understood by its trustees, workers, volunteers and beneficiaries?

1.1 Does the charity regularly review the governing document, policies and plans to ensure they are up to date and developing in line with both the charity's work and the times?

1.2 How does the charity define 'success' against the stated Objects, activities and values?

1.3 How truthfully does the charity communicate its success to its donors and beneficiaries?

2. Is the charity compliant with the legal and accounting regulations that affect it?

2.1 When did the charity last submit its inner workings to outside legal and accounting input?

2.2 Does the charity understand and observe all regulations that affect the arena, and the way in which it operates?

2.3 Does the charity strive to apply 'best practice' to its operations and output?

2.4 How does the charity respond to complaints or negative experiences, e.g. employment claims by departing staff?

3. How effective are the governance and management when benchmarked against other comparable charities?

3.1 Does the board have the right mix of skills, experience and knowledge for the charity?

3.2 Does the charity provide ongoing training and evaluation for trustees and staff?

3.3 Do the trustees work together harmoniously and effectively, and solely for the charity?

3.4 Are the staff and volunteers valued, empowered and held accountable?

3.5 Is the Chief Executive/pastor understood, supported, valued and accountable?

3.6 Are the managers empowered and guided to work effectively and within correct boundaries?

3.7 Does the charity have appropriate and robust systems in place to control risks, assets, expenditure and other liability?

4. How accountable is the charity to donors, beneficiaries and the authorities?

4.1 Is information disclosed on a 'need to know' basis or is the charity open and transparent?

4.2 Does the charity provide a forum to enable its beneficiaries and members to influence and vote for change?

4.3 Are the accounts and annual returns accurate, clear, full and filed on time?

4.4 Does the charity open up its programmes to allow review by outside professionals or donors?

4.5 Do the staff and volunteers have input to this evaluation on the charity's effectiveness?

5. How effective is the charitable activity (programmes, services, products etc.) in achieving the charitable Objects?

5.1 How effective in terms of financial cost?

5.2 How effective in terms of resources (people and/or assets applied)?

5.3 Could more be achieved or could the activity be more effective if the charity worked together with other like-minded charities?

5.4 What performance indicators are built into the programmes and activities?

6. Is the charity reactive or proactive?

6.1 How does it respond to change that is imposed on it, for example by legislation?

6.2 Does the charity foresee change in the needs of its beneficiaries and therefore voluntarily respond by adapting to meet those changes?

6.3 Are the plans and policies regularly reviewed in order to adapt them to meet changes?

6.4 Does the charity interact with other charitable bodies and learn from or work with them where there is significant advantage in so doing?

6.5 Does the charity keep up to date and make good use of technology?

Charities meeting best practice criteria can apply to the Charity Commission for their endorsement of the charity's quality standards in areas such as accountability, governance, structures, conflicts of interest policies and their ability to manage their staff and volunteers.

APPENDIX 1 WHAT TO DO WHEN

1. A trustee retires or resigns

Written notice should be given by the trustee leaving, and that notice should be recorded in the charity's minute book. A formal Deed of Retirement is suggested as being appropriate, particularly if property is involved. It is also necessary to notify the Charity Commission.

If the trustee is one of those named on the title of the charity's freehold property, then the Deed of Retirement will need to be registered at the Land Registry to remove that trustee's name. Professional advice will need to be sought if the trustee is a named party to the charity's lease or a party to the charity's mortgage deed, as it may be more difficult to extricate the leaving trustee from such an arrangement. If the trustee was a party to the charity's bank account, then the mandate will need to be changed

In the case of a charitable company, notice of the retirement or resignation will need to be filed at Companies House (Company Form 288b).

NB: the charity must consider whether the retirement or resignation will reduce the number of trustees to below the minimum number as stated in the charity's governing document. If it does, then immediate steps need to be taken to appoint a replacement trustee to ensure that the charity can continue to function (see also section 9).

2. The charity needs to appoint a new trustee

When a suitable candidate has been found, it is wise to take up at least two character references on the potential new trustee. The charity should also take steps to ensure that the proposed trustee is not disqualified from acting in that capacity (see section 9).

A Criminal Records Bureau (CRB) check must be undertaken where there is a legal requirement to do so and should be undertaken where there is a legal entitlement to do so (see Section 9).

The charity should ensure the proposed trustee fully understands the charity and the responsibilities that they are taking on.

Specific requirements
- Check the governing document to see who can appoint a new trustee (if there exists no one with the right to appoint a new trustee, then an application should be made to the Charity Commission).
- A formal Deed of Appointment is recommended, particularly if the charity owns property.
- The Charity Commission should be notified.
- Consider whether any freehold or leasehold property belonging to the charity held in the names that include an outgoing trustee should be transferred into the name of the new trustee.
- Ensure that the appointment is recorded in the charity's minute book.
- The bank mandate may need to be changed.

If it is a charitable company, then notice needs to be filed at Companies House (Company Form 288a). See also section 9.

3. Trustee numbers fall below the minimum permitted

The governing document of the charity will specify the minimum number of trustees necessary to form a quorum. Failure to maintain that number means that the charity cannot operate lawfully. The practical application of the failure is that decisions made by the board (save perhaps for the decision to appoint an additional trustee or director) are invalid. The Charity Commission have the power to co-opt additional trustees to make the charity board quorate, if the existing trustees are unable or unwilling to do so.

4. There is a dispute between board members

Not every dispute is unhealthy! Whilst board members should strive for 'unity in diversity', this is not always achievable, and there are therefore occasions when a conflict can negatively affect the function of the board and compromise the ability of the charity to achieve its stated charitable purposes.

Steps that might prevent disputes escalating include:

- ensuring that each member of the board clearly understands his or her role and area of responsibility;
- periodic reminders from the chairman of the trustees that the board acts jointly and a trustee does not have power individually unless it has been specifically delegated by the board;
- focusing the board on serving the charity and achieving its charitable objectives;
- reminding any defaulting members of their agreed responsibility under a trustee code of conduct (see section 24).

Notwithstanding the above, if a dispute escalates to the stage where it is threatening the unity of the board and potentially undermining the charity itself, then additional steps may include:

- bringing in an outside independent mediator;
- considering the removal of the trustees in dispute from the board (check the governing document to ensure that correct procedure is followed).

The Charity Commission do have a limited power to intervene, but they will do so only in cases where:

- the way in which the charity is being run is putting significant assets of the charity at risk;
- the charity's income is not being used for its charitable purposes;
- the trustees are not acting in accordance with the charity's governing document or charity law;
- there is a serious danger of the name of the charity being brought into disrepute;
- the administration of the charity has broken down and the charity is not working effectively.

The Charity Commission will not get involved in doctrinal disputes, employment matters or disputes between the charity and other people who have entered into contracts with it (see also section 19).

5. Payment is to be made to a trustee

The general principle is that a trustee must not benefit in any way from their connection with the charity. There is an exception to this rule where the governing document specifically allows a payment to a trustee or allows them to do business with the charity.

A trustee in breach of this rule can be made liable to repay to the charity any salary or benefits they have received. NB: this applies even if the trustee has resigned as a trustee before or at the time they took up the employment, unless the charity can clearly show that the trustee has not obtained the employment by reason of them being a trustee and that there will be no ongoing conflict of interest.

If the governing document does not allow a payment to be made, yet the charity wishes to make such a payment, then the Charity Commission in certain circumstances have the power to authorize such a payment, providing that the charity's trustee can demonstrate that there is a clear advantage to the charity in the payment being made to the trustee.

The Charities Act 2006 (see section 3) has extended this exception further, allowing payment for goods or services that a trustee provides to a charity over and above the trustee's normal duties (see also section 7).

6. There is non-attendance or non-involvement by a trustee

Charity trustees have a duty of care to use reasonable care and skill to ensure that the charity is well run and efficient, and to consider taking external professional advice on matters where there may be a material risk to the charity.

Given the above and the general level of responsibility on charity trustees, it is considered that trustees who are habitually absent from board meetings (say, missing three or more consecutive meetings without good reason) are seriously abdicating their responsibilities and should be asked to leave the board (or removed if they do not agree).

Trustees who, whilst they may attend board meetings, fail to 'engage' or identify positively with the charity's work may also be a negative influence on the board. It is advised that steps be taken to identify the reason for the board member's non-involvement. For example, some trustees serve out of a sense of duty, or have perhaps been seconded to the board in an *ex officio* capacity.

One way in which boards can ensure that each member is engaged and fully focused on the interest of the charity is for the chairman to conduct board appraisals with individual members of the board on an annual basis. Such appraisals can either be based on an informal discussion, or formalized, perhaps by using a pre-agreed questionnaire. The board chairman also needs to be evaluated, and this is perhaps best done by two other senior members of the board using the same approach as that for the general board members.

A board member who was formerly engaged and enthusiastic and who becomes withdrawn (perhaps through a negative experience with the charity) will need sensitive handling, particularly as any sense of injustice may quickly spread to other members of the board and senior staff (see also section 7).

7. Trustees claim they are not consulted

Trustees who validly make this claim are in a very serious and vulnerable position! Given that trustees are ultimately responsible for what happens in a charity, the board is negligent if it allows a situation to arise whereby a Chief Executive or a senior management team are making all the decisions without the knowledge or involvement of the trustees.

Clearly, trustees in this position have a simple choice; either they can resign *en masse* (with the attendant turmoil that it will cause in the charity until the new board is appointed), or they can address the issue involved and ensure that the correct method of governance and accountability is thereafter implemented.

A governance audit may be helpful in order to understand fully who is exercising power within the organization. Ultimately, it is a question of how seriously the charity trustees are prepared to take their responsibilities (see also section 7).

8. One trustee cannot agree with a majority decision of the board

Trustee boards take decisions acting collectively and as a team. The decisions do not need to be unanimous, as a majority decision is sufficient (unless the charity's governing document says otherwise).

If one or more of the trustees cannot agree with a majority decision on an issue, and the issue is a significant one, the dissenting trustee(s) will need to consider:

- whether the decision in question is of such fundamental importance to the charity or the trustee that their continued involvement on the board has been undermined;
- if the decision involves the expenditure of a large sum of money or the entering into of a major contract, whether the dissenting trustee is

prepared to shoulder ultimate responsibility with the rest of the board if the decision goes wrong. If they are not so prepared, then they may need to resign immediately.

- that the minutes of the board meeting clearly record their dissenting opinion and vote on the issue in question.

It is suggested that a wise and skilful board chairman would, in the instance of a major decision, come alongside the dissenting trustee(s) to ensure that any reaction does not undermine the decision itself or the ongoing work and the reputation of the charity (see also section 7).

9. The trustees wish to delegate their responsibilities

Subject to the provisions of the charity's governing document, trustees usually have the power to delegate certain responsibilities to a sub-committee or to individuals. Responsibilities that can be delegated include:

- the implementing of a decision that has been made by the board;
- the investment of assets;
- raising funds for the charity.

Notwithstanding any power to delegate that is contained in the governing document, the trustees have final responsibility for everything that is done in the charity, including things done by those to whom a responsibility has been delegated.

The person or group to whom a responsibility has been delegated should always make the fact of that delegation known to any third parties that they deal with, thereby reducing the risk of them being held responsible by the third party (see also section 6).

10. It is difficult to recruit new trustees

Charities that are finding it difficult to recruit new trustees may consider:

- advertising the opportunity together with brief details of the role, in general and denominational publications;
- approaching specific people in either the geographical area or the particular sector that the charity is involved in and asking them either to make the need known or to suggest potential candidates;

- the appointment of a custodian trustee for the church building and trust;
- possible merger with another like-minded charity.

11. The trustees wish to make an *ex gratia* payment

Fundamentally, a charity's funds can be spent only in accordance with the governing document and in order to further the stated charitable Objects.

An *ex gratia* payment is one where the trustees, although not having a legal obligation, nevertheless feel there is a moral obligation on them to make a payment to a party, yet there exists no power under the governing document for the payment to be made, nor can the trustees justify it as being exclusively in the interests of the charity.

Charity trustees wishing to make an *ex gratia* payment must first seek the consent of the Charity Commission. In addition, the Charity Commission have the power to authorize a payment that the trustees have no legal obligation or power to make, but believe that such payment will result in benefit to the charity.

Trustees who take the Charity Commission's advice on such matters, and proceed in accordance with that advice, are generally protected from any personal liability for breach of trust (provided they have not misstated the facts or withheld material information from the Charity Commission before the advice is given).

An example of a possible need for an *ex gratia* payment would be where a charity received a gift in a will that, because of a legal technicality or an oversight on the testator's part, resulted in a larger gift than the testator really intended, and, as a result, some other person will be deprived of money or property that the testator intended them to receive. The charity may be legally entitled to keep the whole of the gift, and the trustees may conclude that they have a moral obligation to make a payment out of the monies they have received to ensure that the testator's original intentions were complied with. In these circumstances the trustees will need to get the prior written consent of the Charity Commission before the *ex gratia* payment can be made.

12. The governing document of the charity needs amending

In the case of a charitable company, any alteration of the Memorandum and Articles of Association that: (1) changes the Objects clause; or (2) states what is to happen to the assets of the charitable company upon its dissolution; or

(3) authorizes a benefit to be obtained by either the directors or the members of the company, is ineffective unless the Charity Commission have given their prior written consent.

If the Charity Commission consent to the alteration, then the charitable company will need to pass the appropriate resolution and file a copy of that resolution together with the revised Memorandum and Articles of Association with Companies House and the Charity Commission.

The governing document of an unincorporated charity is likely to contain provisions concerning any intended alteration of it. Whilst the legislation is silent on the point, it is considered advisable for the trustees of an unincorporated charity to seek the Charity Commission's consent before altering the governing document in any of the three areas listed above.

The Charities Act 2006 gives the trustees of unincorporated charities powers to pass a resolution to alter the administrative parts of their governing document, for example to vary the number of trustees needed to form a quorum at meetings.

13. The charity runs out of money

As we have seen in section 24, a charity can be insolvent even though it is holding substantial monies (for example, if those monies are held on a special trust and cannot be applied for the general day-to-day expenditure).

Charities who have taken the steps outlined in section 24, yet nevertheless find that the charity has reached a stage whereby there is no reasonable prospect of sufficient income being generated in the short term to enable the debts to be discharged as they fall due, should consider the following:

- immediately take professional advice (accounting and legal);
- consult with a Licensed Insolvency Practitioner;
- consider whether the charity should approach other charities with a view to being taken over;
- investigate whether the charity has any other assets that can be realized to provide temporary respite while a more permanent solution is explored.

The Charity Commission will appoint an Interim Manager (formerly known as a receiver/manager) only as part of an Inquiry into a charity and where they feel it is necessary to protect the assets of the charity, or to resolve a badly administered charity or to prevent further damage to the charity's name or reputation. The Charity Commission will not appoint an Interim Manager just because the charity is running out of money. Indeed, they apply a 'proportionality' test before such an appointment, to ensure both that the charity has the necessary funds to pay for an Interim Manager, and that any negative results from the appointment do not outweigh the anticipated gain.

Prudent trustees should ensure that they have taken appropriate steps long before the charity actually runs out of money. Indeed, failure to do so may call into question their conduct (be they trustees or directors), which could in turn result in personal liability attaching to them.

14. You discover a 'problem'

Depending on the nature of the 'problem', trustees should consider whether it is an issue that just affects the internal workings of the charity, or one that affects the charity's beneficiaries or the public at large.

If it is internal (e.g. a personality issue), the trustees should endeavour to resolve the issue using their personal skills and experience and ensure that the charity is well run and efficient.

If the problem is one that affects the potential beneficiaries or the public at large (e.g. fraud or mismanagement), then the trustees will need to consider:

- involving outside professional input (lawyers, accountants, HR specialists);
- whether the matter should be reported to the statutory authorities (Companies House, social services, police, etc.);
- asking the Charity Commission to assist the trustees in investigating the issues, and working with them to put things right.

Failure by the trustees to respond properly to a problem situation could result in the trustees being made personally liable for any debts or losses that the charity faces thereby.

Charity trustees may wish to consider establishing a 'whistle-blowing' procedure for staff and volunteers. The charity itself would benefit from having a process whereby allegations of fraud, abuse, health and safety breaches, poor employment practice, and malpractice in general, are notified before the charity suffers real harm. A written policy statement from the trustees making it clear that reports of malpractice are welcome and will be taken seriously and handled discreetly is an important and necessary component in a successfully run charity, particularly where staff and volunteers work amongst vulnerable people or in difficult and challenging circumstances.

When a problem is discovered, the facts and circumstances surrounding the issue and the trustees' proposals for resolving it need to be recorded properly in the charity's minute book. If the charity then takes outside professional advice, copies of such advice should be included with the minutes so that a paper trail is in place should the trustees' actions be subsequently questioned.

15. The charitable purposes for which the charity has been set up are no longer possible

If the charity's Objects are no longer relevant, they can be changed, and where charities themselves do not have the power to make that change, the Charity Commission can assist.

In some cases a charity may need to change its Objects completely and in other cases it may be sufficient for the charity to change the way that it works (see section 26 as to how these amendments can be made).

In the case of a small charity, the law empowers the trustees to amend the trusts of the charity and the Charity Commission publish helpful guidance notes on the subject.

As an alternative to the above, the trustees may consider that there are other like-minded charities who are still working effectively in achieving the same charitable purposes. The trustees may wish to consider amalgamating the charity with other such charitable organizations, rather than changing the charitable objective completely just for the sake of perpetuating the original charity. Sometimes it is not the purpose itself that is unobtainable, but rather the existence of some other limiting factor in the particular charity, which is preventing that purpose from being achieved (see section 27).

16. The charity wishes to spend money to do something that is outside the charity's 'Objects'

Consider whether:

- a payment would qualify as an *ex gratia* payment (see Appendix 1, paragraph 11);
- it is applicable to apply for a Charity Commission Scheme (see section 26);
- the Charity Commission have power to make an Order (see section 26);
- a Cy-près scheme is relevant (see section 26);

- an application to the Charity Commission under s29 of the Charities Act 1993 for specific advice is needed;
- whether the governing document permits the charity to make a gift of monies to another charity, which is itself empowered to apply it for the charitable purpose that is not authorized by the donor charity's governing document.

17. The Charity Commission write to say they are coming to visit

The Charity Commission call these 'review visits'; they are not an investigation. The Charity Commission's aim is to examine the charity's activities, its governance and finance, and to understand any issues relating to the charity in order to provide appropriate advice.

In advance of the visit, the Charity Commission will review the charity's accounts and other public documents. They are likely to want to see minutes of trustees' meetings and then agree an agenda for the visit with the charity.

The actual visit itself provides an opportunity for the Charity Commission to speak with the charity's trustees in order to understand fully how the charity operates in practice.

Following the visit the Charity Commission issue a report to the charity, which will highlight any good or bad practices, and offer guidance concerning any issues that may need to be addressed. Their intention is to encourage the charity to participate voluntarily in the review. It is unlikely the visit will last for longer than half a day.

The Charity Commission's selection criteria for a review visit are unclear although the following are suggested:

- If the Charity Commission get a higher than average number of complaints about charities working in a particular sector, they may decide to review other charities in that sector.
- Given that the Charity Commission review annual accounts, they may find issues in a set of filed accounts that lead them to consider a review visit.
- The Commission may be undertaking research into charities working in a particular sector.

The report is not a public document. The charity may well benefit from the review in the long run, as a positive review is a good marketing tool with potential funders and the charity's beneficiaries.

18. The 'leader' will not be accountable

For the reasons set out in section 6, this is not a situation that the charity's trustees can allow to continue for long. Not only does the leader need to agree to be accountable, but also the trustees need to be ready to hold that person accountable.

A review of the reports of Charity Commission Inquiries shows the danger of having a senior person (whether or not that person is also a trustee) acting in an independent way to the exclusion of the charity's trustees. Practical steps to address such a situation could include: (a) attempting to agree areas of responsibility and cooperation between the board and the leader; and (b) the possibility of involving a third party to help bring alignment. If the above steps fail to resolve the situation, the trustees may need to consider the future of the leader and ultimately their own position.

19. There is a claim against the charity

Claims against the charity can come from various sources:

A claim about the services that the charity provides (quality)
A claim from an employee (discrimination)
A claim concerning the charity's work with vulnerable persons (abuse)
A claim concerning the charity's administration/finances (malpractice)
A claim about the way the charity is carrying on its work (negligence)
A claim that the charity is in breach of the law (non-compliance)
A claim concerning the charity's behaviour (nuisance)

Claims concerning the charity's services and their inner workings need to be taken seriously and responded to. Many charities now have a claims policy and procedure that is implemented when a complaint is received.

If the claim concerns an employment issue or one made on behalf of a vulnerable person, then the charity must engage outside professional assistance at the earliest possible opportunity in order to respond correctly to the claim.

If the claim alleges that the charity is in breach of the law then professional help will need to be sought. Charities rely heavily upon their reputation, and registration as a charity implies a degree of trustworthiness and integrity. If a charity is in breach of those standards, then very often the whole charitable sector can suffer if the complaint is not handled correctly.

As a result, a section of the public may end up with a less than positive impression of the way in which charities are administered.

Churches who occupy buildings in breach of the established planning use for that building, or who fail to insulate the property properly to prevent sound becoming a nuisance to adjoining owners, damage the reputation of like-minded charities in the eyes of the planning authorities who have to enforce Planning Acts. In addition, it is a poor reflection of the standards and principles that those churches claim to embrace.

If the charity needs either to commence court proceedings or to defend them, it is good practice to notify the Charity Commission beforehand and obtain prior authorization to use charity funds to meet the costs of legal action. Failure to do so may risk the trustees being made liable for these costs. If court proceedings escalate and a considerable amount of the charity's monies are expended on them, then the trustees risk the Charity Commission's questioning as to whether such expenditure was a good use of the charity's funds. If the Commission are notified at the outset, then such issues are raised by them at an early stage in the proceedings.

20. There is a failure to file Accounts/Annual Return/hold an AGM

Charities that have a gross income or total expenditure in excess of £10,000 are required to prepare an Annual Return and Accounts, and file them with the Charity Commission within ten months of the end of the charity's financial year.

The Statement of Recommended Practice (SORP) outlines the methods and disclosures that are required and both the Annual Return and the Accounts need to comply with these specific requirements.

The Charity Commission actively encourage charities to submit their Accounts and Annual Return on time and to that end they:

- enter the dates that the Accounts and Annual Returns are filed on the charity's entry on the Register (remember that the Register is a public document and can be viewed on line);
- identify those charities that are persistently in default of submitting the Accounts and Annual Returns on time;
- consider taking regulatory action if the charity persistently fails to submit its Accounts on time.

Once the accounts are filed, they cannot be retrieved, and therefore it is essential to ensure that they are approved by the entire board and are correct.

Charities should ensure that their accounts are prepared well before the ten-month deadline following the end of the financial year. To this end the charity can assist by ensuring that all accounting records are in order, bank statements and certificates of closing balances (at the end of the financial year) are to hand, and that all the books are delivered to the Auditor within a few weeks of the end of the financial year. If the Auditors are warned that the books are coming, they can programme the Audit into their work schedule and avoid a last-minute rush to deliver the signed accounts before the end of the ten-month period.

Whilst audited accounts are a historical record, they are likely to be of more benefit to the charity in a management function if they can be produced within a month or so of the end of the financial year. Many charities use the audited accounts as a fund-raising tool (particularly to support major grant requests), and therefore their timely production can only assist.

Depending on the nature of the charitable organization, a failure to hold an Annual General Meeting may not be serious. Charitable companies can pass an elective resolution to dispense with the need to hold an Annual General Meeting, and The Companies Act 2006 may remove the requirement for private companies to hold an AGM.

However, directors of charitable companies need to balance that possible relaxation with their obligation for open and transparent governance. In the circumstances, it may be preferable to hold an AGM to give the charity's members the opportunity to participate.

Unincorporated charities may be required by the provisions of the governing document to hold an Annual General Meeting. Charities that have an active membership (be they an unincorporated charity or a charitable company) will be keen to hold an AGM as that is an important method of accountability and communication to its stakeholders and beneficiaries. If the charity fails to call an AGM, then, depending on the governing document, the members of the charity may have the ability to call and participate in an Extraordinary General Meeting in order to hold the directors/trustees accountable.

21. There is a vote of no confidence in the 'leader'

Charities should be careful before electing to go down the route of dispensing with the services of the leader. The 'no confidence vote' may be on an issue which, although important, is not critical in the life of the ongoing charity. With appropriate support and/or mediation, the trustees should actively consider the possibility of allowing the leader to continue. It is only in the most serious of cases (where there is either gross misconduct or the continuance of the leader in the role is incompatible with the culture and harmony of the charity) that the parties should go their separate ways.

If the board or the members of the charity (if the charity is regulated by members) have lost confidence in the leader then the following options are available:

- If the person is an employee who does not have written particulars of employment, the charity will be in some difficulty, given that they are required as employer to provide a statement of the terms of employment. It is likely that if the decision to terminate the employment were challenged, then an employment tribunal would impose a liability on the trustees for their failure under employment law.
- If the person is hired by the charity under a contract of employment then, depending on the terms of the contract, and after taking appropriate legal advice, the board as employer can consider terminating the contract.
- If the person is not employed (and therefore does not have a contract) then, depending on the governing document, it may be possible to pass a resolution agreeing to dispense with that person's services.
- If the person is also a trustee, then, depending upon the governing document, a board resolution to remove that person from trusteeship may be possible.

In cases of gross misconduct (financial, criminal), the trustees are empowered to take immediate steps to terminate the employment in order to protect the assets, reputation and ongoing work of the charity. If the misconduct is of a moral nature, then advice will need to be taken as to whether the issue is one entitling the trustees to terminate the employment.

22. There is a conflict between the 'spiritual' and the 'legal'

The Charity Commission will not get involved or arbitrate over interpretation of doctrine or spiritual responsibility in the life of a charity. Fundamentally, the trustees are responsible in law for controlling the management and administration of the charity. In the event of a conflict between the 'spiritual' and the 'legal', then unless the issues can be resolved by competent mediation, ultimately the trustees are responsible for the charity. If the trustees are distinct from the persons responsible for the 'spiritual', there is always the possibility that the beneficiaries may side with 'spiritual' leaders, leaving the trustees to administer an 'empty' charity! (See section 6.)

23. The charity wants to undertake a 'mega' project

Decisions concerning projects which are of a size that is out of all proportion either to the normal capacity of the charity or to those projects that the charity has undertaken to date, should be approached in the following way:

- A check should first be made to ensure that the project is consistent with the charity's Objects and therefore permitted by the governing document.
- An evaluation should be undertaken by or on behalf of the charity's board, focusing on the timescale, cost (financial and staffing), and the ultimate benefit of the project to the charity.
- Outside specialist advice should be obtained on both the financial implications and the viability of the project itself. If the project is in a sphere of activity that is not usually undertaken by the charity, then specialist professional consultancy should be taken up.
- A risk assessment should be undertaken and its conclusions built into the project.
- When all the information is to hand the board should make their independent decision as to whether the charity should undertake the project. Proper records of all discussions and reports should be kept (see section 7).
- The charity should decide internally as to who will 'manage' the project (it is suggested that a pastor is not the appropriate person to 'manage' a church redevelopment project) and set up an adequate reporting and accountability structure whilst the project is being undertaken.
- Consideration as to whether the project could be undertaken in stages may be relevant in order to minimize exposure.

24. The risks to the charity are too large

If, following a risk assessment, the charity concludes that the risks facing it on a day-to-day basis are too large to be safely accommodated by the charity, then the options include:

- discontinuing the activity or the particular project that presents an unreasonable risk;
- if it is a specific project, then consider joining with another charity (or charities) in order to reduce the overall exposure;
- the purchase of suitable insurance;
- ring-fencing the risk by using a specially formed company to undertake the project and thereby reduce the overall risk for the charity.

The greatest risk to the charity may be from 'within' rather than 'without'. If the charity lacks strategy, adequate governance, management or experience, then steps will need to be taken to mitigate the risk from those 'internal' issues whereupon the previously perceived risks from 'without' may seem to be manageable after all.

25. The charity has a problem with a key staff member

Carefully review the contract of employment for the staff member concerned. In conjunction with that contract, consider the appropriate response from the charity to the problem that has arisen.

If the charity's disciplinary procedure is to be evoked, the staff member needs to be given the opportunity to be accompanied by a 'friend' to any consultative meeting.

It is important to ascertain the root cause of the problem. It may, for example, result from the omission by the charity to provide a safe and stable working environment or to support the staff member properly, particularly overseas. Consider the impact to the overall work of the charity caused by a disaffected or marginalized key staff member.

Given the nature of the charitable activity, it is likely that many of the charity staff identify very strongly with the objectives of the charity. This, in turn, leads to a sense of ownership in the charity which may be reflected in the fact that the staff member has made a personal sacrifice in order to be involved with it. If there is a breakdown in the relationship between the charity and an employee, it is likely that the sense of betrayal and hurt felt by the staff member will run deep. Charities need to respond very delicately in the whole area of employer/employee relationship. Statistically charities that adopt a more consultative and participatory approach to human resource issues are less likely to have significant problems with key staff members.

26. There is a 'suspicion' of someone or something

If the charity becomes suspicious of a donor's intention they should:

- Report their suspicions to the Charity Commission and/or the police.
- Ensure that none of the charity's assets, premises, staff or volunteers could be used for activities that either may, or may appear to, support or condone any illegal activity.

- Beware lest they commit an office under s19 of the Terrorism Act 2000. If trustees receive information that leads them to believe that a person may be involved in an activity (for example, raising money or using property) for the purpose of terrorism, such suspicion or knowledge must be disclosed to the police as soon as possible.
- Formally seek the Charity Commission's advice under s24 of the Charities Act 2006. Under this section the person who makes a written application to the Charity Commission for an opinion, and who receives that opinion and acts on it, is regarded as having acted in accordance with the charitable trust (i.e. the trustee is unlikely to face subsequent criticism).
- Report to the police and the Charity Commission any fraudulent solicitations received via letter or email (often from overseas).

See section 24.

27. The identity of the trustees is not clear

Enquiries can be made of the lawyers and accountants for the charity to see whether they have any records that may assist. In addition, the Charity Commission may be able to access details from their archives. If the charity has held land, then the title deeds to that land may disclose the last known active trustees.

The Charities Act 2006 allows the Charity Commission to determine who are the members of a charity, but such a determination is not fully binding unless it is endorsed by the High Court. In other words, the trustees so nominated by the Charity Commission can be challenged, and any actions and decisions they have taken can be unravelled, unless their appointment has been ratified by the High Court.

28. There is a 'request' for compliance by an overseas government

Charities working overseas from time to time find themselves facing demands from a national government, which may be directed at one particular charity, all charities working in that country, or perhaps those that come from a specific country or are undertaking a specific kind of work. This can result from insensitive behaviour by the charity; or the government deciding that it does not want details of the social needs of its citizens reported by charities in the West; or outright jealousy that the charity is able to secure grants from international governments, or build and equip schools and hospitals to a better standard that can be done locally. (I have seen first-hand examples of all of these and others, in acting for charities working in various parts of the world.)

When facing a 'request' for compliance from an overseas government that the charity deems unreasonable, the following steps are open to it:

- The board of the charity in the UK needs to be made fully aware of the issue in order to determine whether or not the charity can comply.
- The trustees should consider taking professional advice.
- An application should be made to the Charity Commission for advice and guidance under s24 of the Charities Act 2006.
- The charity may be advised to discuss the issue with the British or EU Embassy in that particular country, as their commercial section may have local wisdom and advice
- Discussions may be conducted with the appropriate government department in the country in question.
- It may be helpful to open discussions with other like-minded charities and NGOs in the country to see whether they are similarly affected. If they are, then there may be opportunity to combine forces in a united presentation to the government on behalf of all the charities/NGOs.

If the above fails to resolve the issue in a satisfactory way, and the trustees (acting on the advice they have received) decide that they cannot comply with the request from the overseas government, then they may opt to adjust their operation accordingly in order to keep on the right side of the law.

Remember the government in a particular country may not share the charity's sense of importance of the specific work being undertaken in that country. It has been found to be unwise to threaten the government with the withdrawal of the organization from the country; that may have been the game plan for the government all along! (See also sections 11 and 20.)

29. The charity is facing an unusual/new challenge

Given that charities operate in a continually changing environment, it is not unremarkable that they may from time to time face unusual and new challenges. The critical issue is how the charity will respond to these. The following issues may be relevant:

- Does the charity's governing document allow the charity to undertake the new challenge being offered?
- If it takes up the new challenge, will that adversely affect the present charitable Objects?
- Does the charity have the expertise in its existing staff to cope with the new challenge?
- If the charity's donors have given monies for the present charitable activity, how will they react if a new challenge is adopted?
- Does the charity need to bring in outside professional support – perhaps on a consultancy basis – to enable it to have the necessary expertise to respond to the new challenge?
- Will the new challenge provide public benefit?

30. The charity can no longer spend 'restricted funds'

Restricted funds are funds held by the charity that are subject to specific restrictions that may have been imposed by the donor, or by the terms upon which those funds were raised. For example, a church that raises funds for a new roof would hold those funds as 'restricted funds'.

Options for the charity if they can no longer spend restricted funds would include returning the money to the donors (if they can be ascertained); or applying to the Charity Commission for a Scheme or an Order authorizing the money to be spent on a wider charitable object within the charity.

As mentioned in section 22, it is a wise move at the start of any fundraising campaign for a specific purpose to agree in writing with the donors that any surplus funds left after the project has been completed can be applied to the general purposes of the charity.

31. The word 'limited' is unnecessary in the charity's title

A charitable company can be exempt from using 'limited' in its name where:

- all profits and income are to be spent in promoting the charity;
- no dividends are paid to its members;
- if the company is wound up, all assets are transferred to a similar organization.

Usually this exemption is claimed at the time the company is formed at Companies House, although it is possible to pass a special resolution to effect this change after the company has been formed.

Many faith-based charitable companies have found it helpful to their charitable Objects to exclude 'limited' from their name.

32. The charity has Permanent Endowment

These are restricted funds where the donor has imposed a condition that they must be held permanently as part of the capital of the charity. The income from the capital is useable in accordance with the donor's instructions. Permanent endowment can be cash, land or buildings. The Charities Act 2006 permits unincorporated charities to spend all or part of permanent endowment as income for the general purposes of the charity as set out in the governing document.

Larger unincorporated charities are also given power to spend capital that had been given for a particular purpose, provided that the value of the capital exceeds £10,000 and the charity has an annual gross income in the last financial year of at least £1,000. The Charity Commission, however, need to be consulted on any resolution that the trustees may pass, and may give directions before the resolution can be implemented.

33. VAT is an issue

Registered charities in the UK are not automatically exempt from paying VAT. Charities may, however, be able to obtain VAT relief when purchasing certain goods and services, even if the charity is not registered for VAT. Examples (but not an exhaustive list) include:

• Aids for the disabled
• Buildings and construction
• Equipment for producing talking books and newspapers
• Medical and scientific equipment
• Advertising and goods connected with the collecting of donations for the charity

To claim this VAT relief the charity needs to complete a special declaration, and an eligibility certificate is then given to the supplier, who will not charge VAT on the purchase so long as all the conditions relating to the relief have been met.

If the charity has turnover from business supplies that is above the current VAT registration threshold, the charity is required to register for VAT as if it were a normal trading business. Once registered, the appropriate VAT treatment will need to be given to income received and supplies made.

Once a charity has registered for VAT, then the receipt of income that is given to the charity is not subject to VAT. The same applies to a grant that is given to a charity, unless part of the grant requires the charity to perform a service or supply goods, in which case VAT is chargeable.

HMRC has detailed information about all VAT and other tax issues relating to charities (www.inlandrevenue.gov.uk/charities).

34. An urgent response is needed from the Charity Commission

There are occasions when a charity needs an instant response from the Charity Commission, particularly on issues relating to possible fraud or money laundering.

The Charity Commission realized that previous turnaround times have not been adequate, and in 2006 they established 'Charity Commission Direct'. This has been set up as a central point of contact for all requests for services from the Charity Commission. In addition, it provides general advice and guidance for which it is possible to speak to an adviser. Alongside this, the Charity Commission have established a quick response unit to give regulatory advice and approvals.

A Large Charities Unit has been established in London to provide regulatory services to charities that have an annual income of over £5 million.

35. The charity works with vulnerable beneficiaries

Charities that are either working with children and/or concerned with the care of vulnerable adults in circumstances where the trustees have access to such vulnerable adults in carrying out their normal duties need to pay special attention to the requirements for Criminal Records Bureau (CRB) checks on the trustees to ensure that a trustee is not disqualified from working with vulnerable people. Currently the Charity Commission's policy is that trustees:

- must be CRB checked where there is a legal requirement to do so; and
- should be checked where there is a legal entitlement to do so.

Fundamentally each charity and its trustees must decide whether they are legally allowed to carry out CRB checks or whether they are legally required to do so. The burden is therefore on the charity and its trustees to ensure compliance. It is an offence to offer a regulated position (e.g. the position of trustee of a children's charity) to an individual who is disqualified from working with children, even if the person offering the position did not know that the candidate was disqualified.

There are two types of CRB check:

1. *A standard check* – this will disclose convictions, cautions, reprimands and any warnings that are held on the police national computer.
2. *An enhanced check* – applicable where there is a greater degree of contact with children or vulnerable adults. The CRB will also look at lists held by government departments to see if a person is on any of those lists as being barred from working with vulnerable groups.

It is considered good practice for the charity to renew the CRB checks every three years. It is not possible for most charities to undertake these checks themselves and therefore 'umbrella bodies' who are directly authorized by the CRB to carry out these checks are used. Groups such as CCPAS have a wide experience of undertaking this work for churches and Christian organizations, as well as a thorough understanding of all the issues relating to child protection.

The Safeguarding Vulnerable Groups Act of 2006 may well bring about further changes whereby some positions within charities will be subject to monitoring by the CRB. Furthermore, it is likely that the application process will be online (see also sections 9 and 18).

36. The charity wishes to purchase a leaving present for a retiring trustee

It is permitted to purchase 'a modest token of appreciation' to a retiring trustee using the charity's funds. Provided that the expenditure is not excessive, it is likely to generate good will with the retiring trustee and everyone to whom he shows the present!

37. It all gets too much!

Despite the noblest aims and ideals of the charity, the commitment and enthusiasm of its key workers and volunteers and the personal affinity that the trustees may share with its charitable Objects, there are occasions during the trustee's period of service when the weight of responsibility, expectation and demand becomes too great.

This can be the result of:

- unreasonable demands that the charity is putting upon the trustee;
- the difficulties that the charity may be going through;
- chronic lack of cash that is preventing the charity from functioning properly;
- personality issues within the board or between the board and key staff;
- ill health;
- the pressures of the trustee's other activities.

Whatever the presenting circumstance, the reason behind it needs to be identified and addressed for the sake of both the trustee and the charity. If a satisfactory resolution cannot be found, it is probably in everyone's best interest for the trustee to consider resigning (or stepping down from trustee-ship for a period).

Solomon (one of the wisest men who ever lived) stated that 'there is a time for everything'. There may come a time when a particular trustee needs to step down from responsibility because it has all got too much, and there may be a time when all of the trustees decide that the charity has run its course and its best years are behind it; that it would be in the best interests of everyone (including the charity's beneficiaries), if the charity ceased and its assets were passed over to a like-minded charity. Perhaps faith-based charities are more inclined to 'stick it out' in the hope that things may change. However, it may be clear to all onlookers that the charity is just perpetuating its existence, living off past glories and really does not have a bright future ahead of it.

APPENDIX 2 DEFINITIONS

AGM	The Annual General Meeting of the charity open to all members.
Alternate director	A person appointed by a director to act on their behalf in their absence. Only possible if the Articles of Association of the company permit this.
Beneficiary	A legal term referring to a person who is eligible to benefit from a charity's work. Usually the beneficiaries of a charity will be defined in the governing document.
Board	Collective term that describes the duly appointed directors or trustees of a charity.
Breach of trust	A breach of any duty imposed on a trustee. For charity trustees, these duties may be imposed by the provisions of a charity's governing document, laws and regulations, or Orders of the Court or the Charity Commission. A duty is something that trustees have to do. It is distinguished from a power, which trustees may or may not choose to use.
Capital	Resources belonging to the charity which the trustees are legally required to invest or retain and use for the purposes of the charity. It may also include permanent endowment.
Chairman	The trustee or director who is appointed to lead the charity's meetings. He/she may have a casting vote in the event of an equality of votes.
Charitable company	A company registered under the Companies Acts, which is established exclusively for charitable purposes and which prevents the distribution of its assets amongst its members. A charitable company has no shareholders and is a separate legal entity from its members and directors.

Charitable Incorporated Organisation (CIO)	A corporate body permitted by the Charities Act 2006, which combines the benefits of being a separate legal entity from its trustees with the administrative simplicity of being regulated by only one body – the Charity Commission.
Charitable purposes	See 'Objects'
Charity Commission	Corporate body set up by the Charities Act 2006, it functions on behalf of the Crown and is not subject to the direction or control of any minister of the Crown or other government department. It replaced the Office of the Charity Commissioner for England and Wales, which was abolished by the 2006 Act. Its objectives are: • To increase public trust and confidence in charities • To provide awareness and understanding of the operation of the requirement for public benefit • To promote compliance by trustees with their legal obligations in controlling and managing the administration of the charity • To promote the effective use of charitable resources • To enhance accountability of charities to donors, beneficiaries and the general public
Charity trustees	The people having general control and management of the administration of a charity (regardless of what they are called). They may also be known as 'the executive' or 'management committee'. In the case of a charitable company, the trustees are known as directors.
Chief Executive	Usually refers to the most senior member of staff within the charity. May also be known as Chief Executive Officer, Director, or General Director.
Community Interest Company (CIC)	A special type of company for those wishing to establish businesses that trade with a social purpose. CICs are outside the constraints of charity status with regard to distribution of profits.
Company Secretary	An officer of a charitable company responsible to ensure compliance with the duties imposed by company law and for the secretarial duties set out in the charity's governing document.
Constitution	The written document that establishes the purpose for which an organization is set up and the principles and rules by which it will be governed. This can be contained in a Conveyance, Trust Deed, Will, Memorandum and Articles of Association, or other written document.
Corporate members	Include companies, local authorities and other public bodies or organizations for which a nominated representative holds a right to vote at the charity's annual general meeting on behalf of the organization they represent.
Corporate trustee	A company or corporation that is appointed a trustee of a charity, e.g. an NHS Trust which acts as a trustee of an NHS charity.
Criminal Records Bureau (CRB)	Organization that provides a disclosure service concerning information held by the police, together with information held under the Protection of Children Act, Protection of Vulnerable Adults Act and lists maintained by the Department for Educational and Skills.

Custodian trustee	A company appointed to have the custody (but not the management) of trust property. A custodian trustee is not a charity trustee and has no say in the administration of the charity.
Cy-près	A legal doctrine under which the trusts of a charity may be formally modified to allow them to be used for a purpose that is as near as possible to the provisions of the original trust.
Designated funds	Funds of the charity that the trustees have 'designated' for a particular project or use, without restricting those funds legally, e.g. monies set aside by the board to renew the charity's IT system.
Directors	Those who hold office of a charitable company whose office is controlled under the Companies Acts. Also known as trustees, and subject to provisions of the Charities Acts.
EGM	Extraordinary General Meeting (sometimes also called Special General Meeting), and relates to any general meeting of the members of the charity that is not an AGM.
Endowment funds	Funds which the charity's trustees are required to invest and use for the charity's purposes. They may be 'expendable' (i.e. useable in their entirety) or 'permanent'.
Excepted charities	A charity that is excepted from the need to register with the Charity Commission, but is to all intents and purposes subject to their jurisdiction, e.g. Scout and Guide associations.
Exempt charities	Charities that are not supervised or monitored by the Charity Commission and are accountable to some other statutory body, e.g. registered friendly societies are accountable to the Registrar of Friendly Societies.
Ex officio trustee	Means trustee by virtue of their office. Normally this relates to positions such as the vicar of a parish, the mayor of a town, etc. Ex officio trustees have the same responsibilities as other charity trustees.
Fiduciary duty	Obligations imposed to promote loyalty or faithfulness, for example, a trustee's duty not to put himself in a position of potential conflict of interest with the charity.
Gift Aid	A gift to a charity by a UK tax payer under this scheme enables the charity to claim the repayment of basic rate Income Tax (if the tax payer pays higher-rate tax, then they will get the additional tax relief). A gift made to charity by a company under this scheme enables the company to set the gift off against its tax income.
Governing document	Any document that sets out the charity's purposes and details of how the charity is to be administered. Sometimes known as a 'Trust Deed', 'Constitution', 'Memorandum and Articles of Association', 'Rules', 'Conveyance', 'Will', 'Royal Charter', 'Scheme of the Commissioners'.
HMRC	Her Majesty's Revenue and Customs.
Incorporated Association	See Incorporated Charity.
Incorporated Charity	A charity that is established as a corporate body. This includes a charitable company, a body incorporated by an Act of Parliament or bodies incorporated by Royal Charter.

Information Commissioner	The independent authority set up to promote access to office information and to protect personal information.
Interim manager	Formally known as a 'Receiver and Manager', interim managers are appointed by the Charity Commission following the opening of a formal Inquiry after the discovery of evidence of misconduct or maladministration in the charity. Their appointment is to manage the charity to the exclusion of the trustees until such time as responsibility can be passed back to a board of trustees to take the charity forward.
Leader	Chief Executive or pastor.
Malpractice	Malpractice in the charitable sector could be where a person who is under a duty to act in a specific manner fails to follow the generally accepted professional standards and, as a result, loss or damage is caused to the charity itself.
Members	An individual or corporate body or other charity who has agreed to belong to the charity. The members' rights and responsibilities will usually be set out in the governing document.
Memorandum and Articles of Association	Effectively a Trust Deed set out in the format required by the Companies Act and which forms the governing document of a charitable company.
Mission or mission statement	A statement designed by a charity to explain why it exists and what it intends to do.
Non-Governmental Organization (NGO)	An organization established for benevolent or philanthropic purposes for the benefit of the public, independent of central local government control, and which does not belong to those who run it or are employed by it.
Objects	The legal purpose(s) for which a charity exists or the thing it was set up to achieve as stated in its governing document. The Objects direct how the charity's assets must be used, e.g. 'The Advancement of Religion'.
Official Custodian for Charities	The holder of this office is appointed by the Charity Commission to hold land or assets as a custodian trustee for charities in respect of any land or assets which are vested in the Official Custodian by means of a Charity Commission Scheme or Order.
Order	A legal document made by the Charity Commission, which can confer new powers on a trustee body, or appoint or remove trustees.
Permanent endowment	The property of a charity which must be held permanently, sometimes to be used for furthering the charity's purposes (e.g. a building), sometimes to produce income from the charity.
Powers	A charity's Powers are the authority that the charity has to enable it to carry out its Objects. Powers are not charitable in themselves and are usually set out in the charity's governing document in a clause immediately following the Objects.
Quorum	The minimum number of people entitled to attend and vote that must be present at a meeting in order that valid decisions can be made. The number of people required for a quorum is usually set out in the governing document.

Register of Charities	A register maintained by the Charity Commission containing the name of every registered charity and other such information as the Charity Commission thinks fit (this is also known as 'The Register'). This other information will include a working name, the Objects of the charity, financial year-end and the name and address of the correspondent for the charity. In practice the register will also include more general information about the charity.
Reserves	Income of the charity that is not yet spent, committed or designated. It does include permanent endowment, restricted funds or designated funds.
Restricted Funds	Funds or property held and administered as a separate trust by or on behalf of a charity, e.g. monies raised by or given to a charity on condition that they are used only for a particular purpose.
Scheme	A legal document granted by the Charity Commission that can change any aspect of a charity's Objects or administrative provisions.
Secretary	The person appointed to be the secretary of the charity or company. If no such person exists, then the person who calls meetings and takes the minutes at meetings.
SOFA	Statement of Financial Activities. A charity's SOFA shows all the incoming resources becoming available during the year and all its expenditure for the year, and reconciles all the changes in its funds. The SOFA should account for all the funds of the charity and should be presented in columns representing the different types of funds.
SORP	Statement Of Recommended Practice for Accounting and Reporting by charities.
Special trust	Funds or property held and administered on its own separate trusts, by or on behalf of a main charity for any special purposes of that charity. It follows that the Objects of a special trust must be narrower than those of the main charity.
Structure document	See Governing Document.
Trading subsidiary	A company limited by shares, owned by the charity and used by it to carry out commercial activities with a view to generating profit for the charity.
Trust Deed	The document setting out the charity's Objects and describing how they will be administered. This can be a Trust Deed, Constitution, Conveyance, Will, Royal Charter, Statement of Rules, Scheme of the Charity Commission, Memorandum and Articles of Association or other formal document.
Trustee board	The charity's governing body, which may also be called the Board of Directors, Executive Committee or Committee.
Unincorporated charity	A charitable trust or a charitable unincorporated association. Its main characteristic is that the charity is not a separate legal entity from its trustees (see Charitable company).
Unrestricted funds	Monies that are expendable in furtherance of the charity's Objects (also known as general funds).
Vision	The goal towards which the charity is working.

Vulnerable persons	Children or vulnerable adults (persons suffering from a substantial learning or physical disability/a physical or mental illness, including addiction to alcohol or drugs/a significant reduction in mental capacity).
Working name	The name or an acronym under which the charity is more commonly known. This name may be completely different from the official name entered on the Register of Charities.

APPENDIX 3 USEFUL ADDRESSES

Centre for Effective Dispute Resolution (CEDR)
International Dispute Resolution Centre, 70 Fleet Street, London EC4Y 1EU
Tel: 020 7536 6060
www.cedr.co.uk

The Charity Bank Limited
PO Box 398, 194 High Street, Tonbridge, Kent TN9 1BD
Tel: 01732 774040
www.charitybank.org

The Charity Commission
Harmsworth House, 13/15 Bouverie Street, London EC4Y 8DP
Tel: 0845 3000218
www.charitycommission.gov.uk

Charity Commission Direct
PO Box 1227, Liverpool, L69 3UG
Tel: 0845 3000218
www.charitycommission.gov.uk

Christian Copyright Licensing International
Chantry House, 22 Upperton Road, Eastbourne, East Sussex BN21 1BF
Tel: 01323 417711
www.ccli.co.uk

Companies House
Crown Way, Maindy, Cardiff CF14 3UZ
Tel: 0870 33 33 636
www.companieshouse.gov.uk

Criminal Records Bureau
CRB Customer Services, PO Box 110, Liverpool L69 3EF
Tel: 0870 90 90 811
www.crb.gov.uk

Directory of Social Change
24 Stephenson Way, London NW1 2DP
Tel: 020 7391 4800
www.dsc.org.uk

Evangelical Alliance
186 Kennington Park Road, London SE11 4BT
Tel: 020 7207 2100
www.eauk.org

Fundraising Standards Board
Hampton House, 20 Albert Embankment, London SE1 7TJ
Tel: 0845 402 5442
www.fsboard.org.uk

Global Connections
c/o Transform Products Limited
Caswell Road, Sydenham Industrial Estate, Leamington Spa
Warwickshire CV31 1QF
Tel: 01926 48 77 55
www.globalconnections.co.uk

HMRC Charities
St Johns House, Merton Road, Bootle, Merseyside L69 9BB
Tel: 0845 302 0203
www.hmrc.gov.uk/charities

Information Commissioner's Office
Wycliffe House, Water Lane, Wilmslow, Cheshire SK9 5AF
Tel: 01625 545 700
www.informationcommissioner.gov.uk

Inland Revenue (IR)
IR Charities, Room 140, St John's House, Merton Road, Bootle,
Merseyside L69 9BB
Tel: 0151 472 6036 / 6037 (general enquiries)
www.inlandrevenue.gov.uk

Institute of Chartered Accountants
Chartered Accountants' Hall, PO Box 433, London EC2P 2BJ
Tel 020 7920 8100
www.icaew.co.uk

Institute of Fundraising
Park Place, 12 Lawn Lane, London SW8 1UD
Tel: 020 7840 1000
www.institute-of-fundraising.org.uk

Listed Places of Worship Grant Scheme
PO Box 609, Newport, South Wales NP10 8QD
Tel: 0845 601 5945
www.lpwscheme.org.uk

The National Council for Voluntary Organisations (NCVO)
Regent's Wharf, 8 All Saints Street, London N1 9RL
Tel: 020 7713 6161
www.ncvo-vol.org.uk

Office of Public Sector Information
Admiralty Arch, North Side, The Mall, London SW1A 2WH
Tel: 01603 723011 (general enquiries)
www.opsi.gov.uk

Office of the Scottish Charity Regulator (OSCR)
2nd Floor, Quadrant House, 9 Riverside Drive, Dundee, DD1 4NY
Tel: 01382 220446
www.oscr.org.uk

Office of the Third Sector
35 Great Smith Street, London SW1P 3BQ
Tel: 020 7276 6400
www.cabinetoffice.gov.uk/third_sector/

Performing Rights Society
Causeway House, Bocking End, Braintree, Essex CM7 9HB
Tel: 01376 552525
www.braintree.gov.uk

Phonographic Performance Limited
Upper James Street, London W1F 9DE
Tel: 020 7534 1000
www.ppluk.com

Regulator of Community Interest Companies
CIC Team, Room 3.68, Companies House, Crown Way, Maindy,
Cardiff CF14 3UZ
Tel: 029 20346228
www.cicregulator.gov.uk

UK Intellectual Property Office
Concept House, Cardiff Road, Newport, South Wales NP10 8QQ
Tel: 01633 814000
www.ipo.gov.uk

Wales Council for Voluntary Action
Baltic House, Mount Stuart Square, Cardiff Bay, Cardiff CF10 5FH
Tel: 029 20431700
www.wcva.org.uk

Other useful resources

Circles of Support and Accountability
Tel: 0870 774 6354
www.ccjf.org/what/circles.htm1

Lucy Faithfull Foundation
Tel: 01527 591 922
www.lucyfaithfull.co.uk

NSPCC
Tel: 0808 800 5000
www.nspcc.org.uk

Sanctuary
Tel: 0870 991 1876
www.sanctuaryuk.com

Stop It Now!
Tel: 0808 10000 900
ww.stopitnow.org.uk

Contributors to this book

A. J. Bennewith & Co
Chartered Accountants, Hitherbury House, 97 Portsmouth Road, Guildford,
Surrey GU2 4YF
Tel: 01483 539 777
www.bennewith.co.uk

Churches Child Protection Advisory Service (CCPAS)
PO Box 133, Swanley, Kent BR8 7UQ
Tel: 0845 120 4550
www.ccpas.co.uk

The Wellers Law Group
Tenison House, Tweedy Road, Bromley BR1 3Nf
Tel: 020 8464 4242

8 Grays Inn Square, London WC1R 5SQ
Tel: 020 7242 7265

5 Lloyds Avenue, London EC3N 3AE
Tel: 020 7977 1260
www.wellers.net

Wellserve Financial Ltd
Tenison House, Tweedy Road, Bromley, BR1 3NF
Tel: 020 8290 7995
www.wellserve.co.uk

INDEX

cash flow 113, 115, 151, 200–201, 210, 218, 228–229
casting vote 61, 276
Centre for Dispute Resolution 180
cessation 244, 247–248
chairman 2, 47, 52, 56, 59–63, 84, 93, 95–96, 254–257, 276
change of use 110–111
charitable
  activities 23, 40, 104, 184, 186, 210, 235, 245, 251, 268, 271
  body 72, 245, 251
  collections 26, 32, 36, 206
  company
    constitution of 18, 42, 83, 89, 104, 184, 246–247, 276
    definition 2–4, 13, 18–19, 25–26, 29
    duty of directors 20, 55, 71, 80–81, 226–227, 230–231
    name 43–44
    organization 13–24
    procedure 61, 83, 96–99, 185
    purpose, see Object(s)
    requirements 58, 63, 68, 77–79, 84, 86–87, 93–94, 207, 252–253, 258–259, 265, 271
    resources 32, 277
    status 4, 11–13, 28, 35, 38–39, 115, 187, 219
    trust 1–2, 13–14, 16, 51, 104, 248, 269, 280
Charitable Incorporated Organisation 13, 19–20, 25, 31, 36, 247, 277
Charitable Uses Act 1601 1
Charities Act
  Charities Act 1960 2, 3, 103
  Charities Act 1992 3, 209
  Charities Act 1993 3, 44, 72, 103–105, 107–108, 159, 262
  Charities Act 2006 1–5, 16, 19, 21, 25–37, 65, 69, 76, 90, 206–207, 225, 231, 238, 242–245, 247–248, 255, 259, 269–270, 272, 277
Charities Aid Foundation 202
Charities and Trustee Investment (Scotland) Act 2005 18
Charities Bill 3
charity
  Charity Commission 268–270, 273
    approval/consent 16, 18–19, 66, 83, 103, 105–107, 180, 218, 229, 240–241, 245, 259
    Inquiry 226, 232, 234

    intervention/investigation 46, 53, 67–69, 80, 181–183
    jurisdiction 12, 26, 31–34, 49, 67, 225, 231–232, 239, 242, 258
    opinion 42, 182, 269
    Order 69, 106, 108, 240–242, 260, 271, 279
    powers 21, 83, 90, 171, 205, 253–255, 258
    role 37–39, 44, 62, 66
    Scheme 43, 106, 182, 205–206, 212, 240–241, 243, 261, 271, 278–280
    visit 40, 76, 88, 262
  shops 23, 219–220
  Tribunal 25, 27, 31, 33–35
cheque 11, 20, 44, 50, 67–68, 85,
Chief Executive 47–48, 52–53, 57, 62, 64, 71, 96, 186, 196, 224, 234, 250, 256, 277, 279
child/children
  abuse 166, 170, 172–173, 177
  care organizations 81
  childbirth 136, 145–146
  protection 87, 189–190, 274
  working with 40, 81–82, 87, 166–177, 190, 273–274
Child Protection Policy 190
Children Act 1989 167
Children Act 2004 167
Christian Action 21
Christian Aid 19
Christian Copyright Licensing International 121, 123, 283
Christian organization 3, 6, 28, 76, 121, 162, 274
Church in Wales 35
Church of England 6, 35, 195, 242
Churches' Child Protection Advisory Service 168, 176, 286
Citizens' Standards on Public Benefit 30
claim 113, 115, 170, 189, 229, 232, 234, 236, 263
  copyright 119–121
  damages 113, 115, 170, 189, 232
  discrimination 127–128, 135, 137–140, 142
  employment 124, 130–133, 144, 148–150, 182, 187, 227, 250
code of conduct 59, 63, 207, 225, 254
collaboration 244–246
collectors 206–207, 209
commercial participator 208–209